GENERATIONS
AND
IDENTITY:
THE JAPANESE AMERICAN

HARRY H. L. KITANO, PH.D.

PROFESSOR OF SOCIAL WELFARE AND SOCIOLOGY
ENDOWED CHAIR, JAPANESE AMERICAN STUDIES
UNIVERSITY OF CALIFORNIA, LOS ANGELES

JANUARY 6, 1993

160 Gould Street
Needham Heights, MA 02194

Printed in the United States of America

10 9 8 7 6 5 4 3 2 1

ISBN 0–536–58370-6
BA 4058

GINN PRESS
160 Gould Street/Needham Heights, MA 02194
Simon & Schuster Higher Education Publishing Group

TABLE OF CONTENTS

Section II

PREFACE

Take skin color, race, values and culture of one group. Mix them into a dominant group with different skin color, race, values, and culture. Present abstractions such as a Bill of Rights and a Constitution, and talk about tolerance and equality, but block entrance into the mainstream. Add strain and hostility between the two groups. Outcome—problems of identity, and a summary of the Japanese American experience.

The Japanese came to the United States from Asia; their skin color was not white; they looked different, and they held different values and different cultural life styles. And there was a war which exacerbated the problems between the two groups, including being placed in camps, and issues of an identity. Then finally, there was peace, and redress for the forced incarceration. This is the story that will unfold in this volume.

This is a new book, but builds upon my first book titled *Japanese Americans: The Evolution of a Subculture*, first published in 1969. Much has happened to Japanese Americans, as well as to the rest of society since that time—the struggle for Civil Rights, the assassination of the Kennedys' and Martin Luther King; the election of Senators and Congressmen of Japanese ancestry; good relations between the United States and Japan interspersed with periods of Japan bashing, and even redress for those who were forced to live behind barbed wire during World War II.

But America is a dynamic society so that time and change are facts of American life. The individual changes, the family and community change, and the society changes. Groups like the Japanese American reflect these changes, so that one underlying theme of this volume is that of change.

Another theme is that of diversity; that what was once thought of as a relatively homogeneous group can no longer be viewed in this manner. Each Japanese generation has gone through a variety of experiences and have been exposed to different facets of American life so that change and diversity go hand in hand. The change is linked to the constant search for an identity.

The final theme of this volume is that change and diversity operate in a broader context. Happenings in Japan and the United States, and the relationship between these nations provide the background for understanding the Japanese American. Therefore, we will present selected events in Japan, and in the United States to provide the context for understanding the treatment and the behavior of Japanese Americans.

Initially, I had thought of including sections on the Japanese in other parts of America, that is in Canada, Central and South America. However, the inclusion of those of Japanese ancestry who have emigrated to other than the United States calls for another volume at some later date.

I would like to acknowledge the assistance of the following in the preparation of this third volume: Professor Dennis Ogawa of the University of Hawaii, especially in regard to the chapter on Hawaii; the valuable research assistance of Lianne Urada and Mieko Yoshihama, both graduate students at UCLA; Margaret Benjamin for typing assistance, and my wife Lynn and my daughter, Christine.

A special dedication goes to the hard working Nikkei Bruin Committee, composed of the following: Dr. Harold Harada, Herbert G. Kawahara, Ms. Frances Kitagawa, Jun Mori, Frank K. Omatsu, Dr. Paul Terasaki, Minoru Tonai, the late Dr. Robert Watanabe, Ms. Ruth Watanabe, Dr. James Yamazaki and Father John Yamazaki. They have contributed and given back to the university and to the community in the best tradition of good citizenship. They have provided the leadership for funding the first Endowed Chair for Japanese American Studies in any major university.

Thanks also goes to a number of Academic Senate Research Grants which helped to fund my research and writing efforts.

This new volume will also provide a number of personal experiences, since many of the events, including a search for an identity, parallel that of many Japanese Americans.

Los Angeles, California
January, 1993

DEDICATION

I would like to acknowledge the assistance of the following in the preparation of this third volume: Professor Dennis Ogawa of the University of Hawaii, especially in regard to the chapter on Hawaii; the valuable research assistance of Lianne Urada and Mieko Yoshihama, both graduate student at UCLA; Margaret Benjamin for typing assistance, and my wife Lynn and daughter, Christine.

A special dedication goes to the hard working Nikkei Bruin Committee, composed of the following: Dr. Harold Harada, Herbert G. Kawahara, Ms. Frances Kitagawa, Jun Mori, Frank K. Omatsu, Dr. Paul Terasaki, Minoru Tonai, the late Dr. Robert S. Watanabe, Ms. Ruth Watanabe, Dr. James Yamazaki and Father John Yamazaki. They have contributed and given back to the university and to the community in the best tradition of good citizenship. They have provided the leadership for funding the first Endowed Chair for Japanese American Studies in any major university.

Thanks also goes to a number of Academic Senate Research Grants which helped to fund my research and writing efforts.

This new volume will also provide a number of personal experiences, since many of the events, includin a search for an identity, parallel that of many Japanese Americans.

Los Angeles, California
January, 1993

SECTION I

CHAPTER 1

INTRODUCTION

The experiences of Japanese Americans in the United States can be likened to a ride on a roller coaster. There have been periods of highs as well as stretches of lows, although on balance there have been more historic lows than highs. But it would be safe to say that it has not been an even and smooth ride, and as for the future, one can predict continued bumpiness.

Part of the reason for the unevenness is America's relationship with the Japanese nation. No matter how different Japanese Americans are from those born and reared in Japan, it remains difficult, perhaps even impossible for many Americans to separate the two. Therefore when relationships between the United States and Japan are smooth, the image of Japanese Americans is positive; whereas when relationships are negative, the perception of Japanese Americans suffers. Japanese Americans have constantly felt the effects of Japan bashing, so that a variation of the saying, "when mother feels cold, the child puts on a sweater," is "when there is hostility between the United States and Japan, Japanese Americans feel the heat."

Another factor deals with America's relationship with its other minorities. The term "model minority" has been used to characterize Japanese Americans (as well as other Asian American groups) to point out to other minorities that they too can achieve some level of "success." Japanese Americans, who might have been expected to accept these words of "praise" at one time in their history, are among the first to raise critical questions—what are the motives behind the praise?, what are the measures used to define success?, and why was this "model minority" put into concentration camps just a few decades ago?

Terms such as the "middleman minority" illustrate the precarious role often held by Asian Americans—a position above some minorities,

3

but below the dominant white group. The scapegoat role is all too familiar to groups who have found themselves caught in the middle. The Jews in Germany, and the Chinese in the Philippines were caught and became targets from both the elites and those in power from above, and from the masses below (Kitano, 1974).

The socio-economic, and political systems, all related to power, also play an important role in the lives of the Japanese Americans. Recessions, depressions and economic good times have an effect on all Americans, but the ability of opportunist politicians to seize on public disaffection to shape perceptions of the Japanese American has been a part of American history. For example, Reynolds (1927), surveyed the files of an early California newspaper and found that the general attitude towards the Japanese Americans was irritation verging on hostility, and that there was a correlation between newspaper attacks and periods of election years and economic depression. It is clear that the perceptions of the majority group, influenced by socio-economic and political events serve as another important factor in explaining the Japanese American experience.

ROLE OF JAPANESE AMERICANS

But, what about the role of Japanese Americans themselves in determining the ups and downs of their existence? Do victims play a role in determining their fate? Surely their culture, their organizations, their values, their family structures, their motives for immigration and their resources have had some say in their adaptation. Therefore, "what the group brings with them," is another factor in understanding their past, present and future in America.

But, the minority group does not exist in isolation so that it is the interaction between the dominant and the minority group that adds further explanatory power. As with most instances where there is a power differential, the influence of mainstream images is more influential. For example, prior to World War II, whatever the Japanese American did, majority group explanations took a negative slant. If the Japanese American worked hard and wanted to become a part of the mainstream, "they were too pushy and didn't know their place in the society"; if they preferred to worship separately and eat ethnic foods, "they weren't real Americans," and if they were forced into segregated housing and lived together they were "too clannish." World War II defined them as "dangerous enemies," to be placed in concentration camps, but several decades later they became a "model minority." Japanese Americans had changed, but not as much as the labelling from the dominant society so that their behavior is the result of the interaction between the majority and the minority, with the balance of power lying with the majority.

This is not to discount the "culture" of the ethnic group. The values, expectations and behaviors brought over from the old country are important, but contact with the mainstream leaves its mark on any immigrant group. As a consequence there is the emergence of a Japanese American who is different from a Japanese growing up in Japan, and who will also reflect the regional ambience of the American society. Imagine the birth of quadruplets—one raised in Tokyo, the second in Honolulu, a third in Los Angeles, and a fourth in New York. They would all look the same (some may even doubt that claim), but the chances are that each will reflect the "culture" of their local surroundings. Add Canada, Brazil and Chile, and one will appreciate the diversity spawned through different experiences. And yet, there may also be constant threads reflecting the "roots" of the ancestral culture.

Further, generational influences are important as well as social class, urban-rural settings and personality so that no one single variable can explain the complexities of the Japanese American experience. Terms such as acculturation and assimilation reflect the influences of the dominant culture, while the term, ethnic identity reflects the influences of the ethnic culture. It is inevitable that the Japanese American of today, as well as yesterday and of tomorrow is a product of a variety of influences.

VISIBILITY

The one constant in the Japanese experience up to now has been that of visibility. By possessing facial features, a body type and skin color different from the white majority, the issue of "melting" or "blending," in conjunction with American racism has created barriers that have yet to be resolved. The picture of a tall, blonde, blue eyed individual as the American prototype may be questioned, but its influence continues to create problems for those who do not possess such features. The rising rates of interracial marriage and the birth of bi-racial children may in the long run have an effect on the American prototype, but "looking different" in a race conscious society means that issues of identity, of "passing," of acculturation, assimilation and of acceptance remain, even though the individual may now be a fourth or fifth generation Japanese American, far removed from the ancestral culture. Even today, Japanese Americans hear such comments as, "Where did you learn to speak English so well?", or "Where are you really from?", when in reality most have been born and reared in the United States, have never been to Japan and in common with most Americans, are basically monolingual.

WHERE ARE WE NOW?

The question of where Japanese Americans as a group are at the closing decade of the twentieth century brings forth a variety of answers. Some see the roller coast on a high—that Japanese Americans are doing well educationally and economically and that their campaign for monetary redress and a presidential apology for the wartime evacuation has been successful. They can point to Japanese Americans in the halls of Congress, of high numbers attending prestigious universities, and a rising number of professionals and college professors.

Others take a less optimistic view—that in spite of high educational attainment, income figures remain lower than for the whites and that there is a glass ceiling on occupational mobility. Japanese Americans hold good jobs, but the higher echelon positions are still non-existent. Executive positions and those positions calling for decision making and for developing policy are still out of the reach of most of the group.

Then there are those who feel that racism and hate crimes remain as major problems still to be addressed, and that progress has been minimal. For example the newspaper, Pacific Citizen (1990) cites a Los Angeles County report that hate crimes against Asians hit a record level in 1990. Unfortunately, the report is not ethnic specific so that there is no mention of incidents involving Japanese Americans, but "Japan bashing" is common, so that it is probable that Japanese Americans were one of the major targets.

Then there is an aging population, as well as Japanese Americans with mental, economic, health and social problems. These issues remain relatively well hidden, and perhaps the cliche that Asian Americans have no problems is reinforced because they seldom are seen at dominant community facilities. The perception that Japanese American families prefer to handle their own problems may have validity, but there may come a time when family units can no longer afford to take such a stance.

RASHOMON PERSPECTIVE

An appropriate generalization is that we are dealing with the Rashomon perspective, which is based on the classic Japanese movie where different perceptions of a single event are made by different actors. The search for one reality and for one truth is elusive and illusory. Views of reality are shaped by position, experiences, emotions and needs, with variations in time, place and situation. A perception from one position may be valid from that point, but an observer from a different angle may provide a different perspective. Although we hope to cover various points of view in this book, it is obvious that our version of "reality" has been shaped by position, past experiences and socialization. The notion that only one view represents the truth and reality is difficult to defend, unless we assume that one actor has a monopoly on wisdom. What is more likely is that the "truth" is composed of power, of marshalling valid arguments, of providing convincing evidence, and the ability to influence decision makers (Kitano, 1991).

GENERAL BACKGROUND

It will be useful to briefly summarize the general background of the Japanese in the United States. The major Japanese immigration to the United States began in the 1880s (there was also a flow of laborers into the then territory of Hawaii), and continued until 1924 when all immigration from Japan and other Asian countries was blocked.

The initial immigrants, called Issei, or the first generation were relatively homogeneous in terms of age (young), sex (male) and general background, having originated in what may be thought of as rural Japan. They were later to be joined by females from Japan so that marriage and the beginning of family life was a part of their history.

Most Issei found employment as agricultural laborers or in small businesses, either working for other Japanese or establishing small shops of their own. In both agriculture and in small business, there was a general tendency towards serving fellow ethnics or other minority populations. They developed their own organizations, retained many of the Japanese customs, and most lived lives apart from the mainstream community. The few surviving Issei have achieved senior citizen status; my mother has lived to the ripe old age of 103, but finds that none of her peers are still alive.

The children of the Issei, the American born Nisei, or the second generation were generally born between 1910 and 1940 so that by the 1990s, many had also achieved senior citizen status. This generation, influenced by their parents' attitudes towards education, availed themselves fully of American educational facilities and became more "American," or perhaps less Japanese, than their Issei parents. But opportunities for this group were greatly restricted by prejudice and discrimination, especially up through World War II so that there were constant discussions concerning the desirability of integration, of assimilation and of pluralism. Or to put it more accurately, whether to become American or to retain their "Japaneseness" in the face of a hostile environment.

The discussions took on an even more meaningful flavor with the outbreak of World War II. All Japanese Americans, whether citizen or alien were evacuated from their homes along the West Coast and placed in "relocation centers," a euphemism for American's version of a concentration camp (Daniels, Taylor and Kitano, 1986). The evacuation had incalculable consequences, such as the destruction of the economic position of the group, the disruption of family life and the loss of homes and businesses. The question of remaining loyal to the country that had put them behind barbed wire was an especially trying one, given their treatment.

The evacuation, from 1942 to 1945, took away their West Coast residences and scattered them throughout the country, but by the 1950s, the majority had returned to the West Coast, especially to California.

The Sansei, or the third generation children of the Nisei were generally born during and after World War II, so that they provide the bulk of the young adult and the "adult marrieds." This population is almost totally acculturated, subject to certain distinctions which will be discussed in a later chapter.

GENERATIONAL STRATIFICATION

The background of the Japanese group, influenced greatly by discriminatory legislation which banned immigration from 1924 until after World War II, provides a convenient stratification by generation. The distinction by generation is especially familiar to Japanese Americans—the Issei, primarily Japan oriented; the Nisei, acculturated but with bi-cultural tendencies and the Sansei, primarily American in orientation. However, with advancing generations, such as the Yonsei (fourth) and Gosei (fifth), generational meanings may be fading so that an overall term, the Nikkei has come into use describing all Japanese born in the United States.

Another convenient category for describing the Japanese experience is chronological; the period between the initial immigration in the late 1880s to the cessation of immigration in 1924; the period between 1924 up to World War II; the wartime evacuation from 1942 to 1945, and the postwar period up to the present.

THEORETICAL MODELS

There are a variety of ways of explaining the relationship between the early Japanese immigrant and the dominant society. One central factor was racism and as Rex (1983) suggests situations involved in racism have the following three elements:

1. There is exploitation, oppression, and conflict which goes beyond what is considered as normal and peaceful in market situations;

2. The exploitation, oppression, and conflict is between groups rather than individuals and;

3. That the more dominant group justifies the ongoing system, using some form of deterministic theory, such as genetic or cultural superiority.

The Social Darwinist perspective indicates that racial differentiation leads to the improvement of races. Although it is difficult to identify any coherent body of theory that could be identified as Social Darwinism, Banton (1983:47) sees the following which he calls Selectionist Theory:

1. Evolution may be assisted if populations are kept apart so that they can develop their special capacities.

2. Racial prejudice and discrimination keep racial groups apart.

3. Racial categories are influenced by evolutionary processes through inheritance and selection.

The sociologist Park (Park and Burgess, 1921) wrote in the 1920s that man was a bearer of a double inheritance. There was racial inheritance, which was transmitted by interbreeding and biological inheritance, and a cultural one, which was transmitted through communication as a member of a social group. Banton (1983) summarizes the main features of Park's perspective:

1. Migration brings together, often in unequal relations, people who are racially different.

2. Because of competition, individuals become conscious of their features by which they are assigned different statuses.

3. People who are in the more dominant positions are unwilling to provide "equal opportunity" for those in less desirable positions. Instead, they tend to look down upon those who are less fortunate as a different category and therefore suited to belong to the "inferiors."

4. Prejudice serves the privileged group; it protects their interests and reinforces the "superior" to the "inferior" category.

Gordon (1964) presents a model of assimilation and integration into American life. He posits a variety of stages, including structural, marital, and identification assimilation. In a later publication (1978), he sees four types of societies with regard to ethnic orientation: (1) racist; (2) assimilationist; (3) liberal pluralist, and (4) corporate pluralist. Liberal pluralism refers to societies where majority group programs for racial equality are more voluntary as against corporate pluralism, where there is a official recognition of racial and ethnic groups as legally constituted entities with official societal standing.

There are a variety of other theoretical models; Cox (1948) provides an early Marxist analysis of American race relations; Blauner (1972) introduces a domestic colonial perspective; Bonacich (1972) writes about the "split labor market" which sees ethnic conflict as a part of the capitalist economy, while George (1984) present a variety of perspectives including ethnic group, caste, colonial and Marxist models.

The domination model (Kitano, 1991) and the domestic colonial model will be discussed in more detail in Chapter 2 and 13.

ORGANIZATION OF THE BOOK

The book will be divided into several sections. The first section will deal with a history of the Japanese in the United States. It will be divided into several chapters; Chapter 2, which draws heavily upon my book, *Japanese Americans; The Evolution of a Subculture*, will cover the period from early immigration to 1924; Chapter 3 will emphasize the period up to World War II and Chapter 4 will address the wartime evacuation (1942-1945). Chapter 5 will be devoted to the closing of the camps and Chapter 6 will cover up to the present time.

Section II of the book addresses the following: Chapter 7, the Community and it culture; Chapter 8, the Community and its organizations; Chapter 9, the Community and its families. Chapter 10 will be a chapter on Hawaii, and Chapter 11 will discuss ethnic identity and the role of women.

Section III includes, Chapter 12, the present status of Japanese Americans, and Chapter 13 will provide a summary and conclusions.

BIBLIOGRAPHY

Banton, Michael (1983). *Racial and Ethnic Competition*. Cambridge: Cambridge University Press.

Blauner, Robert (1972). *Racial Oppression in America*. New York: Harper and Row.

Bonacich, Edna (1972). "A Theory of Middleman Minorities." American Sociological Review 38 (October 1973): 583-94.

Cox, Oliver (1948). *Caste, Class and Race: A Study in Social Dynamics*. New York: Monthly Review Press.

Daniels, Taylor, and Kitano (1986). *Japanese Americans, From Relocation to Redress*. Salt Lake City, Utah; University of Utah Press, xxi, 216p.

George, Herman Jr. (1984). *American Race Relations Theory*. Lanham, Maryland: University of Maryland Press.

Gordon, Milton (1978). *Human Nature, Class, and Ethnicity*. New York: Oxford University Press.

Gordon, Milton M. (1964). *Assimilation in American Life*. New York: Oxford University Press.

Kitano, Harry H.L. (1991) *Race Relations*. Engelwood Cliffs, New Jersey: Prentice Hall, Inc.

Kitano, Harry H.L. (1974). "Japanese Americans: The Development of a Middleman Minority," Pacific Historical Review, November, Vol. XLIII, No. 4, 500-519.

The Pacific Citizen. (1990). Los Angeles, California, Sept. 14, Page 1.

Park, Robert, Burgess, E.W. (1921). *Introduction to the Science of Sociology*. Chicago: University of Chicago Press.

Reynolds, C. W. (1927). "Oriental-White Relations in Santa Clara County," Stanford University, Ph.D. dissertation.

Rex (1983). *Race Relations in Sociological Theory*. London: Routledge and Kegan, Paul.

CHAPTER 2

BACKGROUND OF IMMIGRATION

There is no one, simple answer to the question of why people leave their homes to go to another country. The most often mentioned reason deals with economic issues, so that the combination of hard times at home and better job opportunities in the new constitute a major "push and pull." But then there is the accompanying question, "Why doesn't everyone facing poor employment prospects leave for better opportunities abroad?" So additional explanations are necessary, such as personal and family problems. I have heard (in hush hush tones), of men leaving wives and families in order to start a new life in the new country or of "running away" from disorganized and ineffective families. Other reasons include avoiding the Japanese draft, poor position concerning family inheritance, a search for adventure, better educational opportunities, and boredom and dissatisfaction with the relatively rigid roles available in the Japanese society. Some even indicate that getting on a boat and leaving for a foreign country "just happened," and for many females, it was their duty to join their husbands, or husbands to be in the new country. Therefore, although the economic motive may have been the strongest, reasons for moving from one country to another cannot be reduced to any one variable.

The "push-pull" model is the most commonly used explanation for immigration. Pushes away from the home country—poverty, unemployment, hard times, family and personal problems, combined with the pulls of the new—jobs, better opportunities, and a new start indicate the direction of the movement. An additional factor is that of available transportation, especially in terms of time and cost.

There are other models of immigration. Cheng and Bonacich (1984) view immigration, race and ethnic relations in the context of the world economy. Capitalistic systems require cheap labor; cheap labor lies in less developed countries, so that migrant workers, contract laborers and immigrants provide an important supply of workers. Therefore, the flow of labor and migration is from the less developed countries to those with advanced technologies so that laborers left Asia to come to America, rather than from America to Asia. It should also be emphasized that when Europeans and Americans went to Africa and Asia, they went as conquerors and colonists, rather than as immigrants, so that they maintained their culture and life styles.

But for those immigrants who come as laborers, there are a number of universal questions which have seldom been answered satisfactorily. Will they be given opportunities to become an integral part of the dominant society or will they be restricted to the lowest part of the stratification system? If their labor is no longer needed, what will happen to them? And finally, if they have children, what will their future be?

Questions to the host culture are variations of the above. Will they erect barriers and boundaries through prejudice, discrimination and racism, which will keep the newcomers at a perpetual disadvantage, or will they provide an open society so that the newcomers will be able to achieve a degree of equality? As we will see in the case of the Japanese, they did not enter an open America—formidable barriers were placed in their search for a better life.

JAPAN

There were a number of important events in Japan, which provides a background for understanding Japanese immigration. The Meiji Restoration in 1868 opened the trend towards westernization. Prior to that time during the Tokugawa Period (1603-1867), Japan was essentially closed, both to people coming into the country and for people going out. The Meiji Restoration meant the collapse of feudalism, adoption of western science and learning, new economic and financial policies, a new national defense structure, changes in fiscal policy including the establishment of banks, and compulsory education (Yanaga, 1949).

This period also saw Japan involved in international relations, including the Sino-Japanese War (1894-1895), which was the prelude of Japan's exertion of hegemony over Korea in 1910; the Russo-Japanese War of 1906, which saw the first defeat of a European power by an Asian nation in modern history. However, although the government clamped on rigid censorship on the grounds of military necessity, and the public was given only what the government wanted them to know, victory was at a tremendous cost. There were severe economic, financial and manpower strains which strained the nation to almost a breaking point (Yanaga:313).

Although most of the world applauded Japan for her overwhelming victory, public opinion in the United States, which had been previously been favorable towards Japan for over fifty years, began to change. The emergence of a strong Japan was seen as a threat to the interests of the United States and other European powers in China and Manchuria, so that it cast a blight upon American-Japanese relationships, including questions of immigration and Japanese expansionism. Japan had entered the "modern" world, and was viewed as a "non-white" competitor to the established white powers of that era (Yanaga, 1949).

Internally, there were labor problems including the depression of 1897 which brought a wave of shutdowns, unemployment and government suppression of the labor movement which had active links to socialism. It was a period of rapid change and unrest which provided fertile grounds for potential immigration.

THE EARLY YEARS

In terms of the history of our country, Japanese Americans are relative newcomers. Whereas the first colonists from England arrived in the 1600s, significant immigration of the Japanese began several centuries later. Therefore, they arrived in the United States that had already been settled for over 200 years, carrying with it the stamp of England, and other Anglo Saxon traditions.

Feagin (1989) emphasizes the importance of this "British stamp"; they were the original settlers; they came here as *colonists* which included the invasion and subordination of the native population, and they had numerical superiority for the first few decades. The political, legal, economic and social welfare systems were based on English models. The English language, religious values, the work ethic, the emerging capitalistic system, the pursuit of profit, and music and art tastes were all linked to the English tradition.

Later arrivals would have also been colonists if they had conquered the English who were already here, and placed them in subordinate positions. But history shows that the later groups came here as *immigrants*, which meant playing subordinate roles, some temporary, others almost permanent as they faced what the English colonists had developed. It is important to remember this background, for this is the society that immigrant groups entered and encountered, so that questions of goals, of adaptation, of acculturation, integration, and pluralism can best be understood in this context.

There is general agreement that although there were isolated cases of Japanese landing somewhere along the West Coast in earlier times, the first significant immigration began in the late 1880s (Daniels, 1962; Kitano and Daniels, 1988; Ichioka, 1988; Takaki, 1989, Chan, 1991). They were largely young men, eager to work hard at whatever opportunities were offered, but also unfamiliar with the new country, its language and its culture. As one consequence, getting to know and help each other—the social and economic support systems, based on ethnicity were important, so that terms such as group cohesion and group organization were important in aiding the transition from the old country to the new.

In 1900, the census counted almost 25,000 Japanese, primarily on the West Coast; by 1920, there were more than 110,000. In accordance with the "roller coaster" relationship between the United States and Japan, welcome soon turned to unwelcome. By 1924, with the passage of an Immigration Act, the United States closed its doors to Japanese, as well as to other Asian immigrants. The image of being overrun by "yellow hordes" was too powerful of an emotion to be resisted by the American public and politicians alike.

THE CHINESE AND THE JAPANESE

Looking back over one hundred years ago, it is no surprise that the initial welcome soon turned into unwelcome, since the Japanese followed and were recipients of the treatment of the Chinese. However, the peace treaty between the United States and Japan signed in 1854 opened on an optimistic note between the two nations:

> There shall be a perfect, permanent and universal peace, and a sincere and cordial amity between the United States of America on one part, and the Empire of Japan on the other, and between their people respectively, without exception of persons and places (Lanman, 1872:24).

And for several decades after the treaty, cordiality and friendship prevailed. When the first Japanese ambassadors arrived in San Francisco in 1872, they were greeted with enthusiasm and good will. Fashionable ladies flocked to admire the ceremonial robes of the visitors and entertained them at lavish dinners and dances. Newspapers praised the Japanese as products of an intelligent nation and prescribed that no impediment nor difficulty, either social, moral, political or religious be placed in their way. There was curiosity and respect; not fear of a rising Asiatic power. Part of the reason for these attitudes may have generated from the fact that Admiral Perry and his black gunboats had opened the doors of Japan in their visit in 1853, and permanently changed the Japanese way of life. It was natural that many Japanese looked to the

United States for the knowledge and technology that might help them become a modern nation, and it was to the United States that many young Japanese came for early education and training.

The majority of the first Japanese who came were from the upper classes and most of them attended schools and universities along the Eastern seaboard. They were generally industrious, studious, and shy. An excerpt of a letter from one of them to his father illustrated one attitude toward American life:

> I am over 21 years old, but mentally a boy. After I have studied for 5 or 6 years longer, I may be fitted for parties, drinking and smoking and dancing. . . . I do not think these are accomplishments in which my country is anxious to have me successful (Lanman, 1872:71).

Census figures placed the number of Japanese in the United States in 1880 at 148. Most of these were students who would eventually be returning to Japan. However, the initial contact of some Americans along the Eastern Seaboard with Japanese who represented the nobility and upper classes may have been important in shaping the experiences of the Japanese who later settled in this area.

From 1885 on, thousands of young Japanese men came to Hawaii and the West Coast, especially to California. In one sense they came to the "wrong state at the wrong time." They came after the "Chinese problem" had been "successfully" solved. It should be recalled that full-scale Chinese immigration occurred after the discovery of gold in California in 1849 and as early as 1852 the governor of California advised that restrictions be placed against them. His reasons have a universal racist ring—Chinese coolies lowered the standard of living, they were inassimilable, they were heathens, they came only to take American money, and, unless checked, they would eventually overrun the state.

Cases of violence against the Chinese were common. For example, there was a massacre in Los Angeles in 1871. The problem started when two police officers, seeking to break up a Tong war were seriously wounded and another killed outright.

> A mob of a thousand persons armed with pistols, guns, knives, and ropes immediately marched into the Chinese section, seized victims without any attempt to discriminate between the innocent and guilty, overpowered the officers of the law who were seeking to disperse the crowd, and hanged at least 22 Chinamen (sic) before the evil business came to an end (Cleland, 1922:48).

There were other large scale killings such as in Rock Springs, Wyoming in 1885 when twenty-nine Chinese were murdered, their homes destroyed, and their belongings scattered (Crane and Larson, 1940).

At any rate, the cry of "the Chinaman must go" became a popular rallying point, particularly in California. In 1879, 154,638 Californians voted for Chinese exclusion, and only 883 voted against it (Gulick, 1914:35). Although immigration legislation was the province of the Federal Government, the feelings of Californians regarding the Chinese was clear. The California strategy was two-fold; first was the use of local harassment in order to make life intolerable for the Chinese and second, to use whatever legal means at their disposal. The former technique, although more dramatic and emotional, was never as effective as the latter, as the Japanese were to discover during World War II. Institutionalized discrimination with legal backing is permanent and damaging, and has a deleterious effect on all members of the oppressed group.

By the 1890s the effective combination of harassment, massacre, restrictions and local and national legislation had in effect "solved" the Chinese problem. No more Chinese were coming into the country and many were leaving, but between 1890 and 1900, 22,000 Japanese came to the American mainland.

SIMILARITIES AND DIFFERENCES

As Kitano and Daniels (1988) indicate, there were a number of similarities, as well as differences between the early Chinese and the early Japanese. They both had similar phenotypes, so that it was difficult to identify one as either Chinese or Japanese, although there are some canny observers who claim that they can differentiate between the two. Each group was composed primarily of young males, and they worked at physically difficult, low-prestige, and low-paying jobs. The majority of both groups were composed of hard working peasants and farmers who arrived with minimal industrial skills, but who showed a high willingness to work at whatever jobs that were available.

But there were also differences between the two groups. Perhaps the most important was the different stages of development between the two countries. China, in the early part of the twentieth century was a weak nation that was growing weaker, and was often at the mercy of more powerful outside nations. Japan, on the other hand, had begun the trend towards modernization with the Meiji Period (1869), which included compulsory education, industrialization and the growth of military power. As a consequence, the Japanese immigrant had behind them a government that demanded growing respect, whereas protests from the Chinese government concerning the bad treatment of its immigrants was ignored. However, it should also be noted that the Japanese government was more interested in protecting their image and prestige as a nation, rather than the civil rights of its emigrants to America (Ichioka, 1988; Kitano and Daniels, 1988).

Another important difference was the beginning of family life for the Japanese. Although many came to Hawaii as "contract laborers," and others with a sojourners orientation, permanent settlement was also on the minds of many. My father, who came in 1906 had permanent settlement on his mind, for in spite of racism and discrimination, he felt that he had a better chance to make a living in America than in Japan. As a consequence, there was the influx of Japanese women, often referred to as "picture brides," because many of the initial contacts were through the exchange of photographs. The image, as perceived in pictures, and the actual reality of seeing one's soon to be spouse in person must have come as a shock to many.

Although it is interesting to hear some of the chuckles from present day American audiences when mentioning marriage through the exchange of pictures ("quaint," "awful," and "strange" are typical comments), there were rational reasons behind this procedure. As Chan (1991) indicates, there was the expense of the long, boat trip to Japan to find a bride, and there was the fear of Issei males losing their deferred military draft status if they remained in Japan for over thirty days. There were also friends and relatives involved in the process of selecting brides so that the would be couples were not totally unknown to family members (marriages in Japan are typically between families, rather than individuals), and even today, dating and marital relationships may begin through an exchange of photographs.

Anti-Japanese groups became concerned about the influx of these brides, especially since they began to have children, so that tales, some bordering on fantasy about the alleged fertility of the Japanese added another page to the growing book of racist literature. The Japanese consul in San Francisco, responding to the anti-Japanese sentiments, recommended to Tokyo that it suspend the issuance of passports to picture brides, and in 1920 the picture bride influx was suspended (Chan, 1991:108).

The important factor in the history of Japanese immigration is that the arrival of wives, including the "picture brides," meant that there was the beginning of family life and American born children—the second generation Nisei. For example, in 1910, there were approximately 4,500 Nisei, but by 1920, there were almost 30,000 (Chan, 1991:109). High birth rates for young couples, especially for those involved in agriculture are not unusual, but added fuel to the demagogic charges that they "bred like rabbits."

DISCRIMINATION

It is important to differentiate the various types of discriminatory practices, since each plays a role in maintaining separation and disadvantage in relation to the mainstream. Feagin (1989:15) suggest four types of discrimination—isolate, small-group, direct institutionalized, and indirect institutionalized.

Type A: Isolate Discrimination

Isolate discrimination refers to harmful actions taken by a majority group member against members of the minority. It was common and widespread in the early part of the century, and no doubt still exists today. A waitress may serve the Japanese individual gruffly; a salesperson may be rude or indifferent, and old-timers, such as my father, have told me of being pushed off the sidewalk because it was "reserved for whites." Although on a theoretical level one can indicate that these individual acts are not that significant, in an overall look at race relations, it is irritating, and is a constant reminder to the victim that he or she is of inferior status.

Type B: Small-Group Discrimination

Small-group discrimination refers to harmful actions taken intentionally by a small number of like-minded dominant group individuals against members of a minority group. The actions may be overt—floggings, lynchings, and church bombings are examples against blacks in the South. The massacres against the Chinese is another example of this category.

Or, small group discrimination may take the form of programs, such as the Exclusion League five-point program adopted in 1919 which recommended, (1) the cancellation of the Gentlemen's Agreement, (2) the exclusion of "picture brides", (3) the exclusion of all Japanese as immigrants, (4) the conformation and legalization of the policy that Asiatics shall forever be barred from United States citizenship, and (5) an amendment to the Federal Constitution providing that no child born in the United States shall be given the rights of citizenship unless both parents are of a race eligible for citizenship (Yanaga, 1949:440).

Small group discrimination is especially effective if their message becomes a popular one and influences dominant group members and politicians to take a more active stand in maintaining the "outsider" status of minority group members. The first four items of the Exclusion League program became a part of Federal policy and item 4 lasted for the next several decades.

Type C: Direct Institutionalized Discrimination

Type C discrimination refers to community prescribed actions that are intentional and have been in practice continuously so that they have become institutionalized. Country clubs, social groups and exclusive schools are examples—none of the many Issei I have known ever dreamed of applying for membership in such groups. Perhaps their only contact was as lower level employees.

Of more importance for the Japanese was a series of legal actions which kept them at a competitive disadvantage with dominant group members. The category of "aliens ineligible for citizenship" was an especially damaging one, since it was based on federal naturalization statutes which made Japanese and other Asians ineligible for naturalization and to become American citizens. The phrase was used in California with the infamous Alien Land Acts of 1913 and 1920, which denied those "aliens ineligible for citizenship" the right to lease or own land for agricultural purposes. The California law in 1920 was passed by a 3 to 1 margin, and soon thereafter, similar legislation was passed in a number of other states, including Washington, Arizona, and Oregon.

Other discriminatory actions included housing restrictions through racial covenants, the lack of opportunity in many occupations, anti-miscegenation laws, and the denial of use of such services as barber shops, medical treatment and public facilities. One consequence of these discriminatory acts was the development of parallel facilities in the Japanese community, which will be discussed further in the chapter on the Japanese community.

Type D: Indirect Institutionalized Discrimination

Types A, B, and C discrimination are directly linked to prejudice. Type D is different in that discrimination is not directly linked to prejudice, although the differentiation is often difficult to ascertain. Regulations on seniority (last hired, first hired), and "objective standards," such as scores on college entrance examinations may not be directly linked to prejudice but may be effective in limiting the opportunities for minority group members.

There are various combinations of the categories. The picture of the dominant group and their interlocking political, economic, and social organizations with their intentional and unintentional practices, the desire to protect their privileges, and a mixture of prejudice and racism, provide a cumulative picture of the barriers of discrimination that were a part of Japanese life (Kitano, 1991).

The anti-Japanese movement was fed by a series of other discriminatory incidents. An especially visible one occurred in 1906 when the San Francisco School Board attempted to force Japanese pupils to attend the long-established segregated school for the Chinese. The matter came to the attention of President Theodore Roosevelt who mediated the dispute himself; he called San Francisco officials to come to the White House and influenced them to back down. In turn, he promised to negotiate with Japan to halt further immigration.

The result was the Gentlemen's Agreement of 1907-1908 whereby Tokyo promised not to issue passports to Japanese "laborers." Both governments agreed that those who were established and self-support-ing could bring over wives and other family members. So, instead of male laborers, the next decade saw the influx of Japanese women so that what was once an unbalanced male to female ratio, began to take on a more balanced hue. Many Americans felt that they had been betrayed— that it was their understanding that all Japanese immigration was to be closed.

But the desire to halt all immigration from Japan and Asia was soon fulfilled with the passage of the 1924 Immigration Act which denied the entry of any person of Japanese (or other Asian) ancestry to legally immigrate to the United States. Even a token quota was denied them. The ban on immigration was a major victory for racists, nativists, and exclusionists, and there is little doubt that it was resented by an insulted and bewildered Japan, which, having understood that it was to become an important member of the family of nations, did not now understand this slap in the face. Some of the feelings of Japan are summarized by Ichihashi (1932:313). The country felt that discrimination based on race violated all principles of justice and fairness; that the implication that Japanese could not become assimilated was based on false assumptions; and that furthermore, the United States had violated the "Gentleman's Agreement," one part of which specified that the United States would not adopt discriminatory legislation against Japan.

The 1924 Act undoubtedly strengthened the hands of the militarists and right wing nationalists in Japan. Mosley (1966), in writing about the life of Emperor Hirohito, mentions this act as one important link in the chain of events that eventually led to the Japanese attack on Pearl Harbor in 1941.

In summary, the early years were characterized by unrest and change in Japan; racism in the United States; the initial immigration of male laborers, followed by the Gentleman's Agreement limiting the immigra-tion of "laborers"; the influx of wives who were not "laborers," and the birth of the Nisei, or second generation who were citizens by birth. The immigrants did not enter into an open society, rather they entered into an America which fostered their domination through barriers of racism and discrimination.

Attacks against the Japanese—"Japan bashing," was based on race (inassimilable), on nationality (land-hungry, imperialist, warlike Japan), on culture and styles of life (mysterious, exotic, difficult to understand), on personal habits (sly, greedy, dishonest), on economic competition (cheap wages), on sexual conduct (breed like rabbits), and on whatever other grounds that could appeal to human emotions. The Japanese group was a target for stereotyping and scapegoating. They had very few friends, while their enemies included politicians, labor, management, conservatives, and liberals.

BIBLIOGRAPHY

1. Bonacich, Edna and Cheng, Lucie (1984). "Introduction: A Theoretical Orientation to International Labor Migration," in *Labor Immigration under Capitalism*. Cheng, Lucie and Edna Bonacich (eds). Berkeley, Los Angeles: University of California Press. 1-56.

2. Chan, Sucheng (1991). *Asian Americans*. Boston: Twayne.

3. Cleland, R.G. (1922). *A History of California, the American Period*. New York: The McMillan Co.

4. Crane, Paul and Larson, Alfred (1940). "The Chinese Massacre," *Annals of Wyoming* 12, 47-55.

5. Daniels, Roger (1962). *The Politics of Prejudice*. Berkeley: University of California Press.

6. Feagin, Joe (1989). *Racial and Ethnic Relations*. Englewood Cliffs, New Jersey: Prentice-Hall.

7. Gulick, Sidney L. (1914). *The American Japanese Problem*. New York: Charles Scribner.

8. Ichihashi, Y. (1932). *Japanese in the United States*. Stanford: Stanford University Press.

9. Ichioka, Yuji (1988). *The Issei*. New York: The Free Press.

10. Kitano, Harry H.L. (1991). *Race Relations*. 4th ed. Englewood Cliffs, New Jersey: Prentice-Hall.

11. Kitano, Harry H.L. and Daniels, Roger (1988) *Asian Americans*. Engelwood Cliffs, New Jersey: Prentice-Hall.

12. Lanman, C. (1872). *The Japanese in America*. London: Longmans, Green, Reader and Dyer.

13. Mosley, Leonard (1966). *Hirohito*. Englewood Cliffs, New Jersey: Prentice-Hall.

14. Takaki, Ron (1989). *Strangers from a Different Shore*. Boston: Little Brown and Co.

15. Yanaga, Chitoshi (1949). *Japan Since Perry*. New York: McGraw Hill.

CHAPTER 3

UP TO WORLD WAR II

It would appear that the demands of the most vociferous anti-Japanese backers had been met by 1924. There were no longer any new Japanese immigrants arriving in the United States—that spigot had been turned off, and those that were here were hemmed in by discriminatory barriers or "iron cages" (Takaki, 1979). The "Japanese problem" was ostensibly solved, or at least under control, and a reasonable observer might expect that the hatred and hostility towards the Japanese immigrant might diminish and eventually disappear.

But such was not the case. Previous attitudes, shaped by the mass media were hard to erase. For example, the *Sacramento Bee*, an influential California Valley newspaper printed the following interview on May 1, 1910:

> Now the Jap is a wily an' crafty individual—more so than the Chink . . . they try to buy in the neighborhood where there are nothing but white folks.
>
> . . . The Jap will always be an undesirable. They are lower in the scale of civilization than the whites and will never become our equals. They have no morals. Why I have seen one Jap woman sleepin' with a dozen Jap men. . . . Nobody trusts a Jap.

The vitriol from the press, as seen by these early remarks, was one factor in keeping alive anti-Japanese feelings. Anti-Japanese and anti-Asian movies was another, and politicians found it popular to engage in "Japan-bashing," a current term for an age old sentiment.

But for the exclusionists, the 1924 Bill was only a partial solution, because by 1940, there were still more than 126,000 persons of Japanese ancestry in the United States, and 157,000 more in the territory of Hawaii. And the nation of Japan had become even more of a threat to the hegemony of the Western World so that there was ample ammunition to catch the attention of the American public towards the "yellow peril."

JAPAN

The 1920s and 30s saw Japan involved in international agreements, conflicts, and expansionist policies, accompanied by political maneuvering and military actions. It saw the rise of nationalism, fascism, and Japan's development into a formidable military power.

Yanaga (1949) indicates that Japanese fascism was a reaction against Western influences, including socialism, liberalism, and communism. Western influences were seen as a threat to the pattern of Japanese life and culture. The nation became authoritarian, antidemocratic, suspicious of the League of Nations, and was not afraid of using military solutions.

The ultimate goal of Japan was the achievement of self sufficiency, and for equitable distribution of the world's resources. As such it came into direct conflict with the colonial policies of the Western powers.

A number of incidents placed Japan as the number one enemy of the United States. Japan's expansion into the Asian continent with the invasion of Manchuria in 1931; the China incident of 1937 and the subsequent war in China; Japan's walkout of the League of Nations in 1933, and its friendship with Germany provoked moral outrage in the United States. And the inability of Americans to differentiate between the actions of the Japanese nation and the Japanese Americans meant difficult times for the group residing in the United States.

Friedman and Lebard (1991) indicate that the conflict between Japan and the United States was virtually inevitable, ever since the time that the two countries became the major actors in the Pacific. For the U.S., the Spanish-American War of 1898 which gave America the Philippines made it a Pacific power; for Japan it was the Russo-Japanese War of 1904-05 which made Japan the major naval power in the Pacific. Therefore, conflicts included a combination of geography and location, expansionist ideologies, population growth, (especially in Japan); the search for raw materials, the past colonial experiences of European powers in the Pacific, and ethnocentric ideologies. Both countries also shared in common, arrogance and insecurity which reinforced ethnocentric ideologies based on fear of each other. Both countries were and continue to be commercial regimes with their future tied in trade; thus there were conflicts over markets and resources. This background lead to World War II, and the authors believe that many of these issues remain unresolved up to the present.

In a prophetic volume, dated May 1, 1926, *The Survey* focused on East-West issues. In the introduction, reference was made to looking out expectantly across the ocean, because it was in the Pacific and around the Pacific that things were happening and where the news would be made. The sociologist, Robert Park, the director a Race Relations Survey, was chosen to direct the issue, and the monograph claims that for the first time findings were interpreted in terms of "oriental (sic) migration and settlement, on the land and in industry, singly and in communities, the persistence of ancient institutions and the rise of the native-born of oriental parentage" (p. 135). The volume points out, rather dramatically, that it is across the Pacific where the two frontiers meet; the eastern fringe where the Asiatic is the stranger, the western fringe where the American is the alien.

After 1924

By the late 1920s and 1930s, there were many Nisei, born and raised in America and who were citizens, as compared to the Issei who were permanent aliens, "ineligible for citizenship." But citizenship did not erase the visibility of race, which set them, as well as other "non-whites," apart from the Caucasian mainstream. Nisei could dress, talk and act like the average American—they enjoyed the same "hit" songs, the same movies, and talked and read about issues that were a part of Americana, yet they were unable to escape the racial prejudice and discrimination that was such a central part of the lives of their Issei parents.

Nisei as a group seemed much more vulnerable to racism than their parents—Issei expected to face discrimination and had modest expectations of participating in the mainstream, but Nisei, born and raised in America, had heard and read about equality and justice while attending American schools, and therefore had high expectations concerning their role in American society.

The Second Generation Japanese Problem

The most comprehensive study of the early Nisei was appropriately titled "The Second Generation Japanese Problem." The study was financed by a $40,000 grant from the Board of Trustees of the Carnegie Corporation of New York in 1929. Researchers at Stanford University were to conduct a study of the educational and occupational opportunities offered to American citizens of the "oriental races." The study was essentially that of the Nisei and three monographs were published by Stanford University entitled: *Vocational Aptitudes of Second-Generation Japanese in the United States; Japanese in California;* and *Public School education of Second Generation Japanese in California* (Strong, 1934).

The study was based on personal interviews of 9,416 Japanese living in California in the early 1930s. The family was made the unit for interviewing, and sampling was by specific districts. The largest number of interviews was in San Francisco and Los Angeles, although there was also representation in rural areas such as Walnut Grove, the Fresno area and Santa Clara County. The sample represented 9.94 percent of the entire Japanese population in California. It should be noted that although I have lived and have had contact with numerous Nisei throughout my life, I have yet to run across one who was interviewed by the Stanford researchers.

The basic theme of the interviewees was one of discouragement and despair. For example, Kazuo Kawai, born in Japan but receiving his collegiate training in California, writes in 1926:

> Our community is not self sufficient. We can't stand off and live our own lives. We've got to find a place in American society in order to survive. And yet, no matter what our qualifications may be, evidently the only place where we are wanted is in positions that no Americans would care to fill—menial positions as house-servants, gardeners, vegetable peddlers, continually "yes, ma'am"-ing (Strong, 1934:2).

Strong notes that seven years after this statement, Kawai was appointed assistant professor of geography at UCLA. As far as is known, he was probably the only professor of Japanese ancestry in the University of California system.

Kawai also wrote about the frustration of the Nisei. Nisei began to wonder about the value of education (the development of human capital), so that some questioned the importance of preparing oneself through education in order to maximize one's earnings potential.

> So many of my friends are giving up the fight. "Why get an education?" they say. Why try to do anything at all? Probably we were meant to be just a servile class? (Strong, 1934:12).

Kawai saw the development of a new, shiftless, pleasure-seeking second generation element, rather different from the industrious, hard working Issei. Or, there were some "nicer" individuals who had turned to the church or other sources to drown out their sorrows. They held an unrealistic, optimistic "goody goody" outlook; that if the Nisei stayed in their place, and worked hard in order to please the Americans, the Americans, with their Christian humanity, would throw them a few crumbs to ease their condition.

However, Kawai concluded that the hope for the future lay in those Nisei who got the best education possible, who would hold onto their ideals, and who would work continuously for change. He also felt that in order for the Nisei to succeed, they had to be better than everyone else.

The observations by Strong and Kawai are familiar to most Nisei who grew up in this era. I became a teenager in 1939, and I remember observing my older sisters and their friends as they faced "double jeopardy"—of having Japanese ancestry, and of growing up during the depression years. Discussions of boyfriends, good jobs, education, and the future were tinged with frustration, envy, and a false optimism. Comparisons with Caucasian peers usually ended with unfavorable conclusions—"they" lived in big houses, dressed well, took vacations and were the "in" crowd in schools and in society.

There was frustration concerning the rigidity of Issei parents and the lack of employment opportunities—a good job might mean working in one of the dry goods stores along Grant Avenue in San Francisco, where pay was minimal and one had to dress in suits and bow to Issei owners, even though the worker might have a degree from the University of California.

An interview with Patrick Okura (1991) provided further insights into growing up in the 1930s. Patrick graduated from UCLA in 1933, was a varsity baseball player and was one of the few, if not the only Nisei employee in the Los Angeles County Civil Service system. He related that he tried to convince other Nisei, including those with very impressive backgrounds, to apply for government jobs, but the general feeling was that they stood no chance for employment. Therefore, a generation of very talented individuals continued to work at fruit stands and at small ethnic establishments.

Okura also mentioned that he had heard of Kawai and of the Stanford study, but was not intimately involved in any phase of that project. Given the present impressive growth of UCLA, it was also interesting to hear of the campus as located in the "farm lands of Westwood," and of the inability of the Nisei to find decent housing in the then rural atmosphere. Later to be developed Japanese sororities also found that housing discrimination meant that they could not buy a "house" in Westwood, so that they were a sorority without a house near the campus. By the time that housing restrictions were ended, sometime in the 1970s, housing prices in Westwood were sky high and unaffordable so that the Japanese American (now viewed as Asian) fraternities and sororities still have no "houses." A final touch is provided by one of the interviews by Strong (p. 32) where a Nisei hopes to "get even" for discrimination by declaring he would like to break into Westwood, then an impossible task. But, changes do occur; the 1990 U.S. Census reported that although there was a slight population decline in the Westside of Los Angeles, the Asian population living in Westwood had more than doubled to 13.7 percent (Chazanov, 1991).

Perhaps the best opportunities were in the professions and small business—medicine, pharmacy, dentistry, and "Mom and Pop" stores, where one could make a living, primarily with clients from the ethnic community, or from other disadvantaged groups. Government jobs, teaching and other mainstream opportunities were generally closed; it was only well after World War II that these positions were open to the Japanese. Agriculture was also an important avenue as will be emphasized in a later chapter.

But life, using the common error of *presentism* (using today's reality for interpreting past events), prior to 1941 seemed to be simple. My family was probably typically American; we listened to Jack Benny and Fred Allen; we tried to guess what songs would make the Lucky Strike Hit Parade; we griped about our immigrant parents and generally ignored world events, unless it related to Japan. As long as there was food on the table (my sisters were especially good at introducing American dishes—spaghetti, ham, cakes, and pies), so much so, that I preferred eating American meals (yoh-shoku), rather than Japanese (nihon shoku) food. It is only recently that my taste for ethnic cuisine has become stronger.

Nisei generally knew each other; there were clubs, and organizations that served athletic and social needs; there were the segregated churches, both Christian and Buddhist providing for religious and social needs, and there were ethnic festivals, picnics, parades, and language schools that reinforced a cultural identity. But it should also be noted that the bulk of Nisei activities and organizations were based on American, rather than Japanese models.

GO EAST, OR WEST, YOUNG MAN?

Given the lack of opportunity in California, a logical question would be, "Why didn't the Nisei go east towards the Atlantic Coast, or west, towards Japan?" Going east was certainly a possibility, but as Strong (p. 4) indicates, Americans living along the East Coast never understood the West Coast problem with the Japanese. The stereotypes and the lack of personal contact were too strong; Chinese were usually laundrymen and Japanese were foreign diplomats. Yet, Easterners could not tell the two groups apart on the basis of physical appearance. They, along with most Americans, did not believe that "Orientals" born in this country were American citizens. And the idea that jobs would be awaiting Japanese Americans away from the West Coast were clearly unrealistic.

The idea of going East might have been attractive to some Nisei, but most of them were too young, did not have the capital to relocate and were hesitant to leave their families and the ethnic community. There was the fear of the unknown; interestingly enough the wartime evacuation "forced" many Nisei to start life anew, away from the West Coast, and there have been some who told me that they wished that they had made this move much earlier in their lives.

Going west, meant going to Japan. Kawai discusses this possibility, indicating that many Americans (in the midst of the depression), envied him because he had an American education and could "go back" to Japan to find a job. His answer was that how could people go back to a place where most had never been. Then he continues:

> As to having advantage over the people of Japan, we have the wonderful advantage of being quite unable to speak their language or read their papers, of being totally ignorant of their customs, history, or traditions, of holding different ideals, of thinking in different ways (Strong, 1934:7).

He adds that a white American would be excused if he or she did not speak Japanese well, whereas a Nisei, with a Japanese face would be expected to speak fluent Japanese. The Nisei look like the Japanese, but culturally, they are American. Even in present day Japan, Nisei and Sansei, with their Japanese features are expected to speak the language fluently, whereas whites are generally excused for not knowing the language and the culture.

Another option, which included no movement in either direction was staying put and working in the ethnic community, or its variation, working with other ethnic communities. My father opened a hotel in Chinatown; other Issei ran small restaurants and grocery stores in minority areas. However, a common complaint was that very few of the children were willing to take over the family business, especially if the hours were long, the pay was minimal and the status was low.

One solution to the problem of employment was to develop vertical industries, that is to man a whole industry from top to bottom. As Kawai mentions (p. 165), it was impossible to imagine any American working under a Japanese American, no matter how well qualified, so that in order to avoid troublesome contact with American workers, such fields as farming, fishing, and in the hotel and restaurant business, the majority of contacts were within the ethnic group. But there were problems, such as not enough Japanese to support many such businesses, but even more difficult was the cry that if the Japanese catered primarily to other Japanese, they were unassimilable, clannish and underable elements in the American "melting pot."

SACRIFICIAL GENERATION?

The first generation of any immigrant group can be termed a sacrificial generation. They have to adjust to a new culture and to make a living, in one sense "sacrificing" their own lives in order to make life better for their second generation children. It is a common theme; my father constantly reminded me that his life was a sacrifice so that my life would be better. And in many ways he was correct; his moments of enjoyment seemed few and far between, and self indulgence was minimal; rather he emphasized (ad nauseum) that his enjoyment came in the form of seeing his children grow up.

Therefore, it is interesting to note that a writer in the Japanese-American Courier of Seattle (n.d.) also saw the Nisei as a sacrificial generation.

> The duty of this generation (the Nisei) is apparent. . . . The second generation is fitted into a sacrificial position as pioneers to blaze the trail into American life to effect the proper recognition of themselves as genuine American citizens; to help the proper and easier amalgamation of the third generation into American life and not least of all to promote a better understanding between their country and the land of their parents (Strong, 1934:13).

It is unclear whether the third generation of Japanese Americans see themselves as a sacrificial generation for the fourth. The idea of self-sacrifice may come from a variety of sources, including cultural norms that call for suffering, a rationalization for lack of personal success, and probably the strongest—doubts about "making it" in the American society. It is my position that the idea of sacrifice would disappear if America were truly an open society, and where racism and discrimination were non-existent. Therefore, the idea of sacrificing for the next generation could be interpreted as a symptom of blocked opportunities.

COMMITTEE RECOMMENDATIONS

One common American method of dealing with problems is to appoint a committee. The committee will study the problem, gather data, discuss the major issues, then come forth with a number of recommendations. The findings will be published and the hope is that the recommendations will guide policy. But, what often happens is that the findings and the recommendations will then sit on the shelf until another problem arises and another committee is formed. Therefore, it is informative to look at the recommendations of the Strong committee and evaluate their recommendations concerning the "second generation Japanese problem."

Strong (1934:59) saw the following five recommendations as "alleviating the conflicting views of Japanese and Americans."

1. *Restrict immigration from all countries into the United States.* Since the Japanese were already restricted, Strong's view was toward general immigration control. It should be noted that the country was in a severe depression at that time, and the notion that foreigners would take jobs away from "real Americans" had widespread popularity. The belief is still held by many today, but it is also clear that our present day immigration laws have been much more liberal than in the past.

2. *Rigorously exclude all Asiatic laborers from entry into the United States.* Strong's argument indicates a strong racist pattern—that there was already an unresolved race problem with the presence of twelve million Negroes so that the country could not afford to increase its race problems with the importation of Asiatic laborers. He argues that it is not because of racial superiority or inferiority, but because all individuals have racial prejudice. Therefore, when the daily livelihood is threatened by the presence of foreigners, prejudice and racial problems would be exacerbated.

3. *Make naturalization available to all who are permitted to settle in the United States permanently.* Strong's argument is a reasonable one— to force certain groups to live apart was only to invite trouble. However, he realized that laws extending naturalization to the Japanese had little likelihood of passage and it was only well after World War II in 1952 that the Issei became eligible for naturalization.

4. *Extend friendly treatment to Japanese tourists, students and business types who do not plan to permanently settle in the United States.* The idea that "temporary visitors" were welcome, and permanent immigrants were not has been a common pattern throughout the world. Foreigners spending money, then disappearing without adding to the problems of the host society, appear to be one popular way of dealing with inter-group and international relations. However, even tourist-dependent countries often complain about the changes that result in the influx of temporary visitors.

5. *Remove all discriminatory legislation; Japanese were admitted by "our" laws and have a legal right to remain.* Strong indicated that one result of unpopular immigration was discrimination so that the

restriction of Japanese immigration would be one step in alleviating discrimination. However, this recommendation, quite progressive for this era, was not acted upon and only after World War II was there any change in discriminatory legislation.

In general, the recommendations were in tune with the thinking of the 1930s; that the number of "foreigners," especially Asians, were a threat; that there were unresolved racial issues dealing with Blacks, or Negroes as they were called in those days; that the underlying theme concerning discrimination and prejudice were related to the inassimilability of these aliens (they could not melt into the melting pot), and that the restriction of immigration was the best solution. It would be interesting to observe the reactions of the Stanford researchers (none are presently alive as far as is known) to the current demographic changes in California where the "unmeltable Asians" have become the fastest growing population, primarily through immigration.

THEORETICAL MODEL

Table 1 The Domination Model

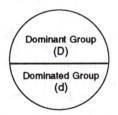

BARRIERS			
	Actions	**Mechanism**	**Effects**
Common actions	1. Prejudice	Stereotypes	Avoidance
	2. Discrimination	Laws, norms	Disadvantage
	3. Segregation	Laws, norms	Isolation
More severe actions	4. Concentration camps	Crisis	Incarceration
	5. Expulsion	Crisis	Exile, refugees
	6. Extermination	Crisis	Genocide

One model (see Table 1) for summarizing the early experiences of the Japanese in the United States is the "domination model" (Kitano, 1991). Weber (1946) saw societies as divided between those who ruled (the dominant group), and those who were ruled (the Japanese in America). There is a tendency for the dominant group to draw lines around themselves in order to restrict interaction except on a "superior" to "inferior" basis.

The initial interaction between the Japanese and the dominant white group begins with the arrival of the immigrant group at the bottom of the structure. The newcomers did not know the language, were unfamiliar with the culture and lacked the necessary capital or resources to compete. Most Issei lacked the education and competitive skills necessary for upward mobility. But most important, even if they had expectations for participating in the mainstream, there were barriers to their mobility.

The three actions which maintain distance and superiority for the dominant group are (a) prejudice, (b) discrimination and (c) segregation. The primary mechanisms that support these actions are stereotypes, laws and norms. The primary effects of these actions are; (a) avoidance, (b) disadvantage and c) isolation.

Therefore, as we illustrated, the Japanese were victims of (1) prejudice through stereotypes (i.e., animal-like, inassimilable, unfit to live with the dominant group); (2) discrimination (i.e., aliens ineligible for citizenship, barring of immigration) and, (3) segregation (i.e., housing restrictions). Therefore, the Japanese American, whether citizen or alien, faced avoidance, disadvantage and isolation.

The domination model emphasizes the process of control and inequality; it also indicates that given these initial stages, far more severe actions can also occur. Once a group has become "victims," crisis conditions (i.e. the minority group becomes a threat to the dominant society) can lead to concentration camps, expulsion and extermination. As we will see, the Japanese attack on Pearl Harbor on December 7, 1941 created a scenario that supports the model, but it is still hard to believe, given the American ethos of liberty and freedom, that an entire group by virtue of "race" could be singled out. All Japanese, whether citizens or aliens, residing along the Pacific Coast were to be herded into "relocation centers," or to put it more bluntly, and as a former inmate, to live behind barbed wire in a concentration camp.

BIBLIOGRAPHY

1. Chazanov, Mathis. (1991). "Census shows decline in Population," Los Angeles Times. April 25, J-1.

2. Friedman, George and Lebard, Meredith (1991). *The Coming War with Japan*. New York: St. Martin's Press.

3. Kitano, Harry H.L. (1991). *Race Relations*. Engelwood Cliffs, New Jersey: Prentice-Hall.

4. Okura, Patrick (1991). Personal interview, Washington, D.C., April 10.

5. Sacramento Bee (1910). May 1.

6. Strong, Edward K. (1934). *The Second Generation Japanese Problem*. Stanford, CA: Stanford University Press.

7. The Survey (1926). May 1. (Robert Park, p. 135)

8. Takaki, Ron. (1979). *Iron Cages*. New York: Alfred Knopf.

9. Weber, Max (1946). "Class, Status, Party," in Max Weber, *Essays in Sociology*, ed. and trans. Hans H. Gerth and C. Wright Mills. New York: Oxford University Press.

10. Yanaga, Chitoshi (1949). *Japan since Perry*. New York: McGraw-Hill.

CHAPTER 4

THE WARTIME EVACUATION (1942-1945)

It is difficult to imagine that over 50 years ago, the United States Government forced over 110,000 Japanese, both citizens and aliens, to move out of their homes along the Pacific Coast. They were first sent to temporary "assembly centers," then to more permanent "relocation centers," both euphemisms for what were really concentrations camps. The "centers" were surrounded by barbed wire fences, had strategically located guard towers, were patrolled by armed guards, and the internees could only leave the gates with governmental clearance.

But, living in today's environment where dissent, challenges to governmental authority and litigation is commonplace, it is hard to believe that such an event occurred. So, I would be skeptical if someone were to ask me the following questions: "Did the American government send a group, including women, children and American citizens to 'prison,' without a formal charge or trial? What about the Bill of Rights and other constitutional safeguards? What about civil libertarians, interested individuals and liberal groups who have usually been at the vanguard in protecting the civil rights of minorities? What about Congress, and the Supreme Court? What about other minority groups? What about the media and the public? What about use of the court system?"

Therefore, the present day answer might well be, "No, how could such an event happen, given the constitutional safeguards, the judicial system, an alert media and a knowledgeable public. This is America, not a tin-horn dictatorship."

But then, I might well ask, (even though it was over five decades ago), was it a dream that I found myself first being removed from my home in San Francisco and shuttled by armed guard to the Santa Anita

37

racetrack, then to a windy, dust covered barbed wire encampment in the Utah desert called Topaz? Was it a nightmare that had me spending my adolescent years and my high school graduation behind barbed wire?

The answer, of course, was that it was not a dream, neither for me nor for 110,000 others, although decades from now, some revisionists might claim that the evacuation of the Japanese, as well as other events such as the Nazi holocaust never happened. And it will only be a matter of time that the last survivors—those who actually experienced this event will have passed away.

But the story of the evacuation of World War II has been well covered. It was the most significant event in the experience of Japanese Americans, and in accordance with its importance, there are books, articles, plays, movies, diaries, and documentaries (see bibliography) regarding this period. Generations of Japanese Americans and others have taken university courses analyzing the why's and wherefore's of the concentration camps; have questioned their parents about their reactions to being incarcerated, and have written innumerable term papers. One general theme from these studies is that "such an event should not have happened; that it was an outrage, but it will not happen again." But events and situations change so that an appropriate addendum might be, "but only if we remain alert and aware."

The purpose of this chapter is to bring an awareness of that period, then to provide a personal account of camp life since I was a victim for three years, from 1942-1945.

BACKGROUND LEADING TO THE EVACUATION

In our model of domination, the "shaping" events that can lead to more drastic solutions between the dominant and the dominated groups are prejudice, discrimination and segregation. The prior chapters provided ample evidence that the Japanese were the primary targets of stereotypes, of legal sanctions and of extreme forms of racism. The Japanese attack on Pearl Harbor on December 7, 1941, provided the impetus for the "final victory" for those who wished to rid themselves of the "Japanese problem." Nevertheless, plans for a final solution were never that clear; instead, the months after December 7 were marked by confusion and contradictory messages, although in the final analysis, the Japanese ended up behind barbed wire.

Immediately after Pearl Harbor, selected enemy aliens, including 2192 Japanese, were arrested by the FBI. Curfew regulations and other precautions were also instituted. These steps might have been sufficient for protective purposes, except in light of the continued battle between

Californians and Japanese. The Hearts papers presented the issue vigorously; for example, the *Los Angeles Examiner* on December 16, 1941, led off with the headline, "Fifth Column Treachery Told," using a quotation from Secretary of the Navy Knox, but omitting the fact that Knox was discussing only rumors against the Japanese. The *San Francisco Examiner* picked up the cry, then the American Legion, then the Chambers of Commerce, then the farm groups, and finally the politicians—"all Japanese are traitors."

Evidence to the contrary was ignored. Bill Henry, conservative columnist for the *Los Angeles Times*, wrote on December 26, 1942:

> The FBI chief says the yarns about the dead Jap flyers with McKinley High School [Honolulu] rings on their fingers, the stories of the arrows in the cane fields pointing towards Pearl Harbor, and the yarns about Jap vegetable trucks blocking the roadway to Pearl Harbor that day are all unadulterated bunk.

But the rumors continued to fly and were picked up on a national level. On January 29, 1942, Henry McLemore, a syndicated Hearst columnist, wrote:

> I am for the immediate removal of every Japanese on the West Coast to a point deep in the interior . . . let 'em be pinched, hurt, hungry. Personally, I hate Japanese. And that goes for all of them.

Austin Anson of the Grower-Shippers Association in Salinas, writing in the *Saturday Evening Post* of May 9, 1942, said:

> If all the Japs were removed tomorrow, we'd never miss them . . . because the white farmer can take over and produce everything the Jap grows, and we don't want them back when the war ends either.

The Japanese handicaps of race and nationality, compounded by social and legal discrimination, isolated ghetto lives, and the outbreak of war, were even too much for the spirit of American democracy and fair play. Very few Caucasians really knew the Japanese Americans; their general ignorance about this group helped to foster and maintain negative stereotypes. The range of those attacking the Japanese was truly remarkable—the American Legion, the State Federation of Labor, the Native Sons of the Golden West, the California State Grange, the leftist parties, and individuals like then California Attorney General Earl Warren and "liberal" columnist Walter Lippmann, as well as the usual racists. The major newspapers in California kept up a constant attack and were joined by local and national magazines. Also as damaging to the future of the Japanese was the silence of the standard liberal organizations. Only some Quaker groups and a few members of the American Civil Liberties Union (ACLU) provided visible support.

Daniels (1975) indicates that the planning steps leading to the evacuation could have been halted, delayed, or diverted if strong voices could have publicly questioned the wisdom and necessity of such a drastic decision. However, in the absence of such actions (it may have been that some of the top government officials privately were against the forced removal, but they never did speak out until years after the incident), the steps leading to the evacuation gathered momentum which culminated in the mass incarceration.

A Smooth Evacuation

On January 29, 1942, the first of a series of orders by U.S. Attorney General Francis Biddle established security areas along the Pacific Coast that required the removal of all enemy aliens from these areas. On February 13, a West Coast Congressional delegation wrote to President Roosevelt urging immediate evacuation of all Japanese, whether citizens or aliens, from California, Oregon, and Washington, and on February 19, 1942, President Roosevelt signed Executive Order 9066, which (1) designated military areas where military commanders could exclude persons, and (2) authorized and building of "relocation" camps to house those people excluded. This set the stage for the evacuation of more than 110,000 Japanese, both citizens and aliens, from the West Coast.

On March 2, 1942, General John De Witt, then commander in charge of the Western Defense Area, issued an order to evacuate all persons of Japanese ancestry (defined as children with as little as one-eighth Japanese blood) from the western half of the three Pacific Coast states and the southern third of Arizona. More than 110,000 of the 126,000 Japanese in the United States were affected by the order. Of this group, two-thirds were United States citizens.

On March 22, the first large contingent of Japanese, both aliens and citizens, were moved from Los Angeles to the Manzanar Assembly Center in California. Prior to this, there was initial governmental encouragement of voluntary movement away from the designated strategic areas, followed by an order on March 27 to halt voluntary emigration.

From then on, all evacuation procedures were controlled by the Army, and by August 7, 1942, the more than 110,000 West Coast Japanese had been removed from their homes. The evacuation proceeded in two stages—first into temporary Assembly Centers at such places as the Tanforan and Santa Anita racetracks in California (under control of the Army and the Wartime Civilian Control Agency), and then to more permanent camps under the jurisdiction of the War Relocation Authority (WRA). The permanent camps and their listed capacities were:

California: Manzanar (10,000)
                Tule Lake (16,000)
Arizona: Poston (20,000)
                Gila River (15,000)
Idaho: Minidoka (10,000)
Wyoming: Heart Mountain (10,000)
Colorado: Granada (8,000)
Utah: Topaz (10,000)
Arkansas: Rohwer (10,000)
                Jerome (10,000)

By November 3, 1942, the transfer from Army to WRA jurisdiction and from the temporary assembly centers to the permanent camps ws complete.

The evacuation was rapid, smooth, and efficient, primarily because of the cooperativeness of the Japanese population, who responded to the posted notices to register, to assemble voluntarily on time at designated points, and to follow all order. The manner in which the Japanese obediently marched to the trains and buses hauling them to camp presaged a conflict-free camp life.

The Santa Anita Riot

But there was some conflict. The writer, then an evacuated high-school student, remembers one such incident. At the Santa Anita Assembly Center, a riot began in response to rumors that a group of evacuee policemen was illegally confiscating electrical appliances and other material for personal use. During this direct confrontation between those interned and those representing the United States Government, there were cries of *"Ko-ro-se!"* ("Kill them!") and *"Inu!"* ("Dog!"). A crowd of around 2000 Japanese, including large numbers of teen-agers, ran aimlessly and wildly about, rumors flew, property was destroyed, and finally an accused policeman was set upon during a routine inspection and badly beaten. The incident was controlled through the intervention of 200 Army MPs, installation of martial law, and stricter security. It was significant that the policeman was non-Caucasian (part Korean), since in most instances of conflict throughout the evacuation period Japanese turned on other Japanese (e.g., generation against generation, or pro-American against anti-American Japanese) rather than the Caucasian administrators.

A letter written by one of the evacuees, dated August 9, 1942, illustrates the significance of this riot to one observer:

Although the censored version of the "rioting" in the newspapers gives a black eye to Center residents by not explaining the extenuation circumstances under which the uprising arose, it seems to have raised their spirits in anticipation of brighter prospects to come. The residents now feel that they shouldn't allow themselves to be imposed upon too much, that occasionally they should assert their rights and not to lie supinely on their backs when injustice is being done. (Kitano, 1964)

PERSONAL ACCOUNT

I was 15 years old when I was sent, along with my family, first to Santa Anita, then to Topaz, Utah. Therefore, I spent three of my adolescent years in camp, including graduation from Topaz High School. I will attempt to answer some of the questions that have been most commonly asked about this period in my life.

Feelings and reactions when the Japanese attacked Pearl Harbor on December 7, 1941.

My brother and I were sort of lounging around that morning when the radio said that unknown planes had attacked the American fleet at Pearl Harbor. I am unclear whether they said it was Japanese, but we immediately went to my father and said planes, probably Japanese had attacked Americans. His immediate reaction was to call us fools for listening to such nonsense (he used the Japanese term, "baka"). That gave us some assurance, so we went to a movie at the old Embassy Theater on Market Street in San Francisco. But sometime during the showing, the lights went up and all service men were told to report to their bases. The "Japs" had attacked America. The next day was one of anxiety, since there was an all student body assembly at Galileo High School. We heard President Roosevelt's speech and the "day of infamy;" I looked for comfort from some of my Japanese American peers, since I thought that everyone was looking at us as if we were the one's who had bombed Pearl Harbor. There were just a handful of Japanese Americans at Galileo and we tried to be as inconspicuous as possible. Fortunately, no one seemed to notice us—there were a lot of students of Chinese ancestry so it seemed that very few could tell the difference, even though our names stood out.

So life continued as normal, with a few exceptions. The FBI came and hauled my father away, so that the burden of running the family business (my father was a hotel keeper) fell upon my older sisters and my mother. We became a tightly knit group—there was a curfew on persons of Japanese ancestry, but since we lived in Chinatown, we felt that no one would notice us. Therefore, one of us would sneak out to buy some pastries at a Chinese bakery on Grant Avenue; we would then sit behind closed shades and enjoy "pigging out." We'd play records (old 78s) on a tinny sounding phonograph, and wonder what other Japanese Americans were doing. I remember liking "jazz" records, while my sisters always preferred the "sweet bands." I particularly liked Count Basie's "One O'Clock Jump" (I think my sisters liked Guy Lombardo), and I carried that record through the whole evacuation period and right on up to the 1970s before it was cracked.

The one story that I remember well was the rumor (as far as I know, it was never established) that some Nisei football players at the University of San Francisco (USF) were accosted by some whites, and the footballers had beaten up their assailants. We told and retold that story constantly—it gave us a feeling of pride—that we were not totally defenseless.

Evacuation Notices

When the first notices went up on the telephone poles, I was sure that the Nisei were not to be evacuated. After all, weren't we American citizens? But it became clear that all persons of Japanese ancestry were to be included. Panic and anxiety became the order of the day, fed especially by my mother, who was sure that we were going to be taken away and shot. She told us to put away our "good clothes," and put on our oldest—if we weren't killed, we would be cast away in some dirty old area.

I don't remember much else of this period except that I took what I thought was the most valuable—the Basie record, a radio-phonograph (we had to turn in our console radio because it received short wave and was therefore considered as contraband, and instead had to trade for a small portable model) and an old, beat up trombone which I had inherited by joining the Japanese Association band. These were to prove important to me at a later time. But the embarrassing thing was that when we were told to assemble to go the camps, it was on Van Ness Avenue, several blocks from Galileo High School. The thought of having my classmates seeing me as a prisoner, waiting to be jailed, was too much and I remember trying to hide my face when high school students strode by. One or two came up to me to express their regrets; others made airplane like noises as they were shooting down the "Japs."

The reactions of some of my high school instructors was varied. My ROTC director (I was in the ROTC band) didn't even know that I was of Japanese ancestry and seemed not to know that I was going to be evacuated. He kept asking me why I was dropping out of school and I kept giving evasive answers. My high school principal was much more supportive; I never knew him personally, but since I had to get his signature I was able to see him. He wrote me a note—"To whom it may concern," which said that I was a superior student and should be given every consideration.

From Citizen to Prisoner

The first feeling of being a prisoner occurred almost immediately. After assembling and answering a roll call (the ability to mispronounce Japanese surnames was state of the art), we were bussed to the train depot, I think it was at 3rd and Townsend, and were herded into some old-fashioned railroad cars with armed guards. They told us to pull down the shades and to obey the soldiers. No one told us where we were going, how long the ride would be and whether we would be fed. So, it was my first opportunity to live by "rumors;" we were going to be killed; we were going to Arizona; we were being shipped out of California and we were even going to be shipped to Japan.

But it was clear that we were prisoners; we were under armed guard and had to follow all orders.

Santa Anita, The First Stop

The first impression that I had when we were told to leave the train was, "My how dark everyone looked." For we were surrounded by other evacuees, primarily from Southern California who at first looked like Latinos and Indians so that I thought that we were in some strange land, perhaps an Indian reservation. But they all turned out to be Japanese Americans from the sunny southland, and they were just as curious to see what this load of Northern California Japanese were like, just as we were curious about them. San Franciscans had stereotypes about Los Angelenos, not very favorable even in those days, but we soon found that they were just like us. The first impressions of Santa Anita, which was billed as a temporary assembly center while more permanent inland camps were being built, were anything but positive. Our initial housing was in the horse stables and even though there was an attempt to whitewash the walls, it still smelled like a horse stable. Even the name of Seabiscuit, the famous racing horse of that era could not erase the fact that his stall was as smelly as the rest. Dinner meant waiting in long mess hall lines for unpalatable food so that I wondered if the basic necessities of shelter and food were to be marginal for the rest of our lives (we had no idea of how long we would be incarcerated).

But by some miracle, a group of Nisei leaders prevailed upon the administration to use evacuees as cooks so that rice began to be served in a Japanese fashion, rather than in rice pudding and food became much more palatable. Okura (1991), in a personal interview indicated that he lead the group that brought about some of these changes. For people under incarceration the importance of food cannot be overestimated. The clanging of the mess hall bell, three times per day, provides a convenient way of assessing the passage of time, but I found myself continuously hungry. I was at the age where there never was enough to eat. My group quickly found that there were different mess halls, and if one could eat quickly enough, one could go to another mess hall, wait in line and be served another meal, even though there were attempts to restrict residents to one mess hall. This meant that eating with one's mobile peer group was more important than eating with the family, so that one camp norm that remained with me throughout camp life was eating with peers. Another feature was "quick eating," so that one would gulp down one's food so that one could dash for another meal. The ability to eat quickly has carried through for most of my life; I still find that I eat more rapidly than my academic colleagues who find leisurely eating as one mark of a good life. Perhaps writing about this will slow my eating habits down.

One other eating habit was the desire to have a full plate of what no matter what was served, since there might not be another chance. But the servers were primarily male, and it was a constant aggravation to see them serve attractive females with fuller plates than we hungrier males. This feeling and the resultant inequality still re-surfaces in cafeteria lines, and with the same results.

Stratification

The adolescent community quickly divided into local groups. I was a member of the San Franciscans and we ran into groups from Hawthorne, Chula Vista, San Pedro and San Diego. Then there were groups from Hollywood, from Boyle Heights and other Los Angeles groupings with names as the "Exclusive Twenty's." These divisions formed the basis of athletic leagues in softball and basketball so that one of the saving graces of life in the Santa Anita Assembly Center was the recreational organizations. There were organized leagues; it was fun to play after supper in these leagues as a member of the San Francisco Fogs and the Golden Gaters, before large crowds. It was an opportunity to impress friends and relatives, and of course, potential girl friends with one's athletic prowess. Friendships were often formed beyond one's own group; the recognition that we were all in the same situation provided a common bond.

There were attempts to start a school system, but all that I remember was sitting in the Santa Anita grandstand, looking out over the race track and the picturesque mountains, while attempting to pay attention to an older Nisei, who was trying to get us to study without books, paper or any other materials. Since it was voluntary, I dropped out after a few days. The one other organization that still stands out in my mind was becoming a member of the dance band, with the magic name of the "Starlight Serenaders." There were enough individuals interested in music and who had their own instruments so that we were able to form a dance band. I remember at a later time reading a pamphlet put out by some governmental body which referred to this group as a "crack dance band," which was probably typical of the type of "overkill" that was a part of governmental publications on the evacuation. For in reality it was a struggling amateur group; I still recall some of the more "hip" Los Angeles audiences of that time hoping that we would pack up so that they could dance to the "real" music (on records) of Glen Miller, Benny Goodman and Tommy Dorsey. My specialty was to play the trombone solo of Tommy Dorsey's "Song of India," but at an octave lower. The band gave me a chance to develop musical skills which later encouraged a temporary musical career. It also gave me a special identification, beyond that of a San Franciscan and an athlete. I began to talk and walk like a musician (at least what I thought they did) and made friends with those in the band who were older than me. Most other friendships were with fellow adolescents.

Parting

The most tearful events (they occurred regularly) was the closing of Santa Anita as various groups were ordered to pack and to leave to different, permanent "relocation centers" throughout the country. We had developed special friendships with some groups, especially from San Diego and San Pedro, so that it was our wish that we would end up in the same camps. Again rumors became the order of the day; one by one different groups were sent to Arizona, Arkansas, Wyoming and to Manzanar in California and each farewell brought out tears and farewells. One popular song that reflected an overall evacuee sentiment was, "You Are Always in My Heart," a song that can still be heard today. It was an appropriate song, for as we parted we were sure that although we would never meet again, "you are always in my heart." Promises to write to each other and never to forget flowed freely, yet for many of the evacuees, parting was permanent. And then, if there were accidental meetings, the passage of time meant that it was difficult to recognize each other.

Thoughts About Santa Anita

Santa Anita was the first time that I had been thrown into a situation where everybody, except the administration, was of Japanese ancestry. And it was the first time that I experienced such diversity; there were intellectuals who talked about the larger issues of Civil Rights and the meaning of America; there were community leaders who attempted to negotiate with the administration for more decent conditions, but who often became targets of contempt ("administration stooges"); there were athletic types, musical types, responsible, dedicated family men, con men, gangsters, girl chasers, hard workers and a full spectrum of other behaviors. There must have been similar types in the female community so that the stereotypes that I see today in the movies and in the public media about Japanese Americans have little relationship to the reality.

Santa Anita also developed a horizontal community, especially for adolescents, based on age so that group norms and behavior were primarily based on age groupings, rather than the more vertical orientation of a family. Further the stratification was often based on previous locale, so that my group was primarily composed of San Franciscans (even though most of us knew each other only peripherally prior to the evacuation), while other adolescent groups from other areas already came in with already formed relationships. Therefore, for my age group, "acculturation" was to adolescent camp norms, which included eating and survival skills, and almost total ignorance of the larger issues behind the evacuation since we had minimal intimate contact with the older, more wiser elements in the community. The family was only a place where we slept together; it was not a place for questions, discussions and a sharing of experiences.

The most pervasive feeling of Santa Anita was that it was "temporary," so that roots were not established and for me, it was like attending a summer camp, but with some obvious distinctions. Therefore, thoughts about the future, the implications of what had happened to us, the changing role of the family and the specter of racism were distant thoughts. Education (I was a junior in high school) had no priority, partly because there was no school system, so that athletics and music provided the most satisfying moments. My stay in Santa Anita was about seven months—from April to October, 1942, when word came that we were to be moved to Topaz, Utah where we would re-join Japanese Americans from the San Francisco Bay Area.

Topaz, Utah

The feeling of isolation and being a prisoner finally hit me as we filed into Topaz, "The Jewel of the Desert." At least Santa Anita was in California; there were automobiles that went past the gates, and many Los Angeles evacuees had friends to drop in to say, "Hi." But Topaz was in the middle of a desert, without any signs of civilization, and our homes consisted of tar papered, rows of barracks. There was a constant wind, swirling clouds of dust and rumors of scorpions, including some nameless individuals who were said to have succumbed to fatal bites. On the second or third day that I was in Topaz and before the barbed wire fences were in place, my adolescent group decided to walk away from the camp. We had no reasonable explanation for hiking out of the camp limits—where was there to go, except miles of desert? But before we had gotten very far, an army jeep, with soldiers pointing guns at us, ordered us to halt. We were interrogated, our names recorded, loaded on jeeps and unceremoniously driven back to camp. As I look back on the incident today, the frustration was that we were made to feel guilty for violating camp norms and that somehow, we had brought shame on our families. It was a frightening and sobering experience and I always kept a safe distance from the fences for the next three years.

Education

The one institution which brought back a degree of normalcy was the high school. We had a wide variety of teachers, some highly qualified, others of dubious quality; some dedicated, others just putting in time. Some teachers were drawn from the camp ranks, and there were some who came from the outside. They taught under primitive conditions and drew a wide variety of responses from the students; although not appreciated at the time, the best teachers were those who treated us as "normal" students and expected discipline and high standards of performance.

One of the best teachers was Eleanor Gerard Sekerak, a graduate from the University of California and a California "credentialed teacher," which gave her enormous prestige among the camp residents. In her own story (Daniels, et al, 1986) she wonders how she could teach

American government and democratic principles while her classrooms were behind barbed wire. However, she expected class to start on time; homework to be turned in promptly, exams to take place regularly and to observe normal classroom standards. There was an attempt to provide all of the normal activities of a high school; there was a school chorus, a student newspaper, a yearbook, a library, student government, drama, athletics, dances and senior week activities. At times, I resented the atmosphere of study and achievement; there was a phrase that caught on rather quickly, "waste time," which was used to question the emphasis on work and study. "Waste time," was a symptom of alienation—what good would our efforts have on an uncertain future? Why not relax, goof off, and scoff at what "goody-goody" teachers were trying to do? It was always a tempting alternative, so that it took a special effort to try to be a good student. A variety of other activities were helpful in fighting the tendency towards alienation.

The Football Team

One of the more astonishing developments was the organization of a high school football team. By some miracle, football uniforms were acquired, although they were of dubious quality. The helmets seemed to be made of reinforced cardboard, and the pads provided almost no protection, nevertheless, we had a team with uniforms and a coaching staff. Although I had dreamed of trying out for football at Galileo High, like most of my Nisei peers, I had to attend Japanese language school after regular school so that there was no time for after school activities. Now there was ample time for varsity football.

But what good is a football team without opponents? Again, through arrangements that must have entailed a high degree of risk, a football schedule with surrounding Utah high school teams became a reality. We played games against Delta (a home game arrangement where we played in Delta and they came into camp to play us), Fillmore and Wasatch Academy. We won the majority of the games, although we were considerably outweighed. I played tailback at 156 pounds and I remember that I could scarcely move for several days after each contest.

The most vivid memory was our first outside game at Delta where we encountered an all white student body. I thought that I heard a voice whispering, "Here come the Japs." Whether that was the primary motivation for playing beyond our physical limitations can be questioned, but we did manage to win. In a more recent discussion with one of our high school teachers at a reunion, I was told that our administration felt that it would be healthy for us to meet schools outside of the camp and to compete with them on the athletic field. It obviously entailed some risks, especially in football where tempers and emotions could often reach an "out of control" level. Fortunately no untoward incidents occurred, although I still walk with a limp from a football injury that happened over 50 years ago.

Social Activities

My fondest memories go back to the high school social activities, such as dances, the junior and senior proms and the socials. These special occasions meant that one had something to look forward to as a relief from the monotony of camp life. There was an artificial equality—we were all Japanese so that we had equal opportunities to become "big shots", or to remain in anonymity (the usual role in previous high schools); there were no cars, there were no "in places" to take dates, and clothing had very little status implications. Everyone had to walk their dates through the dust and the mud; refreshments had to be scrounged from the various mess halls; there was no place to go after the dances and we faced a number of restrictions. The local "internal security" guards came in regularly to check to see if the lighting was not too dark, and even attempted to enforce rules concerning dancing too close. But the chance to date, to work together on social activities, and to participate in school programs formed lasting friendships which exist to the present day. Camp reunions are often based on graduating high school classes.

Other Events

There were a number of other events which I still remember. One was the infamous questionnaire, referred to as "no-no" or "yes-yes," since answering the question meant (at least in the eyes of the government), that one was either "loyal" or "disloyal" to the United States. Answering "no—no" meant being sent to the camp at Tule Lake for the so-called hardliners who were sympathetic to Japan, but as with all simple dichotomous answers to complicated questions, it covered a wide variety of issues.

The question divided the camp. There were debates, arguments and programs which attempted to clarify the meaning of the questionnaire. My sister got up at one of the meetings and advocated freedom of choice—that it was an individual decision and no one should be forced to answer against his or her wishes. It was an unpopular sentiment, at least in my block, because the cooks refused to serve our family for a period of time. Friendships were jarred, and families were torn apart because of the desire of some government bureaucrat to find a simple answer to a complicated question, while ignoring the situation of the evacuees.

Another incident was the shooting of an evacuee. I only heard about it through the "grapevine," but it was underscored as another incident of army insensitivity. What actually happened in the camps was that blocks and neighborhoods had taken on an important identification, so that occurrences outside of the local area were viewed as distant, and since the victim was not from our area, the shooting was not a major concern. Similarly, there was an incident where a person had wandered away from camp. A group of men, including some high schoolers were instructed to look for the wanderer; I was given a bugle to blow for reasons that still escape me. It seemed like a typical "waste-time" activity, wandering through the vast desert, looking for someone who we did not know, or why he had wandered away from camp. But it was a chance to walk out beyond the barbed wires; as far as I remember nothing came from the search. As in Santa Anita, there was also a dance band in Topaz. We were lead by Tom Tsuji, an accomplished musician and we practiced regularly. We were even given a leave clearance to play to the Japanese community in Salt Lake City, and although it was far from a professional group, we again formed friendships and played for a number of camp dances. Since we were the "only game in town," we could proudly proclaim ourselves as the best band in Topaz.

The Talent Shows

It must be recalled that we were in the era of Judy Garland and Mickey Rooney, where one of their most memorable lines had to do with having a talent show. Talent shows were also a regularly scheduled event in the camps; they were also a continuation of such shows in the community before the evacuation and also were continued well after the end of World War II. As with most such events, the primary purpose was to fight the boredom that was a part of camp life. Unfortunately, there was only a limited amount of talent so that there was a sameness to all of the shows. There was also the process of "leave clearance," whereby individuals could leave the camps through governmental clearance, so that often the most talented performers would leave a void that would be hard to fill. The late Goro Suzuki, who later became Jack Sue, was one such talented performer who left the camps for a professional singing career, and later became a TV performer.

The school library became my primary touch with the outside world. I became a voracious reader of the newsmagazines such as Time (I think I outscored our high school instructor, Victor Goertzel, who held a PhD, in one of the tests of knowledge put out by Time); there were also editions of the San Francisco Chronicle where I could follow the exploits of the Pacific Coast League San Francisco Seals, the University of California football team and the general progress of the War. We were spared reading the vitriolic anti-Japanese articles of the Hearst papers (the library did not subscribe to the Examiner), although there was enough "Jap bashing" in the Chronicle to give us a taste of the climate of the times.

Provo, Utah

During one of the summers, probably, 1943, we were recruited to work on some of the farms in the Provo, Utah area. Several incidents stand out; one was working alongside some native Utahns in a packing shed and finding them very friendly. The work was hard but there was a chance for mild flirting and an opportunity to live a more normal life outside of the camps. However, all of the evacuees were housed in a tent city, so that segregation was still the order of the day. The biggest shock came when we went to the movies; we were told that we could only sit in the back rows. There was a great deal of dissent; most of us decided that seeing a movie was not worth the indignity. I am unclear whether that policy was eventually rescinded by the theater management, as we never went back to the theater.

Towards the end of that summer, a group of young Provo males drove by the tents and fired some rifle shots at us. That was a clear signal to my group that the only "safe home" was behind barbed wire; we piled into whatever transportation that was available and hurried back to camp. We later heard that the youthful assailants were released with a mild reprimand, which meant, at least for me, that life was not fair, especially if one were of Japanese ancestry.

A Typical Day

I suspect that there are no typical days in one's life, but the monotony of living in a camp meant that there were more "typical" days in camp than in most other settings. I kept a short diary, but as I look back on it, an adolescent (at least this one) did not have much to say that was of importance. I would wake up, wash up, meet with my peers Peter, Masa, Tak and Zane in order to be first in line for breakfast. There would be a hard boiled egg, toast, milk, cereal, and apple butter. It was my first encounter with apple butter and even today, apple butter reminds me of camp.

I would then go to school, attend classes, go to the library, then have several hours to kill before dinner. One of the favorite pastimes was to kick a football—often for hours, so that it was one skill that I developed which in the long run, had no value. But it did kill time. Dinner was what we called "slop suey" often a mixture of whatever was available, but never enough. I would then go to the block recreation hall, then back to my barracks after the rec hall closed. There was no place to study or do homework in the cramped one room barracks (for a period of time, my brother, two sisters and my mother shared the room) so that school work suffered.

Comments on Topaz

My general impression of the two years that I spent in Topaz was that of boredom, monotony and the slow passage of time. The most difficult times were at celebrations, such as Thanksgiving, Christmas and New Years. Prior to the evacuation, we used to have family gatherings, with the exchange of presents and family feasts; family celebrations were impossible in the confines of barracks and separate mess halls so that special holidays brought out the loneliness and the isolation of camp life. This was especially ironic since there was snow on the ground and a nip in the air, but there was no family Christmas tree, no large exchange of presents and no feeling of a special holiday.

But in most ways, life was certainly simpler, especially in comparison to present day happenings, such as high school graduation. Although there were ceremonies, including speeches and the honor of graduating under difficult conditions, there were no other activities. In contrast, present day high school graduates spend a handsome amount of money; the rental of a suit and a gown, the dates, the corsage, the invitation, the dinner, the limo, the hotel suite, the graduation dance, the after graduation celebration, the liquor and the presents. At Topaz High school our graduation was simple and inexpensive; the major cost was our freedom.

We lived in an artificially created egalitarian society. For those who worked, the standard salary was $16 or $19 per month; one source of excitement was the chance to buy articles from the Sears Roebuck Catalog through a governmental clothing allowance. I forget what the actual allotment was, but no matter what most of us chose, Sears sent us the same thing so that we eventually ended up looking very much alike. A heavy black jacket and a pair of jeans became the standard wearing apparel in high school.

The question of acculturation meant becoming familiar with camp norms and behavior which were functional to the camp situation, but were less functional for life on the outside world. Lining up for almost everything, eating quickly, developing an attitude of "waste time", and putting forth a minimal effort to just get by were adaptations to the camp situation. There developed a feeling of cynicism concerning the role of government and of local, ethnic leadership. The one saving grace was that the camps were temporary so that most of the norms were not internalized; if the camps had lasted for a longer time, the effects on the internees would have been even more disastrous.

Although at the time I did not realize the influence of this event, in later years, to have gone through this unique experience has become a source of identification. At first it was negative; I repressed the memory, and even made believe that it had never happened. If asked where I went to high school, I might answer to Galileo, then onto the University of California, skipping those several years while I was incarcerated. More recently, as this period has become a target for discussion, I can play the role of the "insider,"—an actual victim who suffered through these years. Although I would never wish to have such an event occur to me again, one of my primary identifications is as a Topazans, with instant bonding with others who went through the same experience.

BIBLIOGRAPHY

1. Anson, Austin (1942). *Saturday Evening Post*, May 9.

2. Daniels, Roger (1975). *The Decision to Relocate the Japanese Americans*. Philadelphia: J.B. Lippincott Co.

3. Henry, Bill (1942). *Los Angeles Times*, December.

4. Kitano, Harry H. (1964). *Personal Collection.*
5. Okura, Patrick (1991). *Personal Interview.* Washington, D.C., April 10.

CHAPTER 5

CLOSING OF THE CAMPS:
THE IMMEDIATE POST WAR ERA

In a previous publication (Kitano, 1976), reference was made to Urashima Taro, the Japanese Rip Van Winkle. As a young lad he leaves on a long journey, and when at length he returns, he finds that everything has changed. His old friends are gone, and no one remembers him, although a few recall having heard legends about him.

If Urashima Taro had began his journey in 1942, as the Japanese were being herded into camps to face an almost hopeless future, he might have expected upon his return in the 1990s, to find that his fellow Japanese had been deported en masse to Japan (a poverty stricken, defeated nation at that time), or perhaps to have been confined to permanent reservations, or at best, to be a struggling minority.

Instead, he rubs his eyes in disbelief, for he finds quite another situation. The Japanese are back in California and are also scattered throughout the United States. They appear prosperous and successful, especially when compared to pre-war days. There are Japanese Americans in Congress; Japanese Americans are marrying across racial lines and the Japanese nation has become a formidable economic power. Their former reputation for turning out cheap, shoddy goods has been replaced by an image of exporting high quality goods at competitive prices. And perhaps, the biggest surprise of all—that the former evacuees had been granted redress and reparations so that by the 1990s, survivors were receiving a letter of apology from President Bush and a check for $20,000.

Who would have predicted such a happening, especially if we can hark back into camp life, where optimistic scenarios for the future were non-existent. The dominant mood was that of helplessness—that we were only "Japs," and that no one cared about us. Further, being locked up for several years meant being totally out of the mainstream, so that life outside of the barbed wire fences was an unknown, and what little was known was that it was a hostile world. The nation was at war with Japan; Japan was a dangerous enemy and therefore, Japanese Americans were also a menace.

CLOSING OF THE CAMPS

There were a number of events which hastened the closing of the camps. One involved the handful of Japanese who resisted the wartime evacuation and who initiated court challenges. In their quiet way, these Nisei were heroes—they faced the court decisions without the full support of their ethnic peers, either because many of the evacuees did not know of their efforts, while others feared the possible negative effects on the already suffering population.

Gordon Hirabayashi, a senior student at the University of Washington and Minoru Yasui, a young attorney in Portland, Oregon, both challenged the evacuation orders. Hirabayashi wrote:

> The violation of human personality is the violation of the most sacred thing which man owns. This order for the mass evacuation of all persons of Japanese descent denies them the right to live. It forces thousands of energetic, law-abiding individuals to exist in miserable psychological conditions and a horrible physical atmosphere. This order limits to almost full extent the creative expressions of those subjected. It kills the desire for a higher life. Hope for the future is exterminated. Human personalities are poisoned. . . . If I were to register and cooperate under these circumstances, I would be giving helpless consent to the denial of practically all of the things which give me incentive to live. I must maintain the democratic standards for which this nation lives. Therefore, I must refuse this order of evacuation. (Fisher, 1965)

Hirabayashi was arrested, convicted, and jailed for violating the evacuation orders. The government's treatment of Hirabayashi illustrated some of the incongruencies of the evacuation. Hirabayashi, after conviction, was sentenced to a federal prison in Arizona. The presumably dangerous "enemy" was then given gas stamps and permitted to drive his car from Seattle to Arizona on his own and arriving at the penitentiary, was denied entrance because the orders for his incarceration had still not arrived! (Hirabayashi, 1973)

Yasui was also found guilty, fined $5,000, and sentenced to one year in jail. Subsequent appeals led to a unanimous U.S. Supreme Court ruling of June 21, 1943, which said:

We cannot close our eyes to the fact, demonstrated by experience, that in time of war, residents having ethnic affiliations with an invading enemy may be a greater source of danger than those of a different ancestry. (Fisher, 1965:114)

These were words from the Supreme Court of the United States, and not from nativist or racist groups in California.

Daniels, in an analysis of the records at Heart Mountain, Wyoming, discovered that there were many young internees who refused induction into the armed forces of the United States and preferred to go to prison rather than to take up arms for the nation that placed them and their families in concentration camps. (Daniels, 1971)

Finally, resistance does not have to be either overt or violent. Dominated groups have historically adapted to their status through a variety of adaptations including ritualism and super-patriotism (e.g., interned Japanese purchased war bonds and held Fourth of July celebrations with pro-American speeches), internalization of stress, work slowdowns, inefficiency, strikes and tardiness, aggression, displacement, ethnic humor, withdrawal, and intoxication. All of these adaptations were part of camp life. (Kitano, 1991).

Fred Korematsu attempted a different tactic to avoid evacuation. He hoped to change his name and to alter his features. But the FBI caught up with him; he was found guilty of violating the exclusion order and was given suspended sentence and probationary status. His was a potentially difficult case—his probation meant he was under court rather than Army authority, and therefore at large. But the Army immediately threw him into an assembly center, and his case was finally heard by the Supreme Court, which ruled that Korematsu was excluded not because of hostility to him or to his race but because of the war with the Japanese Empire and the military urgency of the situation. This decision was not unanimous: Justice Black, Rutledge, Reed, Douglas, Frankfurter, and Chief Justice Stone delivered the majority opinion, but Justices Murphy, Jackson, and Roberts dissented.

The most influential case in the cause of regaining Japanese-American liberty was that of Mitsuye Endo of Sacramento, California. In July, 1942, she petitioned for a writ of habeas corpus, contending that her detention camp was unlawful. She represented a test case for James Purcell, a young attorney who questioned that the War Relocation Authority had a right to detain a loyal American citizen for any of the various reasons used by the Army to justify the evacuation. Purcell carried the case to the Supreme Court, and finally, on December 18, 1944, the court ruled that she should be given her liberty. All nine of the justices agreed that the WRA had no right to detain loyal American citizens in camps. It was no accident that, after this ruling, the commander of the Western Defense Area announced that the West Coast mass exclusion orders would be revoked, effective January 2, 1945. (Ten Broek, et al.: 1954)

The Endo case and the continued success of the Pacific war meant the close of the evacuation camps before the end of 1945, and the termination of the entire program by the middle of June 1946. Ironically, it turned out to be difficult to move some of the Japanese out of the camps. They had almost completely adapted to the closed environment. Perhaps, along with the reservation Indian, the reservation Japanese might have come into existence as one result of World War II.

RETURN TO THE COAST

Part of the reluctance of many evacuees to leave the camps derived from their fear of returning to their former homes and hostile neighbors. Secretary of the Interior Ickes reported that by May 14, 1945, there had been twenty-four incidents of terrorism and violence—fifteen shooting attacks, one attempted dynamiting, two arson cases, and five threatening visits. (Bosworth, 1967).

An especially notorious event occurred in Hood River, Oregon, about this time. The local American Legion attempted to exclude all Nisei soldiers names from the "honor roll." They removed sixteen Japanese names, of these, fourteen had served overseas: two had been killed in action against the Nazis, ten had been awarded the Purple Heart, one who volunteered for a dangerous mission in the Pacific and was killed in action. Yet, a headline advertisement in the Hood River Sun (February 2, 1945) read, "So sorry please, Japs are not wanted in Hood River." (Fisher;1965:199).

In such ways, toward the close of World War II, the outlook for West Coast Japanese was gloomy. Although some were returning to their homes in California, most were afraid, and others had simply resettled in other parts of the country. A final attempt was made in California, through a number of escheat cases, to seize property owned by the Nisei under clouded titles. (It should be recalled that since the Issei were ineligible to purchase land, many had put their property under the names of their American-born children.)

The two most critical events occurred in 1946. One was the Oyama case, which involved Kajiro Oyama, an alien "ineligible to citizenship" because of his race, who bought a tract of land for his citizen son, Fred. The California Supreme Court unanimously upheld the right of the state to escheat the Oyama property.

"ineligible for citizenship"

It looked as though the final solution to the "Japanese problem" was at hand. The state could claim much of their land, even that in the hands of the Nisei, and the losses the group had suffered during the evacuation would almost ensure a permanent inferior status. But the constitutionality of the California Alien Land Law was placed under scrutiny, and, although the Oyama case did not involve a direct ruling on this issue, the U.S. Supreme Court reversed the decision of the California Supreme Court on Oyama's citizenship rights. The tide appeared to be turning.

The second and possibly most influential event was the California vote on Proposition 15 in 1946. Proposition 15 was, in effect, an attempt to amend the State Constitution in order to incorporate the entire Alien Land Law of 1920 and to strengthen racist attacks on Nisei property. The voters of California overwhelmingly defeated the proposition.

THE TIDE TURNS

The sharp defeat of Proposition 15 marked the first retreat of the high tide of discrimination and the beginnings of a series of acts designed to heal some of the scars of the last several decades. Politicians, instead of crying for more blood, now began to issue statesmanlike pronouncements about democracy, equality, and justice for all. It is difficult to pinpoint the elements that turned the tide. One was undoubtedly the record of Japanese American soldiers, especially in the campaigns in Italy and France. The 442nd combat team and the 100th battalion, composed of Japanese Americans from the mainland and Hawaii, suffered more than 9000 casualties, had more than 600 killed in action, and became known as the most decorated unit in American military history. There was also a significant contribution by Nisei in the Pacific against Japanese of their own ancestry. Returning servicemen often told and retold the exploits of the Japanese Americans and were quick to rise to their defense. Part of the change may have been reaction-formation and may have come in part through a feeling of guilt. It is possible, too, that the evacuation and many other anti-Japanese acts were foisted on an apathetic majority by a small but active minority. And, unfortunately, part of the diminishing hostility against the Japanese may also be explained by the increased concern over the activities and problems presented by other ethnic and minority groups. The Mexican immigrants and the influx of Blacks created new racial targets.

MOTIVATING FACTORS IN THE EVACUATION

Two questions are involved in any explanation of the wartime evacuation. First, why did the American government intern the Japanese in violation of fundamental traditions? Second, why did the Japanese cooperate so willingly with the authorities during their evacuation and internment?

Plausible answers to the first question were covered earlier-racism, pressure from individuals and groups, the background of anti-Oriental prejudice, wartime conditions, the neutrality of many liberal organizations, and the general lack of knowledge about the Japanese held by most Americans.

WHITE RACISM

It is difficult to avoid the conclusion that the primary cause of the wartime evacuation was West Coast racism. Hawaii, the scene of the initial attack, was theoretically more vulnerable to a Japanese invasion and had a Japanese population of 150,000. Among them were 40,000 aliens, unable to read or write English, but there was no mass evacuation in Hawaii.

There were important differences between Hawaiian and mainland Japanese. The Japanese in Hawaii were a more integral part of the economy, while on the West Coast, Japanese had only a peripheral role or were viewed as an economic threat by some groups. Hawaii was more liberal toward nonwhites, and Hawaiian military leaders had an enlightened view of potential dangers from the Japanese population. Finally, it would have been difficult and expensive to move Hawaii's large Japanese population to mainland camps.

The decision to place the Japanese in camps, surrounded by armed guards and behind barbed wire, came about relatively late. Daniels (1971) reports that when the decision to move the Japanese into the interior was planned, the Army called a special meeting of governors of Western states in Salt Lake City on April 7, 1942. Milton Eisenhower was asked to present information to the select group, and one of the basic questions was what would happen to the "Japs" after the war. Although the United States Government wanted to treat the evacuees with some degree of flexibility, including the possibility of homesteading and communal experiments, the hostility of the Western governors soon quelled any hope for a liberal solution. The emotional cry that no state should be a "dumping ground" for California's problems led to the policy of barbed-wire fences and armed guards.

Canada also treated its Japanese shamefully. Mass evacuations, incarceration, and the denial of constitutional privileges were their fate as well. Latin and South American countries, although influenced by the United States, treated their Japanese with more tolerance, except for Peru and Mexico. Meanwhile, individuals of German and Italian extraction were generally left alone in the United States.

But on the U.S. Mainland, anti-Japanese prejudice was not confined to the West Coast. Bloom and Riemer (1945), comparing attitudes of Pacific Coast and Midwestern college samples, found general agreement concerning the wartime evacuation. Of 2467 students of seventeen colleges and universities tested in 1943, 63 percent on the West Coast and 73 percent in the Midwest felt that the handling of the Japanese was correct. Conversely, only 6 percent of the Pacific Coast sample and 19 percent of the Midwesterners felt that the Nisei should be allowed to complete freedom as in peacetime. Attitudes toward the Issei were even more severe.

The authors also cite a National Opinion Research Center article reported in *Opinion News* on January 23, 1945, which classified responses to the following question: "After the war, do you think that Japanese living the United States should have as good a chance as white people to get any kind of job?" Sixty-one percent of the respondents answered "No," that the whites should have the first chance!

It is difficult to single out a villain to take the blame for the evacuation. General John De Witt deserves his share of the opprobrium for his role as West Coast Theater Commander. He issued the evacuation orders and summed up his feelings at the time with the remark, "Once a Jap, always a Jap." However, Bosworth (1967) reports that the general regretted his actions before he died and felt that he had been the victim of bad advice. Earl Warren, then California attorney general, played a role in the evacuation and may also have been the "victim" of poor advice. John McCloy and Karl Bendersen also played prominent roles. In any case, it does little good to point accusingly. Silence, denials, or the usual rejoinders about "doing one's duty" obscure the truth still, and perhaps it is not really important to affix guilt.

The shock of the wartime evacuation is that for the first time in its history the United States used the concept of collective guilt and initiated group incarceration, even though there was no evidence of prior wrong-doing. The important lesson of the evacuation was that it could and did happen in the United States, and to American citizens.

JAPANESE NON-RESISTANCE

Answers to the second question—why the Japanese did not resist—provide illuminating insights into norms of Japanese behavior. The explanations are both political and psychological.

Prewar Japanese on the U.S. mainland were politically powerless—the Issei were denied citizenship rights, and the Nisei were just reaching voting age. Further, there were no prominent Japanese public figures on the political front or on any other. Therefore, the American public was often only intellectually aware of the evacuation and felt rather detached from the process. It is not facetious to suggest that the Italians could never have been handled in the same manner because of baseball hero Joe DiMaggio. One can well imagine the publicity, the hue and cry for political scalps and investigations, if first- and second-generation Italians, including the famous baseball player, had been sent away.

Economic considerations also help to explain the behavior of the Japanese. There was a short period prior to the evacuation when the Japanese could have migrated to the Midwest and the East, but few did. Most were poor, so that the financial risk of moving to other parts of the country was too overwhelming. Further, the economic structure of the Japanese community—low pay, small business, and high interdependence within the system—meant that very few Japanese could move out or into non-Japanese systems easily. The overall economic picture of the nation, too, was against any easy mobility.

Although there is an interdependence among all of the reason, the social-psychological explanations of Japanese behavior appear to be the most relevant. Future chapters will describe the Japanese-American "culture," its norms, values, and personality, and Japanese behavior. Japanese reactions to the wartime evacuation provide an example of the working of the system.

For example, the community structure with its many small interdependent groups, the critical role of the Issei in terms of leadership, of understanding the system, of wielding power, and of providing for the social control and cohesion of the community, meant that when many Issei leaders were rounded up and incarcerated by the FBI, the system began to fall apart. Many Japanese families were affected by the incarceration, too, so that a group whose primary strength lay in the community and family structure found itself under extremely vulnerable conditions.

The emphasis on norms—the "how to behave in situations" direction of the Japanese culture—also contributed to their docility. Norms and values emphasizing conformity and obedience meant that those in power (e.g., the U.S. Army) were able to use this position to gain the cooperation of the evacuated population.

There were also some primary psychological reasons for Japanese behavior. Many Japanese held low expectations for any sort of "break" in America, so that a wartime evacuation was viewed as a validation of this point of view (e.g., "What else can a poor Japanese expect in America?"); others used the explanation of shi-ka-ta-ga-nai ("it can't be helped"), so that the fate of an individual was tied to forces beyond one's control. Other Japanese used a relatively common Japanese point of view—"I'll become an even better American. I'll cooperate more than 100 percent to prove it." The high need for love and acceptance among many Japanese often leads them to pattern their behavior according to their perception of the expectations of those in authority.

There is also a personality characteristic that is probably not peculiar to the ethnic group but is often found among individuals facing extreme stress. It is the denial of reality—the attitude that says, "It can't happen to me." It is a phenomenon that can be found among soldiers on the battle line and was observable among the Jews in Buchenwald and was present with the Japanese at the time of the evacuation. It was a naïve belief that nothing was really going to happen—that the notices to evacuate really meant something else; that the buses and trains were really not taking them anywhere; that the barbed-wire fences and guard towers were really not for them; and, finally, when in camp, that the situation was not real.

There were no models of resistance or of rebellion—some turned to Caucasian friends, who invariably counseled cooperation. Therefore, with no one to turn to, with their structures and institutions dismantled, with little political or economic power, with cultural norms and values emphasizing conformity and nonconflictual behavior, with a lack of feasible alternatives, and facing the awesome might and power of the United States government, and Japanese marched into camp. Could they really have done otherwise?

CAN IT HAPPEN AGAIN?

Melancholy traces of the evacuation remain today. Rumors that the evacuation camp at Tule Lake was ready for "enemies" were afloat during the McCarthy period and occasionally are heard today. Peterson (1966) mentioned that Chinese citizens wonder if the same thing can happen to them if hostilities develop between China and the United States. The Japanese evacuation set a precedent whereby a wartime emergency can justify the nullification of other constitutional guarantees. Justice Jackson, in his minority dissent on the Korematsu case, warned against the principle of sanctioning racial discrimination in criminal procedure.

> The principle then lies about like a loaded weapon ready for the hand of any authority that can bring forward a plausible claim of an urgent need. . . . I should hold that a civil court cannot be made to enforce an order which violates constitutional limitations even if it is a reasonable exercise of military authority. The courts can exercise only the judicial power, can only apply law, and must abide by the Constitution, or they cease to be civil courts and become instruments of military policy. (Fisher, 1965:181)

Some of the external conditions leading to the evacuation appear to be ever present. There are pressure groups; there are targets; there is hate, discrimination, prejudice, and irrationality; and there is the noncommitted, fence-sitting majority. And periods in our history record what has happened to individuals and groups—the hanging of witches, the treatment of the Indians, and the guilt by association era during the 1950s. But never was there such a mass evacuation of American citizens.

However, when the question of another possible evacuation is raised, we have to ask the question whether we can again find a visible, cooperative, and powerless population; a "population cause" backed by the vast majority; emergency conditions so that the constitution can be suspended; and a mood whereby the very survival of the country is felt to be at stake. If there is massive resistance to an evacuation—tactics of confrontation, all-out court battles, countermobilization, and a sophisticated use of power and counterstrategies—then it is our opinion that something other than a mass evacuation will take place.

A RETROSPECTIVE GLANCE

The wartime evacuation stands as the symbol of both the "low point," and the rallying point of the Japanese American experience. It serves in a similar fashion to some of the dramatic experiences of other groups— for the Jews, the holocaust; for the Indian, "the Trail of Tears," and "Little Big Horn"; for the Armenians, the massacre by the Turks and for the Blacks, the assassination of Martin Luther King. Each of these happenings serve as reminders of past events which will not go away, and also serve as symbols to raise the consciousness of newer generations.

PRESENTISM AND PASTISM

One of the difficulties in explaining both present and past events is that of presentism and pastism. Banton (1983) defines presentism as the tendency to interpret other historical periods in terms of the concepts, values and understanding of the present. Therefore, the current generation, growing up in an era of free speech, dissent, confrontation, and legal redress may find it difficult to understand behavior from a past era where the interaction was based on more conservative norms.

Pastism refers to the tendency to interpret the present in terms of the concepts, values, and understanding of the past. As opposed to presentism, it views yesterday's norms as the present day reality. Therefore, it is difficult to face the changes that have occurred over time. Some Nisei find it burdensome to talk about the wartime evacuation and to support the redress movement because of the fear of upsetting the group in power and of being treated in the manner that they experienced in the 1930s and 40s.

The most appropriate course is to discard simple, moralistic labels to understand the complexity of the wartime evacuation. There can be no single explanation of the events leading to the event, and the reaction of the Japanese to their forced incarceration.

Many of the incongruities remain to the present day. For example, the picture of former evacuees holding a reunion and inviting their former head "jailer" to speak and presenting him with a scroll of honor (can one imagine the surviving Jews of the Nazi camps holding a reunion to honor the memory of Eichman?) is as real as the memory of those evacuees who rioted, who were shot dead, and who were buried in the camps. Perhaps these disparate events remain as the best commentary of that period, which will continue to hold the interest of Americans for generations to come.

SUMMARY OF THE EVACUATION

The evacuation provides an appropriate example of the Rashomon perspective. Each actor—from those who put the Japanese into the camps, to those who managed the camps, to those who actually experienced the event have their own perceptions and explanations.

The following summary statements deal with the implications of the evacuation.

1. The evacuation was a model of disruption. It is difficult to imagine an event more denigrating and humiliating than iden-

dehone (margin note)

tifying an entire group by race, and herding them behind barbed wire under armed guards. It had an effect on all facets of Japanese American life.

economics (margin note)

a. It destroyed the economic basis of the Japanese American community. Jobs, property, and businesses were lost, leases were voided and goods were sold at panic prices.

b. It altered occupational and educational goals. Especially hard hit where those Nisei who were in college or starting their occupational and marital careers.

*- family
- rules
- relations* (margin note)

c. There were dramatic changes in family life. Family roles and the relationship between parents and children underwent drastic change.

d. Acculturation to camp life meant adjusting to primitive, overcrowded conditions with meager resources. As in most such "prison like" settings, adaptation to the norms of camp did not prepare one for life outside of the camps.

Bond (margin note)

e. There was a strong bonding pattern among many of the inmates. Living together for 24 hours per day and sharing a unique experience has lead to strong friendships which have lasted to the present. The proliferation of camp reunions is one indication of this pattern.

f. As a corollary, others reacted negatively to the enforced intimacy, and have kept away from all ethnic activities.

g. Some 5,000 Japanese of both generations, embittered by their treatment, opted to be sent to Japan.

h. It is expected that suffering accompanies wars, but for the Japanese Americans, it came not from the enemy, but from their own government.

Perhaps the most significant learning for me was that no one from the outside, especially the government, was going to do our group any favors. If we wanted anything done, we would have to rely upon our own power and our own resources. Therefore, it was important to work together, especially with our fellow ethnics and whatever sympathetic allies that we could garner, if we wished our voices and concerns to be heard.

BIBLIOGRAPHY

1. Banton, Michael (1983) *Racial and Ethnic Competition.* Cambridge: Cambridge University Press.

2. Bloom, Leonard and Riemer, Ruth (1945). "Attitudes of College Students Toward Japanese Americans," Sociometry 8, no. 2 (May 1945): 166.

3. Bosworth, Allan R. (1967). *America's Concentration Camps.* New York: W. M. Norton & Co.

4. Daniels, Roger (1971). *Concentration Camps U.S.A.* New York: Holt, Rinehart and Winston.

5. Fisher (1965). *Exile of a Race.* Seattle: Ford T. Publ.

6. Kitano, Harry H.L. (1973). *Private conversation with Gordon Hirabayashi in Tokyo,* June 25.

7. Kitano, Harry H. L. (1976). *Japanese Americans: The Evolution of a Subculture.* Engelwood Cliffs, New Jersey: Prentice Hall.

8. _____ (1991). *Race Relations.* Englewood Cliffs, N.J.: Prentice-Hall, Inc.

9. Myers, Dillon (1971). *Uprooted Americans.* Tucson: The University of Arizona Press.

10. Peterson, William (1966). "Success Story: Japanese American Style," The New York Times Magazine, January 9, 1966.

11. Ten Broeck, Jacobus and Barnhart, Edward and Matson, Floyd (1954). *Prejudice, War and the Constitution,* Berkeley, Calif.: University of California Press, 1954.

CHAPTER 6

THE POSTWAR PERIOD

It would have been difficult to be optimistic about the Japanese American future if camp life had continued for any length of time. Feelings of degradation, of inferiority, of being prisoners and of being unwanted would have been strengthened, and low self esteem could have become permanently internalized. Even a short time behind barbed wire created doubts, but one saving grace was the procedure where one could apply for leave, and were released after governmental clearance.

I applied for such a leave and followed the path of three of my older sisters and an older brother by leaving camp in 1944.

> My first feelings were that of relief, fear and anxiety when at the age of 18, I received governmental clearance to leave Topaz. Now that I think back, it was a "gutsy" move; I was leaving a "safe" home by myself into a totally unfamiliar and unknown world. Armed with less than $50 in my pocket, a high school diploma, a letter to the War Relocation Authority (WRA) and a one-way train ticket to Milwaukee, and with no marketable skills, I left my "home." I am not sure that if faced with the same situation today, I would have left.
>
> Feelings of being alone and anxiety came about immediately as I boarded the train at Delta, Utah. The train was overcrowded and filled with GI's; I immediately thought that they would make some comments about "Japs" being on the train. Much to my relief, everyone was deeply involved in their own worlds—many were even making love, a rather shocking sight for me, coming from the restricted camp environment, so that I was totally ignored. Memories of the rest of the trip to Milwaukee and the days in that city remain hazy, although I vaguely remember that Woody Herman and his band were playing at a downtown theater and hearing them in person was like being in heaven.

The WRA office found me a job making silos in Port Washington, a few miles from Milwaukee. I found myself living with a German family; I learned very quickly about rural life in a small town. Food was plentiful and servings were enormous, a rather drastic change from camp cuisine; there was genuine friendliness (I had the strange feeling that perhaps this had to do with the Axis alliance, but I never pressed the issue), and I also discovered that I was not suited for hard, physical work. I therefore thought about using my music background, so I answered several ads in Downbeat magazine (a publication for and about musicians) and was hired sight unseen by Tiny Little, a dance band working out of Worthington, Minnesota. There was an interesting coincidence that aided my transition into my first professional job as a musician. While in camp, I often listened to the radio late at night (very softly as not to disturb the family), and the desert air does strange things to radio waves. There was a station from Tijuana that came in loud and clear, and they would play a record by Jay McShann called "The Jumping Blues," over and over again. The first song that Tiny Little's band played was "The Jumping Blues," so I felt a surge of excitement because of my familiarity with the song. However, even though I played competently, I was given an immediate "two weeks notice", meaning that I was hired unseen, and fired by being seen. However, the manager was thoughtful enough to refer me to another band that was just forming so that I spent several years traveling through Minnesota, Iowa and the Dakotas, playing dance music with such territory bands as Bennett-Greten and Vern Wellington.

There were a number of incidents that gave me insight on the role of being a racial minority and "Asian" (I had changed my name to Harry Lee; I thought that a Japanese surname would be a definite handicap) in an all white orchestra. One of the bands that I played with hired me as a replacement for a black musician (who turned out to be Oscar Pettiford, probably one of the best musicians of that era); there were also heated discussions about Jews. I remember one member of our brass section arguing that Harry James, the famed trumpeter could not be Jewish because he played so well. In terms of acceptance, it appeared that I was less of a threat than blacks or Jews.

I enjoyed life as a musician—it was fun to play with professional musicians of varying quality—to travel from town to town on one-nighters, especially after having been cooped up in a camp for several years—to eat out at restaurants with big steaks, and to live an independent and carefree life.

But I also know that I could never fit in—I was offered several opportunities in bands from Chicago; I felt that I could probably be a good "front man" (band leader), except my ancestry stood in the way. I suspect that I would have continued as a musician if I were White or Black.

There was also this internalized message—that I should go to college and "better myself." Therefore, when my parents were released from Topaz and resettled in Berkeley, I was soon to join them and attend the University of California.

BACK TO CALIFORNIA

Perhaps the most important factor in the immediate post World War II era was the gradual opening up of employment opportunities, especially away from California. As one Nisei said about life in the Chicago area:

> One thing that surprises me is that I haven't met any discrimination out here yet. In some of my job hunting they might have discriminated but nobody got nasty . . . I guess I would still be nothing if I was back in Frisco. I'd probably be an errand boy yet. Now I can say that I am a welder (Thomas, 1952:296-97).

Or as a prominent newspapaperman and author, William Hosokawa, who held a major position in a major Rocky Mountain newspaper said in an interview in 1964:

> I think it works several ways. I'm almost certain that a major Los Angeles or San Francisco newspaper would not appoint me to this position. I'm even more sure that if I were a newspaperman in those cities I'd never apply to expect to fill this position (Kitano, 1964).

But the immediate postwar period saw the gradual movement of Japanese Americans back to the West Coast. Even though there was a subtle underexpectancy among many Japanese on returning to California, it was a time of recouping the losses suffered during the evacuation. Many turned to gardening; two of my brother-in-laws with almost minimal skills in this area found it an acceptable interim occupation while working towards more professional futures. The ethnic stereotype in this case was positive so that gardening proved to be both a temporary and a permanent career for many.

There was also a token payment, estimated at ten cents per dollar to repay some of the property losses suffered by the group. The Federal Reserve Bank of San Francisco in 1942 estimated that the total property loss for evacuees was $400,000,000. By October 1, 1964 the government had authorized payment of $38,000,000 to 26,560 claimants. (Bosworth, 1967).

Popular feeling, politicians and public policy began to reflect changes in a positive direction towards Japanese Americans. The controversial McCarran-Walter Immigration Bill, passed in 1952 and opposed by many liberal organizations, was favorable to the Japanese—it provided an opportunity for naturalization and eventual citizenship for the Issei and a token quota for Japanese immigration. Anti-miscegenation laws, which in 1880 made marriages between Asians and whites illegal were overturned in California in 1948 (Perez v. Lippold). The United States

Surpreme Court eradicated anit-miscgenation laws throughout the country in 1967 (Loving v. Virginia).

Therefore, the decades following the closing of the camps in 1945 showed a gradual trend of removing the restrictions and barriers which had prevented the group from achieving any degree of equality. It was a time for "catching up" so that hard work, including holding multiple jobs became a life style. The GI Bill was an important factor in helping many Nisei achieve a college education. Although there were still many areas where Nisei could not compete, there was a growth of job opportunities in an expanding economy.

CHANGING ATTITUDES TOWARDS JAPAN

Perceptions towards defeated Japan also began to change. In a Gallup poll taken in November, 1944, 13 percent of the American respondents favored total annihilation of the Japanese population. Statements such as, "Let the bastards starve" were commonplace (Friedman and Lebard: 1991, 95). But by 1948, the perceived danger of the Soviet Union altered United States policy so that rather than punishing Japan, America wanted a strong Japan to help defend the Pacific against communism. Therefore, America chose to revive their former defeated enemy.

Several personal incidents come to mind to illustrate some of the changes and some of the newer issues that arose in the decade following the concentration camp period.

> I returned to Berkeley and enrolled at the University of California. Initially, the registrar indicated that I was a non-resident, therefore I would have to pay non-resident tuition. I tried to explain that leaving California was certainly not voluntary and that my parents had moved back to Berkeley after release from Topaz. The contrast was even more pointed since I had enrolled at the University of Minnesota as a freshman in 1945, and their enlightened policy was to waive the "out of state" tuition for evacuees. I was close to tears in trying to explain my plight to an unsympathetic bureaucrat; evidently others had fought against this injustice too because through some unknown process, the University finally gave me resident status.
>
> We could not gauge the sentiments of the California public towards us, therefore, the cardinal ruled seemed to be—be as inconspicuous as possible. I believe it was in the spring of 1946 that I enrolled as a student and became a member of the Cal Band. Anyway, it was only a few days later when the basketball team won an important game and the students were yelling and the band was leading the students out of the pavilion onto the street. And being a trombone player, I was in the front line and the only visible minority; I was

overcome with embarassment and tried to be invisible, with band hat pulled over my face, and wishing that I was a thousand miles away.

In another incident, there was this young Nisei, David Takahashi (now deceased), who would pull out a Japanese "bento" (rice, chopsticks and some Japanese food), right in the middle of the all male Cal football rooting section. Although such an incident would probably be accepted and even applauded today since "sushi" is an "in" food, it was a source of great stress to myself and my Nisei colleagues. We would move away and pretend that he was not one of us so that one could picture this lone Nisei, eating with chopsticks, surrounded by a small group of Nisei pretending that he was not our friend. We were in turn surrounded by a large group of vociferous white students who made us feel extremely self conscious. We felt like outsiders who did not belong.

OTHER TARGETS

Previously, I had mentioned that one of the reasons for the relative acceptance of the Japanese American back into California was the emergence of other target groups. There was the "Sleepy Lagoon," murder case, and the "Zoot-suit Riots," against Mexican Americans in Los Angeles in 1942 and 1943, and a heavy influx of blacks during World War II which created racial tensions. As a consequence, Japanese Americans were no longer the primary target of racist actions during the late 1940s and 50s; although there remained discrimination and prejudice, the major targets were Blacks and Mexicans (Daniels and Kitano, 1970).

While I was a student, I also continued my musical career.

One of the more interesting incidents was my application for a Musician's Union Card in San Francisco. There were two musician's unions at that time; I believe it was Local 6 for whites and Local 669 for blacks. The officials were unsure which local was the most appropriate for me so they finally left it up to me. I think I joined Local 6 but most of my contacts were with black musicians.

I played for an all black band, which booked out of Oakland, and there was one job that called for the band to play in Redding, a small town north of Sacramento. I had been out of camp for several years, but still was self-conscious about being of Japanese ancestry in California. Imagine my surprise when the band leader turned to me and said, "Lee, could you go to that restaurant to see if they would serve our band?" It dawned on me that being Asian meant better treatment than being black. I think that they brought out sandwiches for the band.

There were a number of important legislative actions affecting the Japanese Americans during this period. The McCarran-Walter Act of

1952 was the first general immigration act since the 1924 Act which had prohibited Asian immigration. Although it was a continuation of the national-origins model, it also removed all racial and ethnic bars to immigration and naturalization and provided for family reunification. Although opposed by most liberal groups, the act gave Japan a token quota of 185 per year. Even more important, Japanese aliens, previously classified as "aliens ineligible for citizenship" were now eligible for naturalization. My father and mother were both naturalized under this act; it was the only overt demonstration of "Americanism" that I remember.

Between 1952 and 1964, nearly 63,000 Japanese, more than 5,000 per year came to the United States. The majority came as nonquota immigrants, that is as parents, spouses, children, or siblings of United States citizens (Kitano and Daniels, 1988).

HOUSING DISCRIMINATION

Housing discrimination remained as a major hurdle. It was both formal and informal; formal in that the real estate industry kept certain areas closed and informal in that the wishes of sellers often meant that the Japanese were not viewed as desirable neighbors.

A survey on housing among Japanese Americans in the San Francisco Bay Area found the following: that the Nisei had adequate housing in terms of space and physical facilities; their houses were generally old, and often in older neighborhoods; that they had experienced discrimination and would expect to continue finding it when they go house hunting or apartment hunting. The majority indicated that they would continue their search for better housing, in spite of the barriers caused by the real estate industry. As their occupational status rises, the pressure for better housing in better neighborhoods will no doubt continue (Kitano, 1960).

The following personal incident on my move to Los Angeles in 1958 illustrates the then existent problem in finding suitable housing.

> Upon my move to UCLA in 1958, I followed the advice of my family and friends who counseled going through a Nisei real estate agent in order to avoid the embarassment of discrimination. I had heard of Ty Saito, a UCLA graduate who had started his own company, and he found me a home in a new tract in Culver City. I think I was one of the first Japanese Americans in that tract, but after I moved in, there was a mass movement of Nisei into the area. I think that was a common pattern in those days—a breakthough by a Japanese American would be followed by many others who wanted to be sure to go into an area

where the chances of being accepted were high.

One day, my colleague at UCLA, Professor Joseph Eaton, thought that I should move closer to the campus to Brentwood where he was living. I told him that sounded good; imagine his surprise when his realtor told him that since I was Japanese, he could not show me a house in Brentwood. Joe was extremely upset about this incident, but I took it as a natural course of events—it was nothing new.

Now that I look back on the incident, it brought to life the answers that I found in my survey of the San Francsico Bay Area: That when faced with housing discrimination, the majority of Nisei answered that they would withdraw because it was not worth the trouble, or that they didn't want to move into a neighborhod where they were not welcome. Only 23 percent of the Nisei respondents indicated that they would fight against discrimination (Kitano, 1960).

The contrast with the 1990s is startling. Now, the major obstacle for Japanese Americans is cost, not race. A visit to San Francisco shows that the previous all white areas in the avenues and the Sunset district are now thoroughly Asian, although the irony is that the weather is generally better in Chinatown and the old Japan town. In Los Angeles, Japanese Americans are scattered throughout the area, so that what was once a major barrier, is no longer a major problem. Ethnic enclaves, such as in Gardena, are based on voluntary choice, rather than housing restrictions.

THE CIVIL RIGHTS YEARS

A few Japanese Americans joined the Civil Rights struggles of the 60s and 70s. There was the beginning of the "Asian movement," composed primarily of Sansei in concert with other Asian Americans which provided the impetus for Asian American Studies at various college campuses. *Gidra*, a publication which reflected the views of the younger population, challenged Asians to fight American racism and oppression. The newspaper was founded in 1969 and continued until 1974.

In 1990, the original student group published an anniversary edition which again challenged the status quo. The image of the 1990s—that all Asians were college bound rich kids with little or no social consciousness was questioned. There were still too many who were still working and struggling in low-paying jobs, and shunted from better positions because of language barriers and racism.

In 1980, Congress established the Commission on Wartime Relocation and Internment of Civilians to review the facts and circumstances of Executive Order 9066 which forced the wartime evacuation. The commission report, titled Personal Justice Denied (1982) concluded, among other things, that detention and exclusion were not based on militarily necessary. Rather, the decision to evacuate was based on racial prejudice, wartime hysteria, and the failure of political leadership. The commission reported that:

> A grave injustice was done to American citizens and resident aliens of Japanese ancestry who, without individual review or any probative evidence against them, were excluded, removed and detained by the United States during World War II (1982, p.18).

But there were other incidents which indicated that "Japan bashing," and its variation, "Asian bashing," was also on the rise. The Vietnam War and the influx of refugees, the competition with Japanese imports, and the wide trade deficit with Japan and other Asian countries provided ample ammunition for some Americans to act out their prejudices.

A particularly dramatic incident involved a twenty-seven year old Chinese American named Vincent Chin. On June 19, 1982, Chin was beaten up and murdered in the Detroit suburb of Highland Park. There was an initial round of racial slurs, aimed at Chin and his Chinese companions by a forty-three-year old White automobile industry foreman, who had mistaken Chin for a Japanese and somehow responsbile for his unemployment. Chin was eventually beaten up with a baseball bat and died four days later. Although charged with second degree murder, the white pair were able to plea bargain and recied a small fine and placed on three years probation.

The decision outraged the Asian American community. Subsequently the protests forced an investigation; the primary assailant was found guilty of depriving Chin of his civil rights and sentenced to twenty-five years in prison in September, 1984. That conviction was reversed on appeal and in April, 1987 conflicitng testimony and blurred memeories of witnesses resulted in an acquittal of the killer on the federal charge (Kitano and Daniels, 1988:189).

In summary, the history of the Japanese in the United States has been one of "downs" and "ups." Down periods were associated with negative relationships between the Japanese nation and the United States—the most telling was the treatment of Japanese Americans during World War II. The relationship continues; when Japan is viewed as an ally, Japanese Americans benefit; when Japan becomes too competitive, Japanese Americans suffer.

The inability of Americans to differentiate between the various Asian groups also works in a similar fashion. Negative attitudes and relationships with any Asian nation or any Asian American group is reflected in increased negative attitudes towards anyone who looks Asian. Therefore, although what Asian Americans do is one part of the equation, the interaction with the dominant group is the other. And, as history reminds us, the interaction is often based on the relationship between the United States and the ancestral homelands.

BIBLIOGRAPHY

1. Bosworth, Allen R. (1967). *America's Concentration Camps*. New York: W. W. Norton & Co.

2. Daniels, Roger and Kitano, Harry H. (1970). *American Racism*. Englewood Cliffs, New Jersey: Prentice Hall.

3. Gidra (1990). Montebello, California: P.O. Box 3058.

4. Kitano, Harry H. L. (1960). "Housing of Japanese Americans in the San Francisco Bay Area," in Studies in Housing and Minority Groups. ed. Nathan Glazer and Davis McEntire. Berkeley: Univ of California Press, pp.178-135.

5. Kitano, Harry H. L. (1964). Private conversation.

6. Kitano, Harry H. and Daniels, Roger (1988). *Asian Americans*. Englewood Cliffs, N.J.: Prentice-Hall.

7. Personal Justice Denied (1982). Report of the Commission on Wartime Relocation and Internment of Civilians. Washington, D.C.: U.S. Government Printing Office, December.

8. Thomas, Dorothy S. (1952). *The Salvage*. Berkeley, Calif.: University of California Press.

Section II

Section II of the book concentrates on the Japanese American community; its history, its culture, its organizations, and its families. It will also cover the experiences in Hawaii and close with a chapter on ethnic identity. Some of the material, such as the Japanese Community Picnic, is drawn from my volume, *Japanese Americans: The Evolution of a Subculture.*

The overall theme is one of change, brought about both externally (acculturation) and internally (enculturation). The experiences in Hawaii introduces a setting where Japanese ancestry did not mean a small, powerless minority.

The last chapter in this section presents the concept of identity and ethnic identity, and how this variable remains one of the most discussed among the ethnic group.

CHAPTER 7

THE COMMUNITY: ITS CULTURE

When we talk about the ethnic community, the chances are that we will be using a term that is confusing and with a number of different meanings. For example, individuals with widely divergent views talk about representing the community, or claim to have community backing, and politicians proclaim that they always have the interests of the community at heart. Research that has community backing is considered a plus, although there is also talk about community interference, and Schools of Social Work have courses and majors in community organization. It is obvious that relationships with the community are important, but it is also difficult to sort out the similarities and differences in the use of the term.

Ethnic communities, in order to be functional, have several characteristics. Resources, including adequate numbers, qualified individuals, knowledge, and economic sufficiency to meet the needs of its constituency, comprise one ingredient. Another factor is community cohesion, including norms and values, people willing to work together, leadership, and a community structure. Finally, an ethnic community, in order to maintain its viability, should provide services that are not perceived as available in the dominant community. From this perspective, ethnic communities will change as needs, resources, and interaction with the American society changes.

One of the more relevant ways of looking at an immigrant community is to refer to what Massey (1988) terms the migration network. Migration networks were and continue to be especially important for Asian immigrant groups, since most of them arrived with little knowledge of the language and culture of the new country, and were met with indifference, or as we have seen, outright hostility. Therefore, the importance of an ethnic community, bound by kinship, by friendship, by culture, and shared origins cannot be overestimated.

The early Japanese migration network included personal and family ties, village and "ken" relationships, and the commonality of Japanese ancestry which linked new immigrants to former immigrants. There developed as social structure which provided a support system which helped new immigrants handle the emotional, social and economic costs of migration. Discrimination and segregation reinforced the development of identifiable communities such as "Little Tokyo" in Los Angeles, and "Little Osaka" in San Francisco. These communities were able to provide assistance in terms of such basic necessities as transportation, housing and jobs, as well as to provide settings to meet social and recreational needs.

The ethnic community was important in making life more palatable for the early Issei immigrant, especially since the majority institutions ignored their needs and had other priorities. It provided a parallel structure, or what Gordon (1964) refers to as structural pluralism, whereby the needs of the ethnic group were met by ethnic organizations, rather than by the larger society.

THE COMMUNITY IN JAPAN

The roots of the Japanese community organization lie in course in Japan. The Issei had been born into a social system which, although unlike the American system, peculiarly fitted them to adapt to the difficulties they found here. From birth a Japanese was accustomed to put the interests of his family, village, "ken," nation, and emperor ahead of his personal interests. His behavior was dictated by clearly defined rules and obligations. A system of collectivism and ethical interaction provided mutual assistance for group members, and proved effective in protecting the individual from the cultural shocks of both a rapidly changing Japan, and later, of a new land.

Community cohesion was fostered through what Dore describes as honor:

> In Japan, where the local community has always been characterized by great solidarity and the existence of careful mechanisms for the smooth preservation of law and order, the fulfillment of one's duties to the wider community has always been considered as essential conditions for the maintenance of honour (Dore, 1958).

COMING TO AMERICA

There can be a few sights as dismal as the strange shores of an alien land. America, to the new immigrant from Japan, must have seemed from the deck of his vessel a bewildering welter of white faces and tall buildings. As he landed, he was beset by immigration officials speaking to him in an unknown language. His future must have seemed precarious, but only for a little while, because he would soon hear someone shouting "Hiroshima no hito, ko-chi ni oide" (all people from Hiroshima come over here). People from other kens were waiting to welcome their newcomers. They might be friends and relatives, or they might simply be people from the same Japanese county. In any case, the welcoming and socialization of the new immigrant began in the hands of other Issei. He was provided food and lodging, helped to find employment and invited to share recreational and religious activities. Internal factors such as similar language, food habits and common experiences, and external pressure from a hostile American community, served to strengthen the cohesiveness of the organized group into which he had been introduced.

THE ETHNIC CULTURE

The bond that held the Japanese community together was its culture—that is, everything that was brought over from Japan, and the subsequent development, maintenance, and change of that culture in the new country. It would include its economic, political, social, family and religious structures, its institutions, and its norms, values, personality, and behavior. In a social learning sense, the structures and institutions act as agents, shapers, socializers, and reinforcers; the norms and values determine the content, the direction, and the how and what of expected behavior.

FREQUENT MISCONCEPTIONS

To many people, Japanese culture suggests mainly tea ceremonies and flower arranging. As often happens, the quaint, the unusual, and even the trivial become so firmly associated in people's minds that complex explanations of behavior are often built on pursuits that may in fact represent only the interests of a select population. In the same way certain cultural myths develop and are perpetuated by our general ignorance. Things that seem incomprehensible to Western eyes are often attributed simply to the "curious, mysterious, and inscrutable ways" of the East.

For example, one image of the Japanese culture is that suicides are acceptable. We are acquainted with the case of an Issei who recently committed suicide by throwing himself in front of a moving automobile. This act was reported in the metropolitan press as suicide, but the local Japanese American newspapers delicately reported the death as an accident and raised not so much as a hint of suicide. This raises some doubts about whether suicide is socially acceptable in the Japanese-American culture. And, of course, suicide rates within this group are no higher than in the majority.

There is also one other important point to keep in mind as we discuss the Japanese-American culture. Many of its norms are not wholly Japanese in either a literal or technical sense, but they are real in the behavioral sense—that is, these were the messages that Issei passed on to the Nisei and Sansei. Purist savants of the Japanese culture often delight in finding discrepancies between the Japanese meaning of certain norms and their translation by the Issei, with the inference that the Issei understanding was "wrong." But obviously the meaning of these prescriptions in relation to Japanese-American behavior, not the wrongness or rightness of such prescriptions, is the matter of importance.

NORMS

"Norms" are shared meanings in a culture that serve to provide the background for communication; values refer to clusters of attitudes that give a sense of direction to behavior; and personality refers to the characteristics of persons that remain relatively stable and provide the individual with an orientation to the world. The primary purpose of a social norm is to provide a guide for interpersonal behavior so that an individual has an acceptable way of interacting with others and, conversely, is able to judge the acts of others.

Studies of Japanese social norms reveal some of the following features: Japanese patterns of social interaction are highly personalized; there is a definite hierarchy of status positions with a corresponding regard for the importance of status; the status systems are relatively permanent; and behavioral reserve and discipline are highly regarded. Further, certain norms have been incorporated into the Japanese national school curriculum as ethical doctrine, so that exposure to these teachings has been widespread. These codified norms were *on* (ascribed obligation), *giri* (contractual obligation), *chu* (loyalty to one's superior), *ninjo* (humane sensibility), and *enryo* (modesty in the presence of one's superior) (Benedict, 1946; Wagatsuma, 1977).

These norms, if followed and internalized by its members, would tend to produce the following behaviors: An aggressive and probably arrogant ruling class; conforming, obedient ruled classes, and a high degree of order through the hierarchical structure and external sanctions. Further, the norms would be effective if there were supporting networks such as villages, families and neighborhoods, each with similar normative interactions so that socialization procedures could be consistent and effective. The maintenance of such a system would depend on relative stability among classes, high values placed on the system by all members, clear role prescriptions, a desired modal personality structure emphasizing conformity and obedience, and a symbolic "head" (the emperor) at the top of the hierarchy of structures. The Meiji era culture was built on these patterns and many of these norms followed the Issei immigrant.

It would be inaccurate to say that all or even most Japanese behaved in accordance with the prescribed norms, just as it would be an overgeneralization to indicate that most Americans behave strictly according to the prescribed democratic norms of our society. Nevertheless, a knowledge of the Japanese Meiji period norms is important because it provides the background for understanding Issei behavior.

ADAPTABILITY

Probably the one outstanding characteristic of Japanese norms is their adaptiveness to fixed positions and to external realities. Rather than a stream making its own course, the stream follows the lines of least resistance—their norms emphasize duty and obligation; their values include conformity and obedience. Part of the "success" of Japanese adaptation of the United States was their ability to respond to the problem of lower status with those normative patterns learned in Japan. For example, the immigrant's lower status was similar to his role position in Japan so that a transfer of high-status positions to the "white man" and subsequent patterns of deference and humility were relatively easy transitions.

A lower status in the Japanese structure is often associated with humility, a service orientation, and a high sensitivity to the needs of the superior. Some of the consequences of this structure, where rewards and punishments are distributed by the whim of superiors, are hypothesized by Iga (1967).

One characteristic is insecurity, which means that Japanese tend to be indifferent to other people's troubles and tend not to become too involved with others because of their own need for security. Another characteristic is a lack of commitment to abstract and absolute ideals.

Instead, there is a substitution that leads to following of government or other officials, with little criticism of "superiors." The third characteristic is that of opportunism, since authorities define what is right, and the "inferior" is constantly caught in the position of having to adapt to the new variations. Iga feels that these three characteristics of Meiji Japanese culture and personality help to explain the overall lack of Nisei involvement in the civil rights struggles of the Blacks, the present low voting behavior of Japanese and other facets of Japanese acculturation as well.

Conversely, a higher status in the Japanese system may be accompanied by paternalism and arrogance. However, these status differentials with consequent effects on personality and behavior are not only typical of the Japanese system but are probably present in most autocratic structures, and the old adage about power and corruption, and relationships between the "superior" and the "inferior," appear to be characteristic of many cultures.

THE ENRYO SYNDROME

Among the many norms that shape Japanese behavior, the norm of enryo appears to be one of the most important. Even the present generation of Japanese Americans uses the term, whereas other norms such as *giri* and *on* have long been forgotten. The concept originally referred to the manner in which "inferiors" were supposed to behave to "superiors"—that is, through deference and obsequiousness. As with many norms, however, the meaning and the use eventually expanded to cover a variety of situations—from how to behave toward the white man, to what to do in ambiguous situations, to how to cover moments of confusion, embarrassment, and anxiety.

Enryo helps to explain much of Japanese-American behavior. As with other norms, it has both a positive and a negative effect on Japanese social interaction. For example, take observations of Japanese in situations as diverse as their hesitancy to speak out at meetings; their refusal of any invitation, especially the first time; their refusal of a second helping; their acceptance of a less desired object when given a free choice; their lack of verbal participation, especially in an integrated group; their refusal to ask questions; and their hesitancy in asking for a raise in salary—these may all be based on enryo. The inscrutable face, the noncommittal answer, the behaviorable reserve can often be traced to this norm, so that the stereotype of the shy, reserved Japanese in ambiguous social situations is often an accurate one.

Ha zu ka shi is a part of the enry syndrome. It is observed in terms of embarrassment and reticence. The motive for this feeling is centered in "others"—how other people will react to self so that there remains a feeling of shame, a feeling that one might make a fool of himself in front of others. Childhood discipline emphasizes ha zu ka shi—"others will laugh at you"—and the norm is used as means of social control. It may lead to a lack of aggressive behavior and to high dependency because the cues for shame come from the outside, especially from parents. One result of this kind of behavioral norm is the nod of agreement with which a Japanese often implies a "no" answer. This can cause much difficulty, since Americans assume that the nod means "Yes, I understand," whereas it may mean, "I don't want to cause you embarrassment or trouble by disagreeing" or some other variation of the enryo syndrome. American teachers soon learn that even in classes made up of Sansei it is an error to say," All right, are there any questions? If there are none, I assume you all understand," since there will be no questions and often, little understanding.

Hi-ge, also a part of the enryo syndrome, leads to social interaction that is difficult for many Americans to understand. For example, if an American praises the Japanese wife, the husband may respond, "Oh no, it's not true." Or the Japanese husband may introduce his wife as "Here is my stupid wife." Or the Japanese may denigrate his children or himself or others close to him because his norms preclude the praising of self or family. Such praise, especially in public, is considered to be in very poor taste, except in certain formalized circumstances.

The difficulty with the enryo syndrome relates to the possible effects on the Nisei and Sansei. In Japan the messages, the cues, the presence of others who would understand the culture and play the game accordingly (for example, others may then praise children or the family—the entire system—would operate in this manner. However, in America, the full consequences of the enryo syndrome—including its devaluation of self and family—have never been fully understood by the population. It has helped the Japanese "look good" in Caucasian eyes because of its lack of aggression and high conformity, but for the Japanese American the cost of the "goodness" may have been very high. Low self-esteem and a full development of an individual's potentialities would be hindered under such norms.

AMAE

Another concept, that of *amae*, has been described by Meredith (1966), Doi (1962) and Mass (1986) as critical in understanding the basic dependency of the Japanese. The term refers to the need to be loved and cherished, but is difficult to translate accurately into English. It was frequently used by the Issei mother to describe the behavior of her children—sometimes with approval, sometimes with impatience. From the child's side, it was a technique of interaction asking for love, for attention, for approval, and for recognition. It was one of the few acceptable ways that individuals had to cope with the enryo norm.

We conducted a discussion of the term amae with a group of Japanese college students in Tokyo in 1973, and their reactions were diverse and vehement. Some felt it was a negative type of interaction; others thought of it as a positive term, denoting a "softer" type of response between unequal power positions. All agreed that it was used constantly in Japan, and phrase like "begging," "gaining attention," "asking for approval," "coquetry," and the like were broached, but with no agreement as to the most appropriate definition.

Perhaps the critical part of amae is the way it is perceived and responded to in the Japanese culture. If the parent sees the behavior of her child as amae, she may not have to respond by spanking or yelling, since it is understood as an important factor in a relationship, whereas if she defines it in some other way, a different interaction may be involved. The term is currently equated among Nikkei with "being spoiled" and is therefore considered an undesirable action to be restricted or eliminated. But it may also deprive the child of a "soft" technique for gaining attention or asking for a favor.

There are many other ways of handling the power relationships within the Japanese system, and one of the most critical is related to independence and dependence. One goal of socialization in Japan is to establish a dependency on the family, the group, the company, and the mutual responsibility that goes along with such a perspective. Conversely, the goal of socialization in the United States appears to be the establishment of independence and autonomy as early as possible. The conflict between these two goals is often reflected in Japanese-American families.

INDIRECTION

Functional norms help a group to adapt and to survive. The less-than-equal power relationship faced by the Japanese meant that they had to develop ways of dealing with this problem. A technique that is associated with less power is the avoidance of direct confrontation. People, cultures, and countries with less direct power have avoided the "eyeball to eyeball" type of conflict, whereas those with more power—technology, resources, numbers, and firepower—generally welcome the direct confrontation.

The Japanese have had to adapt to less powerful positions constantly. The size of their country, the lack of natural resources, and their smaller stature has usually meant that there is a preference for indirect tactics, rather than meeting force head on. One of their martial arts, aikido, stresses relaxation, deflection, and the interaction of mind and body as sources of inner strength in defending against an outside aggressor. It is an appropriate technique for neutralizing the force of much larger and aggressive individuals. To meet strength with strength means that both sides will be hurt and that the stronger will eventually win, whereas aikido attempts by deflection to use the strength of the aggressor against himself.

Socialization into the Japanese culture takes into account the art of deflection and the avoidance of direct confrontation. We have observed one consistent technique in their child rearing that encourages deflection and cooperation. Rather than the direct confrontation by the more powerful parent against the child ("You do what I say, or else"), the Japanese parent is more apt to use indirect techniques. They may introduce a diversionary stimulus or attempt to bring about cooperation by saying "Let's do it this way," or "A good child will do it this way."

For example, the differential modes can be illustrated by how a Japanese and an American family might handle the case of an eight-year-old son who is watching television beyond his allotted time when he should be doing his homework. In the American family, there might be the direct statement, "Why don't you turn off that TV and study?" If there is not the desired response , it may escalate into a conflict between the power of the parent and the power of the child. Eventually it may be resolved by "showing the child who's boss around here," and power threats like "Turn off the TV or else . . ." are common interactions. In the Japanese family, a different type of interaction (and often just as ineffective) is used. The parent may indicate to the child that "Isn't that a boring program"; or "I think Jun-chan [a close friend] must be doing his homework now"; or mother might say, "I think father wants to watch his favorite program." There may be an attempt to bring in another member of the family, so that father might ask his daughter to tell her brother to study. She may be praised as a good girl because she is studying and not watching television, and this praise and recognition is probably more effective in socializing her rather than bringing about the desired response in her brother. But direct confrontations between parent and child remain rare. One parent may turn to the other and remark how bad children are getting to be, loud enough for the child to hear but not directed to him.

It is difficult to evaluate the effectiveness of these techniques in isolation, for they are within the context of each of the cultures. One of the ultimate weapons used by Japanese parents to get children to behave is the threat of banishment from the family circle. Children are threatened by putting them outside, or in a closet, or in a basement. This appears to be an effective device, whereas such threats may have little noticeable effects on an American child. In fact, the American technique is often the opposite; rather than the threat of banishment, the threat to "keep in" is often used so that a child is told "You can't go out and play" if he has been misbehaving.

Concepts such as losing or saving face, the difficulty of getting clearcut yes or no answers, and the vagueness of the language itself, are other manifestations of the use of indirection in the culture. Although these themes exist in all cultures, they appear to be central to the Japanese system. The indirectness can have both healthy and unhealthy consequences. Among Japanese Americans, the lack of direct statements often leads to confusion, misinterpretation, and misunderstanding, but is also avoids those direct attacks that often lead to irreconcilable differences. The current therapeutic techniques of confrontation, of expression "honesty" and true feelings will be difficult for many Japanese Americans to handle.

VISIBILITY AND A LOW POSTURE

How to deal with visibility—that is, of possessing a phenotype different from the white majority community was and still remains a constant issue. Because of the nature of American racism and the problems faced by the Japanese, one important adaptation of the group was through invisibility. The dictum was, "Don't bring attention to us," and if public attention were warranted, the phrase was then expanded to, "Only for good deeds and not one that would embarrass the community." The same prescription held for families.

The problem of visibility and invisibility is an interesting one relating to figure-ground perceptions. Most movie viewers see the lone Japanese samurai as the main figure—stoic, noble, loyal, with the ability to repress his passions—while in the background are the thousands of others who connive, fornicate, lust, cry, break down, and openly behave with the full repertoire of human emotions. Yet is important to note that generalizations concerning the Japanese are usually drawn from the more visible, single samurai, rather than the numerous others.

The Issei choice of being less visible was shaped by their culture (one knew his/her place in the Japanese social structure and conducted self accordingly) and reinforced through their interaction with the American social structure. Competing on equal terms with the White man usually meant additional discriminatory treatment, so that one strategy for survival was the "low posture" and staying in the background in order not to bring undue negative attention on themselves. Therefore, life styles were conservative, and those visible behaviors that would reflect on the community were discouraged (for example, crime, delinquency, mental illness, flashy clothes, ostentatious spending), whereas behaviors like good grades in school and membership in scholarship, honor, and good citizenship groups were strongly reinforced.

As a result, it was unusual to see Issei and Nisei riding in Cadillacs, purchasing large, expense homes in exclusive districts (even if such were available), and using money in a way to draw public attention. Clothes were often dated and conservative in style, and for many, the less expensive was chosen with the inference that the "best" was reserved for the Caucasian. The unstated inference "Who does he think he is, a ha-ku-jin [Caucasian]" was often strong enough to discourage those who violated the norms. However, for many of the newer generations, a reaction formation to some of the Issei prescriptions has developed. Many demand the "best," translated into the most expensive from the most prestigious stores, so labels have become extremely important.

The desire for invisibility is related to a number of other socialization goals. Japanese are expected to be quiet, conforming, obedient, and to avoid loud, attention-getting behavior, especially in public places. And Japanese students in class—whether in Tokyo or Honolulu or Los Angeles—retain much of the invisibility by their lack of overt participation.

OTHER FACTORS

There was also a strong emphasis on filial piety. It was originally a reciprocal obligation, but many Issei have felt that in the United States it has been somewhat unilateral: the story of Issei parents denying their own needs for their children is common, whereas the converse is less likely to occur.

There were other facets of both the Japanese and Japanese-American systems that may be more closely related to income (and subsequent living conditions) rather than to some other explanation. One concerns sleeping arrangements: in Japan, children sleeping with their mothers (usually the youngest child) and their fathers (the older child) is common, even to relatively older ages. A group of Nisei were asked about their present sleeping arrangements: the emphasis is on separate rooms for each child (even babies), but in their own upbringing, most remembered, some with embarrassment, that they slept with their parents and then with other siblings up to the beginning of school and even later.

The closer living arrangements are related to both economic conditions, and cultural preferences. There may be psychological benefits arising from parent-child sleeping arrangements.

ATTITUDES TOWARD WORK

One of the most salient features of the Japanese culture, which cuts across the parallel structures, has been attitudes toward work. It was and still remains such an important part of the Japanese culture that one anonymous professor is quoted in the *Japan Times:* "Japanese work as if they were addicted to it. Japanese forced to retire because of age face a lonely life because they have lost the most meaningful part of their existence" (Japan Times, 1973:3).

When compared to the Protestant ethic and the value it places on work, the roots of the Japanese work orientation apparently go back much further. The work ethic may stem from the teachings of Confucius and Buddha; other forces that shaped the practice included the very survival of an island culture with limited natural resources where the greatest asset was the people themselves. Some Japanese we have talked to include other explanations, including that of "blood," meaning that they feel it is a hereditary characteristic that can be transmitted.

There is little question that the social structure was designed to take advantage of Japan's human resource. The value of work was part of the Meiji school curriculum, and one of the main reasons behind the dramatic rise of present-day Japan as an economic power has been the productivity of its labor force.

The Issei immigrants brought over this attitude to the United States, and for many, the problem of sheer survival reinforce this perspective. Hard work was looked on as a desirable goal in itself, and there was often a feeling that occupations that somehow appeared unrelated to sheet sweat and toil (music, show business) were less desirable. We know some surviving Issei who still refuse to purchase a completely automatic washing machine because they feel that something is vaguely lacking (work and effort) in the procedure. Work has played a prominent part in the socialization of most Japanese Americans, and it was reinforced in their contacts with the American culture.

It is our belief that the combination of a Japanese culture emphasizing norms, or the "how to behave" aspects of life, coupled with the content of the norms such as in the enryo syndrome, help to achieve understanding of Japanese behavior in the United States. The cooperative, relatively docile behavior of the Japanese during the wartime evacuation is an example of the consequences of socialization with this pattern. Although we have emphasized some of the possible negative effects of enryo, it also has many positive features, and many Japanese must privately wish that Americans would learn more about the practice of enryo.

VALUES

In describing the general values of the Japanese group, we refer particularly to two studies, that of Iga, in which he compares values of Nisei, Sansei, Japanese in Japan, and a California Caucasian group (1966); and a study by the author, which describes value changes in Japanese Americans by generation (Kitano, 1969). More recent, work on values is being conducted by Kawahara (1991) and Kitano (1991).

Iga hypothesizes a number of values thought to be held in common by most Japanese, and then subjects these to empirical test. Each of these values is related to certain personality characteristics. One value derives from the difference between a collective and an individual orientation. Self-needs for the Japanese are deemed to have a lesser priority than group needs—in athletic terms, one can be a team player or play primarily for individual glory. The Japanese tends to be a "team player."

The terms of particularism and universalism are related to group loyalties and identification. The question is, are Japanese values more related to specific institutions or are they related to more universal value systems? The answer for the Japanese is apparently toward particularism. For example, there seems to be no universal concern with religion among the Japanese, and loyalties are instead to the house, the family, and related specific groups. The extension of paternalistic loyalty is seen in the attitudes of self-sacrifice by employees, and in the attitudes of benevolence and obligation on the part of Japanese employers.

Another value is conformism, regard for conventional behavior, and obedience to rules and regulations. Related to this is the frequent development of dependent personalities. Comprising and yielding to others is highly approved, and disruptive behavior is censured. Further, discipline and obedience are mandatory, so that self-control, resignation, and gratitude are highly desirable. Many Japanese also feel that suffering and hard work are necessary ingredients of character-building.

There is also a heavy Japanese emphasis on status distinction and "knowing one's place," so that age, sex (masculine superiority), class, caste, family lineage, and other variables of social status are important in the Japanese culture. Finally, much value is attached to aspiration and competitiveness, but also to obligation and dependency, especially within the family circle.

As with most value system schemata, there are conflicts and incongruencies that are difficult to resolve on the conceptual level. Nevertheless, on the basis of these hypothesized values, Iga feels that the Japanese individual will have certain personality traits: fear of power, insecurity, obedience, cliquishness, and an inability to make forceful decisions.

Iga's findings provided general validation for his major hypothesis. Fro example, the Japanese in Japan were found to hold the most "Japanese values," followed by the Japanese American, then by the Caucasian. Significant differences between the Japanese American and the Caucasian were found among the following: conformity, compromise, success, aspiration, obligation, and dependency. The Japanese American was closer to hypothesized Japanese values on each of these measures.

GENERATIONAL CHANGES

The writer administered an instrument to groups of Issei, Nisei, and Sansei for the purpose of describing value changes by generation. A group of American college students were also given the same instrument for comparative purposes. The attitudes tested were toward ethnic identity, means-ends, masculinity and responsibility, individual-group orientation, passivity, and realistic expectations.

Ethnic identity refers to the degree of Japanesness, and the preference, by generation, for things ethnic over things American.

Means-end refers to forms of ethical behavior wherein the way of doing things is considered as important as the result of doing them. In other words, "how" is as important, or more important than the "why."

Masculinity-femininity refers to the definition and acceptance of clear distinctions between male and female roles. The American culture probably provides a less clear-cut male role, which results in more role confusion. *Individual-group conformity* refers to individual and collective behavior.

Passivity is related to a fatalistic orientation. An individual resigns himself to external conditions as diverse as a wartime evacuation or reverses in business with the Japanese phrase *shi-ka-ta-ga-nai* (it can't be helped) and a shrug of the shoulders.

Realistic expectations refers to the discrepancy between expectations and reality. Expectations are especially difficult to quantify because abilities and opportunities differ widely from individual to individual. However, from this perspective, we have the impression that the Japanese are an "underexpectant" group—that is, the goals are set low so that it is easy to attain them. For example, it is common for a young man, qualified to be a doctor, to choose to become a pharmacist. The consequence of this is that Japanese are frequently overtrained and overqualified for the jobs in which they find themselves. In the long run, both overexpectancy and underexpectancy are dysfunctional—reaching for the unattainable is as immature as not reaching at all.

The data strongly support a point of view indicating a change of values with each succeeding Japanese generation. In each case, the direction is toward acculturation. A further refinement of the inventory resulted in the isolation of nine factors, which we labeled duty and obligation to family, ethnocentrism, trust in parental authority, independence of family, internal locus of control, responsibility and self-reliance, guilt and family authority, alienation from community authority, and social acceptance versus achievement.

In general, the empirical evidence on values supports what we know and observe about the Japanese. There is a higher degree of conformity, obedience, a manifestation of ethical behavior, and respect for authority, and a corresponding low degree of acting out, overt rebellion, and independence.

There are other values that also help to explain Japanese behavior. One is the concept of *ga-man*, which refers to internalization of, and suppression of, anger and emotion. My father often tells of early episodes of discrimination and mistreatment to which he was subjected. A simple walk down the street, in 1919 in San Francisco, often resulted in being shoved into the gutter and called a "damn Jap." But my father would *ga-man*, that is, take no retaliatory action, and the incidents never escalated into serious conflict.

Another characteristic value of Japanese Americans has been competitiveness. This would at first seem to be in conflict with values of conformity and group loyalty, but, as in the case of most values, there are combinations that are difficulty to resolve conceptually. The encouragement of personal excellence—"do the best you can, no matter what you are doing"—can be interpreted to mean both "be a credit to the Japanese group," or, simply, "be best." Interestingly enough, the competitive behavior of most Japanese is seen primarily in relation to other Japanese. Many Sansei prefer to enroll in college classes that have no other Sansei because they will feel more relaxed there. Japanese families have to keep up with the Watanabes, but don't worry so much about keeping up with the Joneses.

Certain rules also seem to govern competition within the Japanese group. An economically successful Issei would more likely drive an Oldsmobile than a Cadillac. The more expensive car would be considered "flaunting his success." It is important to be a winner, but equally important that the winner be humble, modest, and self-depreciating.

But acculturation has modified the older ways, and there is now a wider dispersion of life styles in the Japanese community. Some have the wealth and flaunt it, but others in the same income level prefer more modest life styles. The equating of the "best" with "name brands," "name stores," and the most expensive is strongly felt in the community, and although such styles may be functional for those with the income, they become additional burdens for those less affluent.

For example, Iga (1966) notes that success-aspiration and obligation, both of which the Japanese American values more highly than does the Caucasian, are ideal norms of an older Protestantism, and both values help the group to become successful in America. Some other character-istics in which Japanese Americans are higher than Americans are conformity and compromise. Therefore, a complex of patterns of Japa-nese—American culture, wherein success-aspiration and regard for rapid socioeconomic success are coupled with deference, conformity, and com-promise, may explain why the group at the present time is doing well in America, but has not raised the hostility of the larger society. But the economic success of the Japanese nation has lead to "Japan bashing."

AN "ETHICAL" CULTURE

The American and Japanese cultures have different ways of viewing norms and goals. The American appears more goal-oriented—efficiency, output, productivity, and the bottom line are highly valued, and the primary object is to win or to achieve success. The Japanese system appears much more norm-oriented—the how, the style, and the means of interaction are important—so that playing the game according to the rules is as important as winning it.

The norm-oriented culture may prove to be quite adaptable to external changes (for example, the Issei immigrant, or the behavior of the Japanese during the wartime occupation of Japan), provided that some social structure remains, because interrelationships have meaning in themselves. How to interact with others—superiors, inferiors, and equals—can be relatively easily transferred from one structure to an-other, so that such a system may be less stressful to its members than one that is more success-oriented in terms of goals. For when goals are blocked or are unreachable, or when the lack of success in terms of "output" is glaringly apparent, the individual in such a position may be placed under very high stress.

Our previous illustration of the employer-employee relationship provides an example of the possible difference between the two cul-tures. A Japanese firm will tend to keep an inefficient employee, since

Japanese norms encourage the notion of obligation; the *oyabun* (parent) and the *ko-bun* (child) relationship obtains between employer and employee and is a goal in itself. Conversely, an American firm will not hesitate to fire an unproductive employee—the goals of the system are productivity, and can be summarized in the familiar phrase, "I'm running a business, not a welfare agency."

ASSIMILATION OF THE AMERICAN CULTURE

The present trend away from the Japanese culture in terms of norms, values, and personality means that in the near future there will be almost complete acculturation. For example, although Japanese and Americans have differed in the past in their collective and individualist orientations, the collectivity orientation has diminished among Sansei and at present is similar to that of Caucasian samples. Egoistic behavior and the importance of self over others has developed to such an extent that, in a study discussed earlier, on a question dealing with the family and the nation, the Sansei held more individualistic positions than did the non-Japanese American! Similarly, standards of discipline, paternalism, status distinctions, and other parameters of the "American" value system show that the Sansei are for all practical purposes completely acculturated. Iga (1967) states:

> Their (the Sansei) desire to be assimilated appears to be so complete and their knowledge of Japanese culture so marginal that we cannot anticipated their return to traditional Japanese cultural interests. The only factor which prevents them from complete assimilation seems to be the combination of their physical visibility, and racial prejudice on the part of dominant group members.

But parts of the Japanese culture undoubtedly remain. Traditionalists carry on such activities as the tea ceremony, flower arranging, ondos, and other dances; sukiyaki, sushi, sashimi, and other Japanese dishes have gone beyond the boundaries of the ethnic group.

Certain traditions have been lost. There were the public singing performances of the otherwise restrained Issei parents at festivals and picnics, and the self-conscious present generations have not stepped in to fill the void. Karaoke has become popular, but it appears that newcomers from Japan and non-Japanese are more prominent in performing than Nisei and Sansei. Some values—responsibility, concern for others and quiet dignity—will hopefully survive but other less attractive aspects—authoritative discipline, blind obedience, out of touch rituals, the extensive use of guilt and shame to shape behavior, and the second class role of females—will not be much regretted in their passing.

BIBLIOGRAPHY

1. Benedict, Ruth (1946). *The Chrysanthemum and the Sword*. Boston: Houghton Mifflin Co.

2. Doi, Takeo (1962). "Amae: A Key Concept for Understanding Personality Structure." *Psychologia*, 5. Kyoto: Department of Psychology.

3. Dore, Ronald (1958). *City Life in Japan*. Berkeley: University of California Press.

4. Gordon, Milton (1964). *Assimilation in American Life*. New York: Oxford University Press.

5. Iga, Mamoru (1967). "Do Most Japanese-Americans Living in the United States Still Retain Traditional Japanese Personality?" *Kashu Mainichi* (California Daily News), Los Angeles, June 21.

6. Iga, Mamoru (1966). "Changes in Value Orientation of Japanese Americans." Paper read at the Western Psychological Association Meeting, April 28 at Long Beach, California.

7. Japan Times newspaper article (1973). Tokyo, p. 3.

8. Kawahara, Yoshito (1991). "Asian American and Euro-American Values." Research in progress.

9. Kitano, Harry (1969). "Japanese American Mental Illness," in S. Plog and R. Edgerton (Eds.), *Changing Perspectives on Mental Illness, pp. 256-84*. New York: Holt, Rinehart and Winston.

10. Kitano, Harry H. (1991). "Cultural Sensitivity and Values." Research in progress.

11. Mass, Amy (1986). Amae: Indulgence and Nurturance in Japanese American Families. Los Angeles: University of California (Doctoral Dissertation).

12. Massey, D.S. (1988). "Economic Development and International Migration in Comparative Perspective." *Population and Development Review*, 14: 383-413.

13. Meredith, Gerald (1966). "Amae and Acculturation among Japanese College Students in Hawaii." *The Journal of Social Psychology*, 70: 171-80.

14. Wagatsuma, Hiroshi (1977). "Some Aspects of the Contemporary Japanese Family: Once Confucion, Now Fatherless?" *Daedulus*, 106 (2): 181-210.

CHAPTER 8

THE COMMUNITY: ITS ORGANIZATION

Without supporting structures and organizations, it would be difficult for the "culture" of the ethnic group to be carried on in any consistent fashion. Norms and values have to reinforced, most often by the family, but also by larger units, such as the neighborhood, by the schools and by the community. The purpose of this chapter is to show the relationship between the Japanese American culture and the community structures which served to shape and reinforce its norms and values.

PARALLEL STRUCTURES

As indicated in the previous chapter, nothing could be more lonely than arriving alone in a strange land with few skills, and with little knowledge of the language and culture. In addition, there was hostility aimed at the newcomers because of racial features, so that there was a need for friendly and familiar faces. But even more important than an initial welcome was the need for longer term services, such as jobs, housing, and information.

The development and maintenance of the ethnic community, with parallel services was the saving grace for the Japanese immigrant. The ethnic community filled major needs; one could go to a Japanese doctor, dentist or optometrist; there were ethnically run stores and restaurants; one could consult an ethnic real estate agent and there were places of entertainment which featured ethnic performers. Issei could buy stocks and bonds, read ethnic newspapers and could live their lives without straying afar from the ethnic community. As a result, prejudice, discrimination, and hostility from the white society did not lead to mass alienation, despair, and dependence on the dominant community, although the choices within their community, especially in terms of upward mobility were limited. With their common ancestry, similar values, and background experiences about community life in Japan, hostility and rejection from the outside world strengthened, rather than weakened ethnic solidarity.

ECONOMIC OPPORTUNITIES

One of the most important resources was the economic opportunities within one's own ethnic community. There was a two-way interaction between jobs and ethnic solidarity; economic factors strengthened community ties; community ties provided for economic opportunities. As Bonacich and Modell (1980) indicate, economic factors played an important role in the retention of ethnic ties, so that the linkage between the ethnic community and the ability to make a living constituted one of the strongest bonds in ethnic solidarity.

The period prior to World War II, where discrimination and lack of opportunity in the mainstream was high, the Issei (and older Nisei) lived in a highly organized, internally unified community. There was a heavy concentration in agriculture, where large sums of money were not necessary; lease arrangements were common, and there was a move towards becoming farmers and farm managers, especially among the Nisei. In the urban areas, many were self employed (the mom and pop stores), or in nonindustrial family businesses and in marginal lines of endeavor. They remained competitive through hard work, the use of family labor, efficiency, and long hours. It was a common observation that the Japanese owned stores would remain open throughout the holidays; they also emphasized services, such as home delivery, and stocked ethnically familiar products, such as tofu, soy sauce and saké.

However, their children have seldom followed the path of their parents; the hours were too long, the pay was too little, the jobs had low status, especially for those with college degrees. It is interesting to note that in the 1990s, newly arrived Asian immigrant groups, notably the Koreans, have carried on the tradition of small business and "mom and pop" stores, and there is little doubt that their college educated children will also look for career opportunities elsewhere.

Community cooperation was also a part of the parallel system. The accumulation of capital through voluntary groups, such as the "tanomoshi" (Miyamoto, 1939; Light, 1972) provided a modest amount of capital for business ventures. The vertical integration of businesses within the ethnic community (i.e. there were Japanese owned suppliers, distributors, retailers and customers) meant that all facets of a venture could remain within the ethnic community. There was the control of competition between Issei firms, and recognizing ethnic-group interests above other interests helped to develop a strong ethnic group economy (Bonacich and Modell, 1980).

The community, lead by the Issei, provided the primary source of employment for the Nisei prior to World War II. There was a high Nisei concentration in produce retailing in Los Angeles County; the pre-war stereotype of university graduates working in the produce markets lead to the somewhat cynical observation that the fruits and vegetables in the Los Angeles produce markets were being handled by extremely intelligent workers:

Okura (1991) relates some of his personal experiences:

> Well, a bunch of us Nisei went to UCLA (in the early 1930s), but couldn't live in Westwood because of housing discrimination. So we rented a place and could always find work in the produce markets. The pay wasn't much but we always had good fruits and vegetables.
>
> I wanted to get a job at UCLA; I was lucky because I finally became a teaching assistant to Grace Fernald in the Psych Department. I may have been the first Nisei to be hired as a teaching assistant.

Although Nisei could survive in the ethnic economy, at least there was some type of employment, there was much dissatisfaction (Ichihashi, 1932; Strong, 1934). The discrepancy between getting a college education and hopes for a white collar position, coupled with racism and job discrimination meant that many were forced back into whatever opportunities there were in the ethnic economy. Many of the jobs in "J" town were based on paternalism, low pay, long hours and expectations of loyalty which meant that if and when opportunities became available in the larger community, there was a work force, ready, willing and able to move into whatever opportunities were available.

Unfortunately, the new job opportunities that opened up in 1942 were in the concentration camps of World War II. But it should be noted that for the first time, the Nisei were able to fill such positions as firemen, policemen, accountants, time keepers, teachers, and the full range of jobs (except for those executive positions filled by Caucasians) that were necessary to keep the camps going. There was also the experience of those who relocated into the Midwest and the East Coast where there were job opportunities that were more in line with their education and training.

VOLUNTARY COMMUNITY ORGANIZATIONS

There were a wide variety of organizations in the Issei community, ranging from those involved in business, to area of birth (the "ken"), to informal recreational groups (the most popular was fishing), to those involved in health and welfare. Issei exposure to the American mainstream was limited; segregation, language difficulties and the like meant the development of their own organizations. The most important was The Japanese Association.

The Japanese Association of America was initially formed by the Japanese consulate general in San Francisco in 1909. Tokyo was concerned about the reputation of its emigrants, largely because it felt that its prestige as a nation was involved. Therefore, they tried to exert a degree of social control over the Issei, and attempted to create and nurture organizations which would enhance the good reputation of the nation. Theoretically, all Japanese in the United States had to belong to the association through a local or regional group, with dues from $1 to $3 per year.

To encourage membership, the Japanese government, through its consulates, gave the associations an official role and made them the intermediaries through which individual Japanese residents had to pass if they wished to retain official connection with the Japanese government. Both Japanese law and the Gentlemen's Agreement required the Japanese consular service to issue certain documents to resident Japanese. The responsibility for these certificates was delegated to the association, which in turn could collect fees for their issue (Kitano and Daniels, 1988).

Such items as travel abroad and the right to return, and the ability to bring into the country wives, children and parents were covered by the certificates. But because of its connection with the Japanese government, several problems arose. First, the Issei were not given the highest priority—the reputation of Japan was more important. Therefore, local complaints affecting the lives of the immigrants were often bypassed in favor of international priorities.

A major portion of the activities of a Japanese Association was devoted to intra-community affairs. It established and maintained graveyards, provided translators, placed people in contact with legal and other necessary services, and policed the activities of the Japanese community. For instance, the Japanese Association would try to curtail prostitution, gambling, and other activities which might "give a bad name" to the Japanese. They also sponsored picnics and gave backing to youth groups and youth services. But these organizations had few contacts with the majority community, and those few contacts were limited to formal business or ritualistic occasions involving the leaders only. The Japanese Association might participate with the larger community to the extent of sponsoring a float in a local parade or helping to collect for the Community Chest.

An illustration of one of the functions of the Associations was to issue directives to control gambling. Ichioka (1988) cites a 1918 anti-gambling proposal which included some of the following: To report the names and addresses of all known gamblers; to photograph, publish, and distribute the names of all gamblers to the immigrant press, and to their native places in Japan, and to order hotels to expel gamblers.

Although the Associations had little overt power to control gambling and other "vices" of the Issei, nevertheless they attempted to act as the arbitrators of morality. Gambling remains one of the more popular recreational activities among present day Japanese Americans—the race track at Santa Anita, and the casinos in Las Vegas and Lake Tahoe have more than their share of Asian customers.

There was prestige and status in becoming leaders in the Association. I remember my father buying fifths of whiskey to be distributed judiciously when running for the presidency of the San Francisco group. Conversely, he was the recipient of similar gifts (even though he was a non-drinker) when others were running for office. Although the position was largely ceremonial, it gave Issei a chance to play leadership roles that were unavailable in the larger society.

The height of the Japanese Associations coincided with the age and power of the Issei. They were especially prominent prior to World War II when the Issei were in their prime; they were still visible during the post-war era, but from the 1970s on, the advancing age of the Issei, the Associations also diminished in importance.

THE JAPANESE AMERICAN CITIZEN'S LEAGUE (JACL)

The JACL can be thought of as a second-generation counterpart to the Japanese Associations. It, too, developed in response to the special problems and interests of the Japanese, but primarily of the Nisei. Although its initial function was protective, it served, in a way that the Japanese Associations did not, to accelerate acculturation. It was first begun in 1919 by young Nisei, whose interests were not served by the Japanese Association, and who therefore established local Nisei groups, called by various names such as Loyalty League, or Citizen's League. By the early 1930s, these local groups had consolidated into a national organization, supported by local chapters which cut across religious, "ken," political and special interest ties. The special plight of the Nisei was more than sufficient to override these previously divisive factors. There were problems of citizenship for their Issei parents, of the continuing discrimination and prejudice with which they themselves were faced, and their own problems in the larger society. In addition, the Nisei group was relatively homogenous in age, interests and goals, so that, as is often the case with groups formed in response to special social crises, the JACL developed quickly into an effective organization (Hosokawa, 1982).

In many ways, the JACL was synonymous with the name of Mike Masaoka, who served as the leader of the organization for many years. In his book, *They Call Me Moses* (1987), he comments that one of the challenges for the Nisei was to fight the label of "unassimilability." Rather than giving into this image, he emphasized that the Nisei were products of America so that they should speak English and forget their ancestral heritage; they were to embrace the future and not the past, and to demonstrate their Americanism in such a way that even though they looked "oriental," they were in fact American. Masaoka's strong stand for assimilation and Americanism was sorely tested by the attack on Pearl Harbor.

The gravest crisis with which the JACL had to deal was World War II and the evacuation. Because it was the only national Japanese-American organization, many Japanese looked to it for leadership. It decided to cooperate fully with evacuation orders. In this decision it actually had little choice, because there were few alternatives; the community was disorganized, many Issei leaders had been picked up by the FBI, and all ethnic organizations had been disbanded. Many Issei and Nisei had lost their jobs, and small businesses were in precarious condition. The might of the American government was paramount. For these reasons, it is not likely that JACL could have effected any other course. And it is probable that, whatever JACL might have decided, the Japanese community would have cooperated with evacuation procedures as it did anyway (Hosokawa, 1982).

However, because they had declared themselves willing to cooperate, many JACL leaders became spacegoats for feelings of resentment which later developed. Some had extremely harrowing experiences at the hands of fellow Japanese in the relocation camps, and the JACL is to this day resented by some for its cooperation during the World War II crisis.

The primary importance of the JACL remains its role in the acculturating of the Nisei. It accelerated this process in two ways; first, it broke away from the Issei community, and, secondly, it was modeled after American groups. The early conventions, planned and financed by Nisei, concentrated on Nisei problems exclusively, but the debates and procedures followed American patterns. Most importantly, exposure to local and national issues widened the horizons of the Nisei. A possible measure of the general success and affluence of this group is perhaps provided by the sites of its present meetings. Early gatherings were held in local community halls or churches. Today they are held in expensive resorts, with all the external trappings of any middle-class American convention.

With acculturation, increased affluence, and diminishing hostility from the larger community, the JACL finds itself forced to redefine its functions and goals. Many of the unifying issues, such as redress and citizenship for Issei, have been successfully resolved.

It will be interesting to observe the relation of the JACL to the third and fourth generation of Japanese. The Nisei were able to break away from the paternalistic control of the Issei and to develop their own organizations based on their own perception of needs. The barriers of communication, generation, and culture served to the advantage of the Nisei in this respect, since ready made Issei structures and organizations were not handed down to them. The ability of the organization to attract and serve the needs of the newer generations remains the key to its survival.

RELIGION

Religion, in the American sense of Sunday School attendance, belief in a single faith, and relative intolerance of other faiths, is alien to the Japanese. In general they are tolerant of all theologies and have not institutionalized religion to the extent that most Americans have. This was true in Japan at the time the Issei were growing up there, and appears to be true in Japan today. For example, while in Japan recently, we saw a pilgrim on his way to a shinto shrine, carrying a protestant bible and wearing a catholic crucifix. We were told that this was not uncommon, and that many people like to feel they were "touching all bases." The Issei brought with them to America a similarly flexible approach to religion. Most had gone through no baptismal or confirmation ritual, and were not churchgoers, although most came from a broadly Buddhist background which influenced the ceremonial aspects of birth, weddings and deaths. Otherwise, the focus of any religious training was ethical behavior—how one acted toward parents, friends and strangers.

It is therefore not surprising to find certain discrepancies and inconsistencies in religious censuses even today. Many Japanese claim a Buddhist background but may attend a Christian church. A religious survey by Miyamoto (1939) of the Japanese in Seattle in 1936 showed that most were Protestants. Data gathered at the time of the wartime evacuation show the same thing. Data gathered among Japanese in

Brazil found most of them to be Catholic, suggesting that Japanese tend to adopt the religion of the country in which they find themselves.

Initially, it was believed that religious preference was a good predictor of acculturation. Miyamoto indicated that the Buddhists were much more conservative and more "Japanese" than the members of Christian churches. But this point of view, though historically correct, probably ignores the religious flexibility of the Japanese and of the Buddhist church itself in adapting to changing religious conditions.

EARLY CHRISTIANITY

Although early attempts to introduce Christianity in Japan were not successful, Japanese immigrants in the United States provided a fruitful missionary field. Their adoption of the Christian faith was strongly reinforced by practical considerations, because Christian churches had much to offer the new immigrant. Many found employment through their Church, particularly as houseboys. In fact, this was so common that at one time the Japanese houseboy was referred to as a "mission boy." The churches also provided an opportunity to learn to speak and behave like Americans, and had therefore an important acculturative function. Several other factors contributed to the development of Christianity among the Japanese. The social welfare functions of the Church were congruent with Issei experience, and church attitudes of benevolence and helpfulness toward others were sympathetically received. When the new immigrant was without family, the church served in a family role, supplying the feeling of group participation which the family had provided in Japan. Christianity was also less complicated and expensive than Buddhism when it came to such practical matters as weddings or funerals. Churches often provided mission schools, preschools, and kindergartens. The Christian concepts of ethical and moral training were congruent with those of Buddhism, and, finally, the churches played a strong part in defending the Japanese from legislative and political attacks.

Church activities were particularly important in the acculturation of Japanese women. Women's clubs provided for many a first exposure to American ways—food and fashions, democratic group procedures such as voting, and an opportunity to serve in positions of leadership. Many Nisei remember the unexpected results of mother attending a cooking class—spaghetti, whipped cream desserts, Chinese chow mein and Italian veal cutlets.

These early church activities were usually presided over, in a missionary spirit, by Caucasian ministers and interested congregations.

However, as time went on, the Japanese tended to form all-Japanese congregations. This has by now produced an interesting reversal, in which the educational activities of the Church provide, not lessons in Americanization but lessons in Japanese culture—flower arranging and other culture activities—and are for many the sole contact with their Japanese heritage.

There was one potential source of conflict between Christianity and the Japanese culture. This was the Christian emphasis on individualism, which, on the surface of things, would seem to be incongruent with the cohesiveness of other Japanese social principles. But because, within the cohesive Japanese community lay an inherent competitiveness, the apparent philosophical incongruence provided no real practical difficulties.

Although theoretical differences in the roles played by Buddhists and Christian churches in acculturation can be hypothesized, actual differences are hard to detect. Both churches have Sunday school, Sunday services, and bazaars, social services, women's and youth programs. Buddhist weddings have shortened and resemble Christian ceremonies. Both churches give services in English and Japanese. The ministers of both churches are usually Japanese, although by now, they may be Sansei. In general, although there may have been initial differences in the direction of acculturation, both institutions, both particularly the Buddhist, have themselves changed to the point that they are relatively similar, at least to casual observers. Japanese parents of either religion usually agree that "it doesn't matter what church you go to, so long as you go to church."

NISEI COMMUNITY ORGANIZATIONS

It would be difficult to overlook the vast network of services and opportunities available to the Japanese youth. Some are by definition based on mainstream models—the Boy and Girl Scouts, the YM and YWCA's, and the Campfire Girls. Others, such as Judo or Kendo groups, are strictly Japanese, but all serve to function as agents of socialization and social control.

Probably best known to the Nisei and least known to outsiders were the ambitious all-Japanese athletic league. These tended to concentrate on basketball, a sport which did not require expensive uniforms and facilities, and which, because of considerations such as physical size, limited competition with non-Japanese groups. The all-Japanese leagues were organized into divisions according to age and locality, and held regional and Statewide playoffs. At one time there was a national Oriental championship. The golden age of Nisei basketball was in the late

1930s and again in the 1940s and early 1950s. It offered the usual advantages of participation in a group activity—team and group identification, travel, competition and rewards. Ironically, the Nisei basketball team was often the only group through which a youngster identified with his high school. For example, one Nisei relates:

> "I used to wait for the All-Hi Tournaments. It was the time when all Nisei going to different high schools in San Francisco would get together and compete. We'd have rooting sections, championships playoffs, all-star teams, medals and trophies, and then a big victory dance (Kitano, 1962)."

After the tournament, a Nisei, who might have been named the "most valuable player," and have been much-praised in the ethnic newspaper, would resume his anonymous role among the larger student body of his Caucasian high school.

The Nisei learned far more from these teams than the skills of athletic competition. It was an experience of independence, travel, social interaction and role-playing. Here a boy could be a "big fish in a little pond"; his brothers, sisters, and girl friends would come to see him play; there would be dances, bazaars, and other fund-raising and supportive activities. The basketball teams therefore became primary reference groups for many, and a Nisei would often introduce himself by saying "I'm from the Cardinals," which meant that he was from Los Angeles, or as being from the Zebras of San Jose, or from the Greyhounds—a YMCA group in San Francisco.

The basketball teams served as a vehicles for acculturation. The Issei remained aloof from them, and considered them rather frivolous, so that the Nisei were free to develop in the American pattern. The play, the rules, the goals, and values were all American; only the players were Japanese. In spite of this, any integration attempts were firmly resisted. Big fights were apt to occur if a non-Japanese or part-Japanese player with one of the teams. In the 30s, a great crisis developed when a group called the San Francisco Mikados—perennial champions—left the league to play in a larger community league. "Do they think they're too good for us now?" stormed the other players, parents, ethnic newspapers, and community sponsors. The offending group came back to play in the ethnic league again the following year.

It comes as a mild surprise that Japanese athletic teams and leagues continue to the present day. Increased opportunities in other areas for individual and group participation might have diminished some of the enthusiasm, but there remain a variety of athletic activities that still attract many of the younger members of the community. Basketball, volley ball and the Little Leagues baseball teams provide opportunities for participation where there is a degree of equality in terms of size and athletic ability.

PAN-ASIAN GROUPS

One possible development in the Japanese American community is to participate in pan-Asian organizations. Espiritu (1992) writes about past attempts, such as the Council of Oriental Organizations (COO), to develop pan-Asian coalitions. Most coalitions have been short lived for a number of reasons including issues of power (Chinese and Japanese domination); the constant struggle for resources, domination by middle-class professionals, past nationality differences, generational, cultural and leadership issues, and shifting levels of solidarity. Unity was strengthened by anti-Asian violence.

THE BELLEVUE HOTEL CONFERENCE

One of the most interesting Pan-Asian Conferences took place at the Bellevue Hotel in San Francisco in 1972. The National Institute of Mental Health (NIMH) had responded to the growing unrest concerning the lack of Federal attention for the Blacks, Chicanos and other minority groups by holding a number of conferences with mental health professionals. Patrick Okura, who was the Executive Assistant to the Director, Bertram Brown at that time said:

> Well we only had funds to invite about 86 representatives from across the country to the conference. I had assured Bert that this conference would be different from the ones that were held for the Blacks and Chicanos. It was going to be peaceful.
>
> Imagine our surprise when about 612 Asians showed up at the Bellevue. We had to develop at least 10 more workshops, recruit discussion leaders and were totally unprepared for the confrontational style, including the demand for funds
>
> (Kitano, 1992).

As one of the invitees to the conference, I too was surprised by the interaction between the various Asian American attendees and representatives of the Federal Government.

> The first thing that I remember was that in the opening session, George Woo, then a community activist, but currently an administrator at San Francisco State University, demanded (in colorful language) that all persons representing the FBI get up and leave.
>
> That set the tone of the conference. The Federal officials were characterized as ignorant, as insensitive, as not caring, and as racists.

Attempts to explain the Federal position were met with hoots, shouts, and laughter. There were strong feelings of solidarity, unity and brotherhood among the attendees, so that this diverse group of Asians felt a surge of power in their confrontation with the mental health establishment. The three day meeting came to a close with NIMH Director Brown fleeing in the trunk of a car.

It is to the credit of Director Brown and his staff that they did not take the attacks personally, and instead were able to provide resources for mental health research and training. Under the direction of Royal Morales, over 160 Asian American students benefited from the Asian American Community Mental Health Training Center (1970-82). A large number gained their MSW's from the University of Southern California (USC), and the University of California, Los Angeles (UCLA). The development of social and mental health services to the Asian American communities was one concrete result from that conference.

However, the impetus that was developed several decades ago is no longer visible, so that those who went through that conference feel that another Bellevue Hotel type meeting may be necessary.

Fugita and O'Brien (1991) indicate that Japanese American voluntary organizations have existed without exclusive strong ethnic ties. They can be involved in many aspects of the mainstream community while still supporting their ethnic organizations. For example, Japanese Americans may be scattered throughout a community, such as in Los Angeles; work in mainstream settings and interact primarily with non-Japanese, yet support their ethnic community through such organizations as the Japanese American National Museum, and the JACL. It is primarily a bi-cultural approach.

In summary, the ethnic community provided the following for the Issei:

1. A structure for mutual aid and assistance, and carrying on ethnic norms and values.

2. Opportunities for leadership roles and maintaining a degree of contact with both Japanese and American officials.

3. A parallel opportunity structure in the face of prejudice, discrimination and segregation.

For the Nisei:

1. Development of their own organizations which fostered economic, political, social and athletic opportunities.

2. Fostered independence from Issei organizations.

3. Provided experiences based on mainstream models.

4. Provided a source for ethnic identity, while still participating in the mainstream culture.

The current generations have a much wider range of opportunities, both in the ethnic community and in the mainstream. At the university level, they can "rush" for some of the mainstream sororities and fraternities, as well as join groups that are primarily Asian. Although remnants of the values and norms of the Issei and the old Nisei culture remain, most of their attitudes and behaviors are closer to the American mainstream. Yet, many still participate in ethnic organizations.

BIBLIOGRAPHY

1. Bonacich, Edna and John Modell (1980). *The Economic Basis of Ethnic Solidarity: Small Busines in the Japanese American Community*. Berkeley: University of California Press.

2. Espiritu, Yen Le (1992). *Asian American Panethnicity: Bridging Institutions and Identities*. Philadelphia: Temple University Press.

3. Fugita, Stephen S. and O'Brien, David J. (1991). *Japanese American Ethnicity*. Seattle: University of Washington Press.

4. Hosokawa, Bill (1982). *JACL in Quest for Justice*. New York: Morrow and Co.

5. Ichihashi, Yamato (1932). *Japanese in the United States*. Stanford: Stanford University Press.

6. Ichioka, Yuji (1988). *The Issei: The World of the First Generation Japanese American Immigrants, 1885-1924*. New York: Free Press.

7. Kitano, Harry H.L. (1962 and 1992). Personal collection of interviews.

8. Kitano, Harry H.L. and Roger Daniels (1988). *Asian Americans*. Englewood Cliffs, New Jersey: Prentice Hall.

9. Light, Ivan (1972). *Ethnic Enterprises in America: Business and Welfare among Chinese, Japanese and Blacks*. Berkeley: University of California Press.

10. Masaoka, Mike (1987) *They Call Me Moses*. New York: Morrrow.

11. Miyamoto, Frank (1939). *Social Solidarity Among the Japanese in Seattle*. Seattle: University of Washington Press.

12. Okura, Patrick (1991). Personal interview, Washington, D.C. April 10.

13. Strong, Edward K. (1934). *The Second Generation Japanese Problem*. Stanford: Stanford University Press.

CHAPTER 9

THE COMMUNITY: ITS FAMILIES

Along with the culture and the organizations making up the Japanese community, the family has been an integral part of the Japanese American experience. There is a common perception, which verges on a stereotype, that the "key" to Japanese American success lies in their families. They are thought to be intact, cohesive, and with the ability to inculcate their offspring with important norms and values. However, as we have indicated previously, there are a wide variety of Japanese American families, ranging from those with very "modern" American outlooks, to those retaining a high degree of the ethnic style.

As with most generalizations there is probably some truth to the perception of the strength of Japanese American families, but there remain a number of questions. Are we talking about the Issei, Nisei or Sansei family? What about interracial families? What are some of the family values? What role has exposure to the dominant society and acculturation played in changing the family? The purpose of this chapter is to answer some of the above questions.

THE FAMILY AT A JAPANESE COMMUNITY PICNIC

It is hard to believe that I have not attended a Japanese Community Picnic for over thirty years. But when I was still a student at the University of California in Berkeley in the 1950s, the San Francisco Community held a yearly picnic, and the following is a summary of what I can recall from one such picnic.

On a day in early summer Japanese American citizens gather for their most visible rite, the annual picnic. Here in microcosm may be seen

113

the workings of the Japanese American community as a whole and of the Japanese family through several generations. Thousands of families, congregating in larger groups related to the original ken or province of their forefathers, celebrate their Japaneseness, their sense of a heritage different from the white American culture of which they are a part in day-to-day life. The proportions of these picnics are staggering—ten thousand people are reported to attend the largest of them, in Elysian Park in Los Angeles. It is difficult to think of another American racial or national minority group which maintains a social event of such size and regularity, unless it would be displaced Iowans, whose immense annual picnic in Long Beach, California, provides fair analogy.

The resemblance of the Japanese to the Iowa picnic will be apparent to anyone who has much knowledge of the traditional middle-western institution, and the resemblance should be borne in mind, for, developing as it does from two totally dissimilar backgrounds, the likeness of Japanese to Iowan enforces a critical point about the success of the Japanese in America. The essentially congruent values of Japanese and middle-class American permit compatible coexistence without assimilation.

Picnic day, which is not dictated by tradition, has been settled upon in advance by a committee of leaders of the Japanese community. Before the war, Japanese holidays were often designated, by now convenience and a hope of good weather are primary considerations. The day does not coincide with any other traditional Japanese festival, and opinion among Issei is divided about its origins. Some hold that there was never such a thing as a community picnic in Japan, while others claim they had them all the time.

At any rate, arrangements are made to use some available public park. Japanese merchants are canvassed for donations or merchandise to be used for prizes and favors. They are happy to comply, and derive for their generosity the good will of their fellows, income tax advantages, and the removal from inventory of whatever has been superfluous anyway. Someone donates a loudspeaker system which, within a roped-off area, plays loud Japanese music, formerly of the traditional variety, but now betraying the Western beat that has crept into most popular music from Japan. In fact, this is all right with most of the picnicgoers, for none but the purest Issei ear really enjoys the old music. Similarly, none but the Issei can read with any assurance the large signs written in Japanese characters to guide the picnic-goers in the right direction. But the music and the signs and the gay lanterns have a Japanese feel, and feeling Japanese is what is wanted on this most festive of days.

Our typical family arrives at the picnic and spreads its blankets on the ground near relatives and friends. The littlest children immediately scamper off in the company of their fellows. Teenage sons and daughters, at the age when they are likely to feel self-conscious and contemptuous of the whole affair, have usually not come at all, although a few can be seen holding hands, and dancing rock-and-roll furtively at the perimeters of the gathering. They are generally disapproved. But for the most part, teenagers and young adults are absent. Most will reappear in a few years, when they have become young parents and find themselves an awakened interest in Japanese pastimes and traditions.

The most conspicuous group at the picnic are not the young but the old,—the Issei men—because many are drunk. The picnic is one of the few occasions during the year when workday gravity, sobriety, and decorum are set aside. Now they gather in convivial groups upon the grass, pass the whiskey (overtly if they are single, and covertly if they are married), and indulge a license for "racy" talk. There is, in fact, a faintly Japanese formality to the talk; it is laden with stylized metaphor about sex through gardens and seed, but in any event it represents sufficient departure from the usual conversational conventions to be striking.

The Issei brand of loose talk probably sits unfamiliarly at first upon the tongues of the younger, Nisei men, who have learned the Western variety. But to the Nisei, it is a great satisfaction to be admitted to the Issei group; at least to be invited to drink with the Issei at the Japanese picnic is something akin to a *rite de passage*.

The young Nisei husband, now admitted to the company of men, nevertheless retains his role of son, and is exhibited in this capacity far and wide, especially if he is successful, by his proud, drunk and garrulous father. The picnic is an occasion for boasting about one's offspring, introducing them to friends and acquaintances, and for receiving praise and congratulations for one's good luck and fertility. Later in the afternoon there will be a prize for the Issei who has the most descendents, and much public commendation of the efficacy of his seed. If he is able, the enviable patriarch will make a little modest speech about having been blessed with a fertile garden to plant. For children are a man's pride and blessing. During the races and competitive games which take place throughout the afternoon, much store is set on winning. It is important that a man's son be better than other men's sons, and the spirit of the games is more serious than one might find at an Iowa sackrace. The Issei who referee the games (now aided by older Nisei) are dressed correctly in white uniform and shoes. Prizes are given to all participants, with a grand prize—always a large sack of rice given to lucky winners.

Other forms of entertainment follow the games. These usually include a brief speech by the local consul from Japan, who is all dressed up in black coat and necktie, and is cheered enthusiastically by the rowdy crowd. Some attempt is made to arrange the picnic when the Japanese naval training ship is in port; the smartly-dressed young naval cadets drill and demonstrate Japanese games and entertainment. In recent years most Issei have become too old to do their traditional dances as they used to, but there is increasing interest among Nisei groups in learning them, so it may be that these performances will not disappear. Something will be needed to combat the encroachment of rock-and-roll, the favorite of the Sansei generation.

While the men are drinking, talking, visiting other groups of men, reveling, hoping to make a valuable business contact here, saying a few words to an old friend there, all—gardener and banker, Issei and Nisei, father and son, united in the splendid camaraderie of manhood and drink, the situation is somewhat different for the Japanese woman. As in all endeavors which require the family to eat out of doors, for her it is not such a picnic. For one thing, she is likely already tired and tense. If she is Issei, she probably has been cooking various delicacies for several days before. Visitors, coming to exchange a few words with her husband or her, will be offered a sample and she will be covertly judged by the excellence of her cooking. Her daughter, of the Nisei generation, may have refused to be drawn into this subtle competition, and will have bought potato salad instead of o-su-shi, but, as any woman knows, it is not so easy to escape a practically inherent female tendency to become ego-involved when her cooking is on public display. Even the most advanced Nisei is likely to spend an extra, anxious moment over that potato salad. It is possible too, that she has been in overt conflict with her mother or mother-in-law over the whole matter.

Add to this the facts that she has to sit more or less alone on the blanket, dishing up for strangers while husband and children disport themselves around the park, that critical eyes will be judging not only her cooking but her children, whose good deportment she is not very confident of, since they have escaped her direct intervention and are running around, and that her husband is making a fool of himself with the boys in a fashion more or less unprecedented since the picnic last year, and it will be understandable that the ladies get irritable and priggish. But this does little to mar the fun, and when the picnic is over at sundown, all, even the ladies, feel themselves to have had a wonderful time on this one day of vacation from the white man's world. They no longer leave the park with nationalistic cries of "Emperor Hirohito, banzai," as they did before the war, but they do include one final reproach to white America. At a signal, at the end of the day, all, even the tiniest children, set about picking up every last scrap of litter-every wrapper, every plastic spoon, every paper plate and cigarette butt, every tiniest fragment of potato chip. They leave the park as clean as they found it—cleaner than they found it. In fact, it will not be so clean and tidy again for another year.

There have been several rather unpredictable developments arising from the Japanese community picnics. Those given in the city have not changed too much in ethnic composition, but those in the rural areas have served an unexpected integrative function. For example, a Japanese farmer invites a Caucasian neighbor to the Japanese picnic. Year by year this practice becomes more widespread. The Caucasian child, especially, has become fond of the organized games, races and prizes, and his parents apparently enjoy the overall organization as a contrast to the usual informal small family outings that are his norm for the rest of the year. Therefore, in some instances, the Japanese community picnic has become the rural community picnic, given annually and looked forward to with anticipation. The role of the Japanese has become an ambivalent one—as hosts and instigators they find an enormous amount of work and responsibility. At one recent picnic, the Japanese hosts found themselves barbecuing 3,000 chickens, teriyaki style, so that the picnic has become more work than pleasure.

It appears, that at least in California, all-community picnics have gradually been replaced by family groups and gatherings by smaller organizations. For those who enjoyed the experience, its passage is another indication of the changing nature of the ethnic community.

THE TRADITIONAL JAPANESE FAMILY

The Issei, while growing up in Japan, was exposed to a family system which is often labelled as traditional. There was a hierarchical family structure with the husband at the top and preferences for male heirs; there were appropriate roles based on age, status and sex, and there was an emphasis on obligation, duty and loyalty. The organization was based upon Confucian principles which believed that stable families ensured a stable society (Wagatsuma, 1977).

According to Wagatsuma, the *ie* (family, household, house) was central to the family system and served as the primary unit of social organization. The *ie* was a continuous entity which included all past, present and future members of the family so that it was of greater importance than any of its members and their individual interests and goals. It was a composite of the concrete and the abstract, of the material as well as the spiritual, and included such diverse elements as family name, occupation, property, tradition, family altar, graveyard and expected family behavior.

The continuation of the *ie* was extremely important to a family's future, so that the selection of prospective marital partners was a matter for the *ie*, rather than the individuals involved. The social, psychological, health and physical background of prospective mates and their families was carefully scrutinized so that appropriate matches could be made. Marriages were made for the purpose of producing an heir; love marriages were considered immoral because it asserted individual interests over the welfare of the family unit.

Meiji Japan developed a code of norms to guide interpersonal relationships so that there were specified ways of behaving between lord and subject, father and son, husband and wife, older and younger siblings, and friend to friend. It was important to know one's role in relationship to others so that appropriate obligation, duty and loyalty requirements could be fulfilled. Adherence to these norms was considered a sign of virtue.

The importance of status and role consciousness was built into the Japanese language itself which had specific ways of addressing others depending on their role and status. As Benedict observed, there was great security to be bound by the individual in knowing precisely how one should behave in any given situation:

> If the Japanese loved and trusted their meticulously explicit map of behavior, they had a certain justification. It guaranteed security so long as one followed the rules; it allowed protests against unauthorized aggressions and it could be manipulated to one's advantage. It required the fulfillment of reciprocal obligations (1946:73-74).

THE ISSEI FAMILY

Ichioka (1988) indicates that there were two types of Issei immigration; the first, from 1885 to 1907, followed the *dekasegi* pattern, which involved temporary migration, primarily by single men, but always with the goal of returning home. The second pattern, which began from about 1908 was that of permanent residency, encouraged by influential immigrant leaders who felt that the *dekasegi* orientation encouraged American exclusionists in their goal of denying any Japanese immigration.

The initial Issei immigrant was composed of young, single males who had been exposed to Meiji values. But, they did not have their parents, extended family, and *ie* structure to whom they had to pay their obligations, duties and responsibilities. As one consequence, in common with a young, single male population, isolated from the mainstream, they developed their own life styles which often lead to gambling, a search for sex and other behaviors which were eventually controlled through family responsibilities.

They did not have much money, and upon arrival worked for very low wages. Some immigrants and their families sold, or mortgaged everything they owned to raise fares, while others were financed by family and clans with relatives contributing as much as they could (Ichihashi, 1932).

Most of them came with the idea that they would stay for several years and then return to Japan to start their own businesses. But as Miyamoto (1939) indicates, although many did return, and their "hearts and minds" remained in Japan, a significant number came back and decided in favor of permanent residence in the United States. This, in spite of facing prejudice, discrimination, and segregation.

One factor in their adjustment in the face of hostility may have been their value system which encouraged the acceptance of authority, and of their lower status; a collective orientation and their "other directedness" definition of situations (Iga, 1957:274). Oppression, and belonging to a lower status was apparently not too different, whether it be in their home society or in the United States. In addition, economic opportunities, even at the lowest levels may have been better than what was available in Japan.

The shift from the sojourner style to permanent residence meant the beginning of family life. The young males turned to Japan for their future wives for a variety of reasons. Segregated living conditions, racial prejudice, and cultural barriers, such as language and life styles, limited interaction with American females, and if by chance, relationships were established, there were anti-miscegenation laws which made Asian-White marriages illegal.

There were a number of ways of summoning wives from Japan. Some women, who were already married but had been left behind, joined their husbands in America; other men, who could afford the passage went to Japan to get married. The third method was the picture-bride pattern, an already familiar practice in Japan, whereby an exchange of photographs was a part of the screening process. It would be incorrect to assume that the exchange of pictures was the primary basis for marriage; marriages were primarily between *ies*, so that there were investigations, go-betweens and other procedures that were a part of the process. In any case, the number of Japanese female immigrants grew dramatically; in 1900, there were 410 married women in the immigrant society, in 1910, there were 5,581 and by 1920, there were 22,193 (Ichioka, 1988:164).

Although there were many successful marriages in this early period (at least as measured by statistics on divorce, which seldom approached

2 percent), there were also instances of desertions by wives and wife stealing. Living and working conditions for the newlyweds was primitive. Women had to draw water from wells for cooking, washing and bathing; kindling wood was the source for heat, and in many cases, the wives had to cook for large gangs of workers employed by their husbands. Living quarters were often shacks, and wives were forced to work alongside their husbands from dawn to dusk, and then to carry out their housewifely duties. Tales of wives bearing children, then returning the next day to work in the fields was common (Ichioka, 1988).

One consequence, which shakes the stereotype of the strong family, was that of wife desertion (Yanagisako (1985:34). The early ethnic press regularly carried stories about wives who had disappeared or were stolen.

> All stories contained variations of the desertion theme. . . . A picture-bride deserts right after arriving; another deserts after living with her husband for a spell. An older married woman leaves her husband and children, while another takes her infant with her. A woman and her paramour plot to steal her husband's hidden money. A woman is caught and sent back to Japan, while another is placed in a church-operated women's home. The men with whom women run off range from young laborer's to roving city salesmen, to partners in their husbands' farms or businesses, and even to professional gamblers . . . (these) stories were not imagined by reporters; they were based upon actual incidents (Ichioka, 1988:170).

Absconding couples were treated as outcasts, but the stress of living with unsympathetic and uncaring spouses under primitive conditions meant that desertion remained an option. Even the strongest families faced the strain of poverty, of the changing roles of husband, wife and children; of alcoholism and gambling (Kikumura, 1981), and of trying to survive in an alien and hostile environment.

The picture-bride practice ended in 1920 when the Japanese Foreign Ministry informed its ambassador to the United States of its unilateral decision to cease issuing passports to picturebrides, effective March 1, 1920. The Issei did not take kindly to this decision; there were protests and condemnation of the decision of the Foreign Ministry. However, Tokyo chose to abolish the practice in order to placate the American anti-exclusionists. But there were still 24,000 single, adult males, primarily laborers, who had remained single because they did not meet the financial requirement of $800, and whose primary option was the picture-bride process. It was a case where the diplomatic priorities of the Japanese government took precedence over the welfare of its Japanese immigrants (Ichioka, 1988:175).

The Issei, although relatively homogeneous and sharing some common values, such as the primacy of family obligations and the importance of achievement, still were differentiated by past education in Japan, by urban-rural origin and by family background factors. As Levine and Rhodes (1981) indicate, some were better equipped to deal with the new country than others. Data from the Japanese American Research Project (JARP) indicates that the children from more favored family backgrounds did better in terms of socioeconomic success.

IMMIGRANT ORIENTATION

The Issei came as immigrants, not as colonists, so that even if they were forced to rely on the ethnic community for much of their support, they encouraged the Nisei to seek education and white collar careers. They understood that their own participation in the American mainstream would be limited, but high hopes were placed on their American-born Nisei children. Nisei were American citizens with the advantage of an American education, even though the Issei realized that race and national origin remained as barriers for all Japanese towards equal participation. Like many of any immigrant generation, they thought of themselves as a sacrificial group; their own lives were secondary to the advancement of their children. The phrase, *kodo no tame ni* ("for the sake of the children"), also the title of a book by Ogawa (1978), was a common one. Perhaps it remains a universal theme whereby each generation sacrifices for the next, only to be followed by complaints on how ungrateful the recipients are.

Issei family life was one of hardship, but not total deprivation. Daniels (1985) indicates that although the depression of the 1930s affected most Americans, the Japanese community was less affected by the collapse of the American economy. The types of jobs—in agriculture, and in small business in insulated ethnic communities—protected many from poverty and dependence on public welfare. A Los Angeles County supervisor counted only 25 welfare cases in a Japanese population of 37,000.

There were leadership positions in ethnic organizations, and entertainment from Japan, such as movies, magazines and songs brought moments of nostalgia and joy. Festive occasions were eagerly anticipated and celebrated, and as discussed in the section on the community, the entire family enjoyed the community picnic. Even solemn occasions such as deaths and funerals brought Japanese families together, and weddings were often large and pretentious.

CAMP LIFE AND THE ISSEI

The decline of the Issei family was the product of age, which was inevitable, and the wartime evacuation which hastened the process. Conditions in the camps altered the Issei family in a wide number of ways. One room units in a barrack meant little privacy and almost no home life; family quarrels, crying children and any noise was heard throughout the various units. Community mess halls, lavatories, showers, and washrooms meant adjusting to a communal, rather than a family life style. Mess hall food was served cafeteria style and discouraged family dining and hampering the important ritual of family discussions and interaction at mealtimes.

Dependence on the government for the essentials of life—food, clothing, shelter, and income meant a breakdown in family discipline. The maintenance of family solidarity, integration, and social control became primarily dependent on affectionate ties, and many Issei-run families were weak in this type of bonding. Nisei, formerly dependent on their Issei parents, became independent; some joined the army, others left to start new lives away from the camps and the Issei run family.

In summary, Yanagisako (1985) summarizes Issei marriages and family life, built on the model brought over from Japan as follows:

1. Absence of choice in the selection of spouse

2. Interaction based on obligation

3. Strong involvement in wider family relationships

4. Priority of filial bond over conjugal bond

5. Male dominance

6. Rigid division of labor and other roles by sex

7. Emotional restraint, with emphasis on compassion, respect, and consideration

8. Stability

9. Minimal verbal communication between spouses (and children).

THE NISEI FAMILY

The Nisei family, with exposure to both the Issei model and to American styles provide a number of contrasts. There is more freedom of choice of the spouse, the importance of the concept of romantic love, relative freedom from other family relationships, priority placed on the conjugal bond over filial bonds, greater equality of the sexes, more flexibility in sex roles, high emotional intensity, with an emphasis on sexual, romantic attractions, and greater instability and higher verbal communication between spouses and children (Yanagisako, 1985:122).

The Nisei families were mixtures of Japanese and American influences. Some Nisei families carried on some of the conservative traditions of the Issei model, while others were closer to American family norms. Age was a critical factor; older Nisei spoke Japanese more often than the younger and were more apt to be familiar with things Japanese than their younger cohorts. Variables such as the degree of isolation; availability of alternative models; occupation and location, and the receptiveness of the dominant American community also interacted to influence Nisei family life. Variables within the family such as affective ties, bonding patterns, the effectiveness of socialization, ethnic identity, acculturation, personalities, education, and allocation of roles also influenced the family.

There were a number of guidelines that shaped the life of the early Nisei. Misbehavior often meant the threat of being sent to Japan, which lead to tears and the promise to conform. Another was "never to make a fool of oneself," especially in public which had an inhibiting effect on spontaneous behavior. That, and its companion thought, "don't let others make a fool out of you," were especially strong in my life and had both positive and negative effects on later development. It meant that one could "fit in" without making waves, but also was a strong inhibiting factor in terms of asking questions, and taking risks. It lead to a narrow perspective—I would concentrate and take on tasks that I knew that I could do well—I didn't want to look clumsy and foolish in front of others. It also meant that Nisei were quick to criticize others; the overall effect was to narrow the repertoire of behavior and cut down on spontaneity.

Hosokawa (1969:XV) mentions other means of controlling behavior—*hiito ni warareru*—you will be laughed at by others, and *sonna koto wo shitara haji wo kaku*—such actions will cause disgrace. Teen age rebellion and exposure to Americana often meant, "To hell with what others think of me: I'll live my own life." But it was hard to discard the group and family orientation for the individualism that was the norm for middle class America.

In summary, the Nisei family was shaped by Issei influences and exposure to the American culture. Values, attitudes and behaviors were mixtures of the two cultures; older Nisei were generally closer to the Issei model, while the younger Nisei were more likely to adopt American middle class norms.

The wartime evacuation changed the dependency ties of the Nisei and paved the way for a more independent existence. Nisei were able during the post World War II era to find job opportunities more congruent with their education and training. These opportunities, especially in the Midwest and East Coast, meant high exposure to American family life which lessened the influence of the traditional Issei family model (Kitano, 1988).

THE SANSEI

The Sansei, and the newer generations continue to be influenced by acculturation. In almost every way, except for that of visibility, they are more like their majority group peers. Discussions with current college age Sansei indicate life styles that reflect the influence of the mainstream; skiing vacations, trips to Europe and to Asia, and Caribbean cruises. Nisei parents, who in their growing up years often settled for summer jobs and low cost vacations, talk with a mixture of pride, envy and despair about how lucky their offsprings are. But they also see the comparison of their generation with the Issei where even the thought of vacations was rare.

The perceptions of S.I. Hayakawa reflect some of the generational differences. If Dr. Hayakawa had been appointed to the presidency of San Francisco State prior to World War II, there would have been unanimous acclaim from both the Issei and the Nisei community of that era. He would have been a model of what the family and community desired—a Ph.D. of Japanese ancestry, appointed to the presidency of a large educational institution.

So, at Disneyland in April, 1969, there was a large ethnic assemblage, made up primarily of Issei and older Nisei to honor Hayakawa's appointment to the presidency of San Francisco State. However, while the crowd inside was giving him a standing ovation, a smaller, but visibly younger Asian group was on the outside with signs such as, Hayakawa is a banana—yellow skin but white on the inside, or "Hayakawa is not our spokesman." Such overt expressions of dissent would have been rare several years previous and impossible several decades before (Kitano, 1972).

Levine and Montero (1973) suggest two different Sansei streams, paralleling the choices of the previous generations. One is more traditional, following the traditions of the ethnic culture, while the other is assimilationist. They predict that the Sansei combination of high educational training, and a strong emphasis on socioeconomic success will disperse them geographically which in turn will lead to the destruction of the Japanese overtones of Sansei family life.

Connor's (1974) study of three generations of Japanese Americans in the Sacramento area provides evidence of generational changes in the predicted direction, but despite these changes, the importance of the family and dependency needs among the Sansei still persisted.

Johnson (1977) in studying kinship relations in Honolulu found a persistence of kin solidarity among the Sansei despite their social mobility and increased assimilation. Obligation to parents was less burdensome and more easy to fulfill because the responsibility of aged parents was shared by the entire family unit, rather than by the eldest son. The sharing of filial responsibility by the entire family unit increased kin solidarity.

An illustration of some of the differences among the Sansei reflects the diversity in Sansei life. A Sansei student writes as follows:

A UCLA student, I grew up in Gardena, a Los Angeles suburb, which has a large Japanese population. I was surrounded by Japanese culture; I practice *enryo* (behavioral restraint) and love Japanese food, and my family celebrates the New Year in traditional Japanese fashion. I dress in a Japanese *yukata and zori* (kimono and slippers) for *obon* festivals, can speak Japanese, and avoid such American teen-age fashions as designer jeans.

My family helps one another at home; my two sisters and younger brother help with preparing for dinner, washing dishes, and cleaning house. There is much verbal communication but very little overt expression, such as hugging and kissing. My Nisei mother seems to be old fashioned, and so the thought of a woman asking a man for a date is taboo. I feel that I am the most "Japanized" of the family and that the influences of the Issei and Nisei culture had less effect on my siblings (Taguma, 1985).

There is still a strong Issei-Nisei flavor in areas such as Gardena; there are also influences of Japanese from Japan. There is a large Japanese supermarket with products from Tokyo, as well as the usual American wares, a community center, and many other organizations and services which make for a structurally pluralistic community.

In contrast, another Sansei, growing up in all white area had a different background.

She grew up in all white area of San Diego, and her only contact with the ethnic community was through attendance at an ethnic church. She went through her high-school years with no thought of being different; she felt at home with her friends, who were primarily Caucasian. Culture shock for her was attending UCLA, where she found a large Asian population, including an Asian sorority, which she eventually joined. (In contrast, culture shock for the student from Gardena was to see the large number of nonAsian faces at UCLA). She had not been subject to racism and had never been called a "Jap." Her parents had told her that it would be nice if she married a Japanese American but that happiness was of more importance than marrying within the group. Her older sister had married a Caucasian and was very happy with her choice. She feels closer to her mother; her father is more distant, but they have family gatherings. She feels different from the "Gardena girls," who have a distinctive style that includes their Japanese language, hair, dress, and makeup. The Gardena girls are characterized by participating in all-Asian volleyball leagues, sororities, and ethnic church activities and have a network of friends are mostly Asian, (Amano, 1985).

OUTGROUP MARRIAGE

One of the strongest trends for the more Americanized Japanese generations is that of marital assimilation. As Gordon (1964) indicates, marriage out of one's own ethnic group is related to the degree of structural assimilation, that is, entrance into the social groups of the dominant society. In a number of studies (Kikumura and Kitano, 1973; Kitano, et al., 1984; Kitano, 1988) there was a consistent trend of Japanese Americans in Los Angeles County marrying out of their ethnic group. The great majority of these marriages were to white Americans (see Table 1).

Table 1 shows the outmarriage rates of the Chinese, Filipino, Japanese, Korean, and Vietnamese in Los Angeles County. The Chinese, Japanese, and Korean rates are for 1975, 1977, 1979, 1984 and 1989. The Filipino and Vietnamese rates are for 1989 only.

Japanese rates of outmarriage, defined as at least one mate marrying a non-Japanese, shows the following percentages from 1975 to 1989; 54.8 percent; 63.1 percent; 60.6 percent; 51.2 per cent, and 51.9 per cent. In terms of the actual number of outmarriages the numbers were as follows; 363; 477; 463; 719, and 588. Overall, the highest rate of outmarriage was in 1977, with 63.1 percent; the highest number of outmarriages occurred in 1984 with 719. It appears that the outmarriage rate of the Japanese in Los Angeles has levelled off to approximately the 50 percent level.

Japanese females tend to outmarry more than the males. Their outmarriage rate hovers between 52 and 60 percent; conversely the male rates hover between 39 and 47 percent.

In comparison to the other ethnic groups, the Japanese tend to outmarry at a higher rate than any of the other Asian American groups. Since outmarriage is affected by variables such as numbers, sex ratio and the like, different areas should have different rates. There is a large Japanese American community in Los Angeles; areas with smaller, less cohesive communties will probably have higher rates of outmarriage.

TABLE 1

Outmarriage Rates of Chinese, Filipino, Japanese, Korean, and Vietnamese, Total and by Gender for 1975, 1977, 1979, 1984, and 1989, Los Angeles County

| Ethnicity | Year | Marriages | Outmarriges | | Percent of Outmarriage by Gender | |
			Number	Percent	Women	Men
Chinese	1989	1,836	622	33.9	63.0	37.0
	1984	1,881	564	30.0	56.6	43.4
	1979	716	295	41.2	56.3	43.7
	1977	650	323	49.7	56.3	43.7
	1975	596	250	44.0	62.2	37.8
Filipino[a]	1989	1,384	565	40.8	74.2	25.8
Japanese	1989	1,134	588	51.9	58.3	41.7
	1984	1,404	719	51.2	60.2	39.8
	1979	764	463	60.6	52.7	47.3
	1977	756	477	63.1	60.6	39.4
	1975	664	364	54.8	53.6	46.4
Korean	1989	1,372	151	11.0	74.8	25.2
	1984	543	47	8.7	78.6	21.4
	1979	334	92	27.6	79.6	20.4
	1977	232	79	34.1	73.4	26.6
	1975	250	65	26.0	63.1	36.9
Vietnamese[b]	1989	555	147	26.5	54.4	45.6
	1984	560	34	6.0	74.7	25.3

[a]Data for the Filipinos is limited to 1989.
[b]Data for the Vietnamese is limited to 1984 and 1989.
Source: Los Angeles County Marriage License Bureau.

TABLE 2

Mean Age, Education, Generation, and Number of Marriages Between In- and Out-Married Japanese by Gender in Los Angeles County, 1989

	Female		Male	
	Inmarriage	Outmarriage	Inmarriage	Outmarriage
First Generation (N,%)	108 (59.0)	75 (41.0)*	99 (71.7)	39 (28.3)*
Second Generation (N,%)	17 (50.0)	17 (50.0)	15 (51.7)	14 (48.3)
Third Generation (N,%)	147 (37.1	249 (62.9)*	160 (45.5)	192 (54.6)
Age (M)	30.8	30.4	33.2	32.3
Education[a] (M)	15.0	15.3	15.3	15.8
Number of Marriages[b] (M)	1.19	1.19	1.15	1.21

[a] Education refers to the number of years of education completed.
[b] Number of Marriages refers to the total number of marriages, including the marriage presently being applied for.
* To control for simultaneous alpah rate, $p < .001$ is used as the significance criteria. For variables testing proportions as denoted by percentages, test for significance of difference between two proportions is used. For variables testing means, t-test is used.

Table 2 shows the mean age, education, generation, and number of marriages between in- and out-married Japanese by gender in Los Angeles County for 1989. For females, the rates by generation were: Issei, 41 percent; Nisei, 50 percent and Sansei, 62.9 percent. For males, the rates were as follows: Issei, 28.5 percent; Nisei, 48.3 percent and Sansei, 54.6 percent. Generation is one important predictor of outmarriage; the third Japanese American, whether male or female has higher rates of outmarriage than the preivous two generations.

PREDICTING OUTMARRIAGE

Table 3 shows the odds ratio for variables predicting outmarriage by gender. Compared to the Japanese American female, the Chinese and Filipino are more likely to outmarry, while the Korean female is less lkely to marry out of her group. The Korean male was less likely to outmarry than the Japanese American male.

Generation was the strongest predictor of outmarriage. Compared to the male and female of the first generation, the second generation was more likely to outmarry; similarly the third generation Asian American

TABLE 3

Odds Ratio for Variables Predicting Outmarriage by Gender

Variable	Gender	
	Female	Male
Chinese[a]	1.34*	0.98
Filipino[a]	2.25***	0.89
Korean[a]	0.45***	0.18***
Vietnamese[a]	1.03	1.08
Second Generation[b]	3.11***	3.35***
Third Generation[b]	5.63***	4.57***
Age	1.00	0.97***
Education	1.01	1.00
Number of Marriages (2 +)[c]	1.62***	1.69***

aCompared to Japanese American
bCompared to first generation
cCompared to one marriage
*p <.05. **p <.01. ***p <.001.

was the most likely to outmarry. The number of marriages (more than one) was also related to higher rates of outmarriage.

Kitano, Fujino and Takahashi (in process) summarized the literature and the major theories and models on Asian American outmarriages. The following appear to be the most relevant in marriages involving the Japanese, as well as other Asian Americans:

1. *Relative Group Size, Heterogeneity, and the Sex ratio.*
   The smaller the group, the more unbalanced the sex ratio, and the more diverse the group (i.e. scattered locales, generational differences), the higher the rates of outmarriage.

2. *Acculturation, Assimilation, and Generation*
   Acculturation, assimilation, length of time in the United States, and generation is related to outmarriage. Acculturation and generation are related to the lessening of family controls, the acquistion of more American ways, including an emphasis on individual choice, American dating patterns, values and life styles.

3. *Propinquity, Housing, Education and Occupational Mobility.*
   Physical closeness, such as being with non-Japanese in terms of work, school, housing, and recreation leads to increased equal status contact which is related to outmarriage.

4. *Legal Barriers, Norms*
   The first anti-miscegenation legislation was enacted in Maryland in 1661 which prohibited the marriage of Caucasian females to "Negro" slaves. California's anti-miscegenation law was overturned in California in 1948; the United States Surpreme Court overturned all anti-miscegenation legislation in Loving v. Virginia, 1967.
   More tolerant norms in both the minority and dominant communities towards interracial dating and marriage have also contributed to rising rates of outmarriage.

5. *Hypergamy*
   Females of lower status tend to marry males of higher status (Cretser and Leon, 1982; Davis, 1941). Minority women may trade their youth and beauty for the higher social status of the dominant group.

There is also some evidence that individuals less integrated into their own group (both the majority and minority) will find members of the out-group more attractive.

CHILDREN OF INTERRACIAL MARRIAGES

In areas where there are fewer Japanese Americans, the prediction is that even higher rates of intermarriage will occur. The number of children from these unions is difficult to estimate because the change in surname creates problems of identification. Further, the U.S. census has no clear category for children of interracial unions, so that the safest generalization is that their numbers will continue to grow.

However, there appear to be sufficient numbers to begin their own organizations. For example, there is the *Multiracial Americans of Southern California,* the *Japan International Society* in Los Angeles, *I-Pride* in Northern California, and the *Center for Interracial Counseling and Psychotherapy.* There is also *Harmony* in Britain, the *Japan Afro-American Friendship Association* in Japan and the *Hapa Club* at the University of Hawaii. There is also the *Amerasian League,* founded by Amerasians such as playwright Velina Hasu Houston and Attorney Philip Tajitsu-Nash who are establishing international contacts and providing scholarships for Vietnamese Amerasians to come to the United States (Williams, 1989).

A constant problem for the group is to find an appropriate name, since they are of mixed descent.Terms such as ai-no-ko; haafu, hapa, Eurasian and Amerasian have been used to describe the children of mixed-race marriages, but there is no agreement as to which term is the most appropriate. The chapter on Identity will cover more of the issues related to mixed ancestry.

THE INTERGENERATIONAL FAMILY

The Nisei family is the first three generation family. Parents of the Issei remained in Japan so that the Nisei did not have grandparents to indulge them, but the Nisei have Issei parents and Sansei children, sometimes living in the same household. Household interaction could be a mixture of Issei ways, of Nisei ways and the more modern outlook of the Sansei. Issei grandparents are often accused of spoiling their grandchildren, and permitting behaviors that were taboo when they had parental responsibility; Nisei grandparents face similar accusations from the Sansei.

Each generation has perceptions of the other. Nisei accuse the Issei of being old fashioned, too traditional, "up tight," and rigid; in turn the Sansei use similar terms to describe the Nisei. Issei used to accuse the Nisei of being too American, too materialistic, and too modern; conversely, Nisei use similar terms to describe the Sansei. The term "Yuppie" to describe the young urban professional, has been modified to "Yappie," the young Asian professional.

But the overriding characteristic of the Japanese American family, whether it be Issei, Nisei, Sansei, or Nikkei is its role in socialization and social control. DeVos (1992) in comparing minorities in the United States and Japan indicates that deviant behavior occurs specifically in families where there is a relative lack of cohesion. Separated parents, and families where there is a lack of discipline, supervision, love and affection are related to deliquent behavior. Similarly, in a study of Japanese American delinquents (Kitano, 1967), delinquent children had similar family profiles. It also helped that there was a cohesive community which reinforced the family. But, as we have seen, the community and family that the Issei and older Nisei knew has changed, perhaps for the better?

In summary, the following characteristics of the community, its culture, its organizations and its families indicate the following:

1. That the culture that was brought over from Japan was reinforced by the organizations and the families that made up the community.

2. That the cohesvie ethnic community, with its parallel structures, provided opportunities on the economic and social levels, even though it was characterized by low pay, long hours, limited mobility, and limited interaction with the mainstream.

3. That prejudice, discrimination and segregation strengthened the bonds of the early Japanese American community.

4. That experiences in the United States, ranging from being placed in concentration camps, to acculturation, to time, to American born generations has brought about changes in the Japanese American community, its organizations, and its families. Each generation has moved away from the Issei culture towards the American model, although there has also been a retention of ethnicity.

5. That the diminution of barriers, such as legal discrimination, and a more open society, has been another major factor in affecting change.

6. Certain cultural styles can still be recognized. They include a preference for ethnic peers, family ties, ethnic celebrations, and high educational expectations.

7. The most visible change in the Japanese American family is that of out-group marriage. Studies on those who have out-married and their children will tell us much about the future of the Japanese American.

BIBLIOGRAPHY

---

1. Amano, Karen (1985). "Interracial Marriages: A Comparative Analysis of Views of Japanese Americans." Unpublished term paper. University of California, Los Angeles.

2. Benedict, Ruth (1946). *The Chrysanthemum and the Sword*. Boston: Houghton Mifflin.

3. Connor, John (1974). "Acculturation and Family Continuities in Three Generations of Japanese Americans." Journal of Marriage and the Family. 36:159-165.

4. Daniels, Roger (1985). "Japanese America, 1930-1941: An Ethnic Community in the Great Depression." Journal of the West. 24:35-50.

5. De Vos, George (1992). *Social Cohesion and Alienation*. Boulder, Westview Press.

6. Gordon, Milton (1964). *Assimilation in American Life.* New York: Oxford University Press.

7. Hosokawa, William (1969). *Nisei: The Quiet Americans.* New York: Morrow.

8. Ichioka, Yuji (1988). *The Issei: The World of Frist Generation Japanese Immigrants.* New York: The Free Press.

9. Ichihashi, Yamato (1932). *Japanese in the United States.* Stanford: Stanford University Press.

10. Iga, Mamoru (1957). "Changes in Value Orientation of Japanese Americans." Paper read at the Western Psychological Association Meeting, April 28, Long Beach, California.

11. Kikumura, Akemi and Kitano, Harry (1973). "Interracial Marriage: A Picture of the Japanese Americans." Journal of Social Issues. 29:2, pp. 67-81.

12. Johnson, C.L. (1977). "Interdependence, Reciprocity and Indebtedness: An Analysis of Japanese American Kinship Relations," Journal of Marriage and the Family, 39 (May): 351-363.

13. Kitano, Harry H. (1967). "Japanese American Crime and Delinquency." *The Journal of Psychology,* 66, 253-263.

14. Kitano, Harry (1972). "Japanese Americans on the Road to Dissent," in Seasons of Rebellion, ed. by Boskin, J. and R. Rosenstone, New York: Holt, Rinehart and Winston, pp. 93-113.

15. Kitano, Harry H.L., Yeung, Wai-tsang, Chai, Lynn and Hatanaka, Herb (1984). "Asian American Interracial Marriage," Journal of Marriage and the Family, 46:1, Feb., pp. 179-190.

16. Kitano, Harry H.L. (1988). "The Japanese American Family." Ethnic Families in America. ed. by Mendel, Charles, Robert Habenstein and Rooselt Wright. New York: Elsevier, 258-275.

17. Levine, Gene and Colbert Rhodes (1981). *The Japanese American Community: A Three Generation Study.* New York: Praeger.

18. Levine, Gene and Darrell Montero (1973). "Socioeconomic Mobility Among Three Generations of Japanese Americans." Journal of Social Issues. 29:33-48.

19. Miyamoto, Frank (1939). *Social Solidarity Among the Japanese in Seattle.* Seattle: University of Washington.

20. Ogawa, Dennis and Glen Grant (1978). *Kodomo no Tame Ni-for the Sake of the Children: The Japanese American Experience in Hawaii*. Honolulu: University of Hawaii Press.

21. Taguma, Joy (1985). "What Gardena Means to Me." Unpublished term paper, Los Angeles: University of California.

22. Wagatsuma, Hiroshi (1977). "Some Aspects of the Contemporary Japanese Family: Once Confucian, Now Fatherless?" Dedalus, 106 (2):181-210.

23. Williams, Theresa (1989). "International Amerasian Identity: Toward a Multi-racial/Multi-cultural Existence." Unpublished term paper, Los Angeles: University of California.

24. Yanagisako, Sylvia (1985). *Transforming the Past Tradition and Kingship Among Japanese Americans*. Stanford: Stanford University Press.

CHAPTER 10

HAWAII

It is difficult to understand the omission of Hawaii when there is a discussion of the Japanese American, but such a practice is common. Perhaps there is a feeling that Hawaii is an exception to many of the generalizations concerning the Japanese American, or that it is so small that it is not worth counting. But a glance at population figures shows how erroneous such impressions are; in 1990, 247,486 Japanese in the United States were residents of Hawaii.

The numbers alone do not begin to reflect the importance of the islands. The most prominent politicians of Japanese ancestry come from Hawaii, and the sight of Japanese faces sitting in both the United States Senate and House of Representatives must be a surprise to those who view America solely as a white nation. And the experiences in Hawaii have been different, so that they provide another frame for looking at the Japanese.

For example, the Japanese in Hawaii were never a small, scattered minority in a vast land but were a large, sometimes majority group on a few concentrated islands: they entered into a more racially tolerant society than their peers in California; and they were one of a large number of imported nationality groups. Further, they were geographically close enough to Japan so that homeland influences were much stronger than on the mainland. Therefore, the Japanese in Hawaii offer an opportunity to evaluate the effect of variables like power, a more tolerant social structure, a relative degree of social isolation, and closer ties to the homeland on a Japanese population.

KOTONKS

But the question of different experiences would remain academic if the Japanese in Hawaii turned out to be identical to their mainland counterparts. Most close observers indicate that differences do exist and that a person acquainted with the Japanese can distinguish between those from Hawaii and those from the mainland. There is even a classification system with special terms—the Buddhahead for the Japanese American from the islands and Kotonk or Katonk for his cohort from the continent.

The term *Buddhahead*, according to one interpretation, originated when mainland Japanese Americans first met Hawaii Japanese. During this encounter, the mainlanders found the islanders to be exceptionally stubborn or pig headed. Thus, the English word "pig" was translated into the Japanese word "buta," and the Japanese in Hawaii were subsequently called *Buddhaheads*. In comparison, the term *Kotonk* is largely based on the myth that since the head of the mainlander is so hard and hollow a "kotonk" sound is heard when a coconut hits his head.

Although the audio origin remains the most colorful, the definition also included the feelings the islander had toward his look-alike peers from the West Coast. The mainlander was considered standoffish and uptight, overly concerned about surface appearances, materialistic, too careful about impressing the majority group, too acculturated, and, in one word, too *haolefied* (white).

For example, Ogawa presents one stereotype of the Kotonk as contrasted to the islander. In a restaurant, the islander fights to pick up the check, or at a bar, he takes out cash and puts in on the table. In contrast, the Kotonk carefully ascertains whether he paid the last time, or accurately figures out how much he owes and then adds the required tip. Or if the Hawaiian Japanese had a good time he would say, "Terrific, yeah," whereas the Kotonk might say, "Yes, it was marvelous" (Ogawa, 1973:16).

The term *Kotonk* remains in use today, especially in Hawaii. The mainlander still finds some difficulty in gaining full acceptance into the Japanese-American social system, and his island peers will seldom let him forget his Kotonk background. Conversely, mainland Japanese also hold certain stereotypes about the islanders as "pineapples," but the current ease of travel and the constant interchange have changed the stereotypes, except among the most prejudiced.

There are some obvious differences between the islanders and the mainlanders, whether Japanese or not: variations in language (including pidgin), a healthier tan, and the more casual Hawaiian style of dressing and living. But these differences are regional, and the vastness of the United States incorporates a smorgasbord of life styles. Other differences may reflect rural-urban contrasts, although present day Honolulu is a big city by any standard, including freeways, overcrowding, and pollution.

But subtly, the Japanese in Hawaii make up a powerful group with a number of alternatives not readily available to most of their peers on the mainland. They are more comfortable in their ethnicity; they are freer to retain their life styles by voluntary choice. Yet, they were also freer to acculturate because the barriers toward Americanization were not as rigid as on the mainland. Even more important, their acculturation was to a more racially tolerant island culture, so that many profess surprise when a discussion of racial discrimination, mainland style, is raised. It is the amalgamation of these experiences that has developed the Japanese in Hawaii into something different from their mainland counterparts.

HISTORY

Hawaii was initially settled by Polynesians, believed to be from Tahiti, around A.D. 750 to 1000. Their ability to navigate the vast Pacific was an incredible feat of early seamanship. The Western world first heard about Hawaii through Captain Cook, who in 1778 named it the Sandwich Islands after his patron the Earl of Sandwich.

At the time of Cook, each island was ruled as an independent kingdom by hereditary chiefs. King Kamehameha I gradually brought the islands under his control, so that by the time of his death in 1819 he had established the Kingdom of Hawaii. A "bloodless revolution" in 1893 overthrew the monarchy, and a provisional government under the leadership of Sanford Dole, an American, requested, but was refused, annexation to the United States. The provisional government then converted Hawaii into a republic; it was annexed as a United States Territory in 1898 and became the fiftieth State on August 21, 1959.

Several factors have influenced Hawaii ever since its "discovery" by Captain Cook. First was the early influence of explorers and traders of many nations who visited this independent kingdom for rest, recreation, and trade. Lind remarks that the Westerner, if he wished to remain on friendly terms with the islanders, had to honor the customs and practices of the Hawaiians; conversely, if the natives were to enjoy those goods and services of the foreigner, he too had to use tact, compromise, and discretion. Therefore, the stage up to about 1850 was characterized by mutual degrees of tolerance by both sides (Lind, 1967).

The second stream was the influence of various Western religious groups, starting with the New England Congregationalists who arrived in 1820 for missionary purposes. Although there were disagreements between the traders and the religious people, the two groups of foreigners had much in common, and they eventually supported each other against the native islanders. The Roman Catholic influence began in 1828, and Mormon Missionaries began to arrive on the islands in the middle of the nineteenth century.

A third, and the most important stream, was the importation of "labor" to work on the large agricultural plantations. By this time, the islands were essentially conquered, and business and economic considerations were of the highest priority. Peoples of various racial and national origins, Portuguese, Chinese, Puerto Ricans, Japanese, Micronesians, Melanesians, Polynesians, Germans, Koreans, Russians, and Filipinos, among others, were imported in varying numbers to supply laborers for the expanding plantations of Hawaii, but with little thought for the complex processes of ethnic interaction which were thereby initiated (Lind, 1967:7).

Due to the heavy demand for plantation laborers, Japanese immigration to Hawaii began on a large scale in 1885. Under a three-year contract and with an option to review, thousands of Japanese laborers arrived in Hawaii. Their travel and employment arrangements were handled primarily through private business firms known as *imingaisha* or emigration companies. Between 1894 and 1908 approximately 125,000 Japanese workers came to the islands (Moriyama, 1985). By 1900 the Japanese percentage of Hawaii's population climbed to 39.6 percent (Adams, 1933).

Almost all of the workers were young men who came from poverty stricken regions such as Hiroshima, Yamaguchi, Kumamoto, or Okinawa. Yoshida states:

> This class consists of those who are engaged in agricultural pursuits, either as tenants or as farm laborers. They belong to the lower classes of the Japanese community, if not the lowest of all. They are the real cornerstone of the nation, but they are poor. In this class of emigrants the most conservative, uneducated and innocent persons can be found (Yoshida, 1909).

The Japanese had no intention of living permanently in Hawaii. Their goal was to accumulate a fortune in the quickest possible time and return to Japan. Many soon realized, however, that the plantation wages were too low and they were destined to remain beyond the foreseeable future. Out of loneliness and the desire to have a family, many laborers began to send word back home to their villages asking for a marriage partner and, thus, a large number of women came to America between 1911 and 1919 as "picture brides" (Ogawa, 1978).

It is interesting to note the initial attitudes that some native Hawaiians held toward the Japanese. In an interview between Mr. Kapena, a representative of the Hawaiian government sent to Japan to search for immigrants, and the Japanese Minister of Foreign Affairs Inouye in Japan in 1882, Kapena sounded the following note or racial affinity:

> We believe the Japanese and Hawaiians spring from a cognate race and that Japanese children growing up and amalgamating with our population will produce a new and vigorous race, which will repeople our Islands. . . . We wish to repeople our country with an orderly, laborious [sic], civilized, law abiding and cognate race (Kuykendall, 1967:160).

But the feelings of Kapena were not to be shared by groups already on the islands. Some saw the possibility of Japanese domination and feared that Hawaii might become a Japanese satellite. The Portuguese considered them a menace to their position. Mechanics and tradesmen would soon note with apprehension the Japanese drifting away from the plantations to become possible competitors for lower- and middle-level positions. But as Kuykendall notes, during these early years from 1886 to 1894, the anti-Japanese sentiment was relatively minor, and the Chinese were the main targets. The Japanese were to become victims later (Kuykendall, 1967:172).

Hawaiian history is the story of a tolerant native population quickly losing their lands and their power to the more sophisticated, restless, ambitious, and ruthless *haole* (whites), who then began to encourage the Hawaiian government to import various nationality groups to labor on the plantations. There is a parallel between the Hawaiian experience and the treatment of the native Indian populations on the mainland. Both native groups were overwhelmed; their lands were taken away from them; both were ill-suited for laboring for their conquerors; and both were, therefore, bypassed as newer groups were imported.

RACIAL HARMONY

The ideal of racial harmony has long been a part of the Hawaiian ethos, and in comparative terms, conflicts stemming from race are perhaps less severe on the islands than in most other parts of the world. But it would also be an error to minimize its history of diverse racial and nationality groups; the plantation economy ruled by a small group of white oligarchs and the continual struggle of various immigrant groups to gain some degree of control over their lives.

Generally the theme of harmony has come from a power group perspective, and life must have been pleasant and reasonably tranquil for the ruling elites as long as the lower status groups could be kept under control. One of the strategies was to cut off the immigration of one group before it got too powerful and switch to another group, and then to another, and another. Once in Hawaii, nationalities were often kept in separated plantation camps with a Caucasian overseer, or *luna*. It would be difficult to ignore the racism in such arrangements.

The native Hawaiians were also manipulated toward an anti-Oriental stance. For example, Fuchs writes that many Hawaiians responded to their own frustrations and bitterness by using the Asians as spacegoats. Rather then confronting the haole, who had taken away their land and freedom, the Hawaiians helped the haoles write discriminatory land restriction laws against the Chinese and Japanese in the late 1800s (Fuchs, 1961:82).

It is our hypothesis that as more ethnic histories are discovered and publicized (especially those written in the native language), the picture of harmonious race relations will be discredited. But it is also our observation that the relative harmony among the various groups in Hawaii is so vastly superior to other areas that it still deserves the appellation of a "racial paradise," albeit with flaws.

THE PLANTATIONS

The Japanese entered into the Hawaiian plantations as contract laborers and inherited the bottom position in that system. They were assigned to the poorest houses and were the lowest paid. They were expected to work efficiently and to be highly productive. They served under impersonal Caucasian managers who employed various methods of punishment to control them.

As Takaki points out, the most widely exercised form of punishment was the fine system. Plantation owners developed an elaborate system of fines, which specified a charge for virtually every type of misconduct. Workers were fined $5.00 for damaging a wagon through negligence, $1.00 for insubordination, $.50 for neglect of duty, and $.25 for refusal to do the work as ordered. Besides having to lie in fear of the endless fines, the workers were constantly watched by the *luna*, who often used his whip to keep them in order (Takaki, 1983).

In addition to the severe working conditions, the laborers had to bear with meager and unsanitary housing. According to Hunter, the men lived in termite-ridden, unfit quarters, and from six to forty men were often huddled together in barrack-type rooms. Their lives were controlled by an indifferent and inaccessible plantation management in which the laborers served as specialized functionaries with little personal or individual identities. "They lived in plantation owned houses, bought their food and clothing from plantation owned stores and were treated by plantation paid physicians."

The appalling conditions drove some laborers to gambling and other vices. "Between April 1894 and December 1895, alone, 14,492 Japanese were arrested; 10,109 were convicted. A few . . . put an end to their misery by committing seppuku (self-disembowelment). More of them just quietly despaired, 'Shikata ga Nai, it is no use'" (Hunter, 1971:80-81).

Between fifty and sixty percent of the immigrants eventually did return home, some with economic dreams fulfilled (Ogawa, 1982). Others, however, would remain to toil in the harsh physical conditions of the plantations.

Most owners felt that the Japanese made good workers, except that they were not content to remain on the plantations. There were continuous efforts to harass the Japanese to render them obedient and to prevent them from leaving the plantations.

As early as March, 1883, the Executive Committee of the Republican Territorial Central Committee passed a resolution discouraging the employment of Asiatics in Honolulu because their labor was deemed necessary to the plantations.

Other strategies included "maintaining a surplus, playing race against race, keeping aliens out of the city, restricting government jobs, prohibiting laborers movements to the mainland, working through foreign consults and police officials and intimidation." For example, there was the practice of establishing competing labor camps, so that "now Puerto Ricans, Spanish, Russians and Filipinos would be used to keep the Japanese in their place" (Fuchs, 1961:210).

Faced with adverse conditions, the Japanese laborer could be obstreperous, even to the Japanese consul; he could and did express his grievances in no uncertain fashion. The workers, as Okihiro states:

> Were not simple instruments of the planters but resisted their repression and exploitation by reducing their productivity, depriving owners of their labor by running away, forming permanent communities of settlers, and striking for better conditions and higher wages (Okihiro, 1991:XII).

There were numerous strikes on the plantations including two major ones known as the Oahu strikes of 1909 and 1920. Some of the reasons given for the strikes were indicative of Japanese dissatisfaction with plantation life. The workers demanded the discharge of excessively cruel lunas; they pressed for compensation for injuries; they wanted higher pay and better working conditions; they called for the reinstatement of discharged employees; and they preferred the use of Japanese, rather than white lunas (Wakukawa, 1938).

The Oahu strikes of 1909 and 1920 were important because they were concerted efforts among Japanese working on various plantations to organize and to coordinate their resources. There was planning; the strikes were island wide; and the numbers and duration were unprecedented for those times. Part of the impetus for the 1909 strike came from an article by University of California student Motoyuki Negoro, which showed the disproportionately high profits for the plantation owner when compared to the extremely low paid but very productive Japanese laborer (Wakukawa, 1938).

The strikes often split the Japanese community, since values of loyalty and obligation to the employer, hard work, and gratefulness could not be easily integrated into a militant, adversary position.

The response of management was much simpler and appealed to racism and the American way. The owners felt that the Japanese could not be trusted because they might be allied with a foreign power, although they themselves were allied with the United States. For example, an editorial in the *Honolulu Star Bulletin* dated February 13, 1920, asked:

> Is control of the industrialism of Hawaii to remain in the hands of Anglo-Saxons or is it to pass into those of alien Japanese agitators? . . . Never lose sight of the real issue: Is Hawaii to remain American or become Japanese?

WHICH DIRECTION?

The choice of Japan or the United States was an option for the Japanese residents, but not in the manner in which the question was raised. The possibility of Hawaii becoming part of Japan was a remote one, especially when considering that that nation was just emerging from its enforced isolation of centuries, but for the immigrants there was the unrealistic possibility of remaining "Japanese" or becoming "American." The Japanese language and culture could survive, since there was a large community with ethnic institutions and organizations and one could identify with his Japanese background and heritage as one realistic alternative.

Conversely, there was also the possibility of becoming "American" in a way that could not be duplicated on the mainland and to move toward acculturation and assimilation since the barriers of racism were not so overpowering. These options are clearly indicated in the following biographies of two Japanese in Hawaii.

ETHNIC RETENTION: FRED MAKINO

Makino came to Hawaii in 1899. He felt that the plantation owners were exploiting the Japanese, and rather than fatalistically accepting their position, he felt that the best strategy was for the Japanese to organize and to strike back. He helped the Japanese to found their own unions; he started lawsuits against discriminatory practices; and he was willing to go to jail for his convictions. One of Makino's priorities was to heighten ethnic awareness through promoting ethnic identity and developing ethnic cohesion. He supported Japanese-language schools where Issei and their Nisei children could learn their native language and understand their native heritage. He held that the Japanese values of the Meiji era were superior to those of the Americans and that the Japanese should resist the attempts of the Americans to "rob" them of their culture. He advocated political organization, voting blocs, and the strategy of ethnic power as the most effective means of dealing with the white man. He believed that the maintenance of a strong and cohesive ethnic community based on the Japanese culture was the wisest adaptive strategy. Popularity with and acceptance by the white man were not important in Makino's perception of the world (Jacobs and Landau, 1971).

ACCULTURATION AND ACCEPTANCE: TAKIE OKUMURA

Okumura, living in Hawaii about the same time as Makino, perceived the problems of the Japanese quite differently. He advocated an acculturative position whereby the Japanese could find acceptance by identifying with and acquiring the American culture.

For example, Okumura felt that one of the major barriers toward group acceptance was the maintenance of the Japanese culture. He felt that Japanese living conditions, manners, habits, and customs should be discarded. Therefore, smelly Japanese foods, noisy Japanese festivals, loud conversations in Japanese, and prominent Japanese architectural forms were to be discouraged, since they were hindrances to acceptance. From this perspective, any behavior that might be offensive to the Americans was to be controlled.

The most important guideline for Okumura was the concept of the Japanese as "guests." As such, the Japanese should conduct themselves with as little visibility as possible. Attending American schools, learning the English language, and adopting the ways of the American were the highest priorities. Unpopular actions, such as labor strikes and running away from the plantations, were to be discouraged, whereas to continue to work loyally, no matter what the provocation, was a part of the Okumura philosophy.

Both positions and their numerous variations were viable alternatives for the Japanese in Hawaii. Because of the number of realistic options, it is our impression that in Hawaii there is a wider and more diversified range of attitudes and behaviors than is true for Japanese on the mainland (Jacobs and Landau, 1971).

DUAL CITIZENSHIP

The alternatives of remaining "Japanese" or becoming "American" would also take on new meaning with the birth of the second generation: the Nisei. Growing up in the islands, the Nisei became culturally attuned to their surrounding environment through school and peer group contacts. In Hawaii, the multi-cultural atmosphere influenced the Nisei in the language (*pidgin*) they spoke and the customs they practiced. Although this social process is often viewed as Americanization, such a broad labeling overlooks the fact that the environment of the islands was far from being unidimensionally "American." Hawaii's society was a combination of various cultures and lifestyles.

In addition to being influenced by the school system and the multi-cultural surroundings, the Nisei were strongly influenced by their Issei parents to remain Japanese. The parents encouraged their children to attend Japanese language schools, worship at Japanese temples, and to hold dual citizenship.

Dual citizenship meant that the Nisei, by right of blood, would legally and automatically be a Japanese citizen, and by virtue of place of birth, an American citizen. The impact of this "dual citizenship" on the Nisei has been viewed in both a positive and negative context. Some have argued that this dualism has strengthened the character of the second generation by incorporating both American and Japanese values.

Others have suggested that this dualism has damaged the Nisei by confusing them psychologically. Despite the various interpretations, it is clear that the Nisei were the products of two cultures. When war broke out on December 7, 1941, the Nisei were placed in to a highly sensitive position (Ogawa, 1978).

WORLD WAR II

The Japanese attack on Pearl Harbor was even more dramatic on the islands than on the mainland because it was the actual site of the battle. Residents could hear gunfire, feel the bombs burst, and see the airplanes.

Immediately after the attack, a state of martial law was declared in the territory of Hawaii affecting over 421,000 individuals out of which 157,000 were of Japanese ancestry including 35,000 Japanese aliens and 68,000 individuals possessing dual citizenship. With such a large Japanese population, one would expect a massive movement toward relocation. Yet, despite rumors of a large-scale evacuation of Japanese to Molokai (the former leper colony), the bulk of the islands' Japanese population was not relocated (Office of Chief of Military History, 1945).

A combination of factors mitigated against relocation. First, the Japanese were simply too large of a group to be transported to the mainland relocation centers. And even if they were successfully evacuated to Molokai, the concentration of disgruntled Japanese would pose as a formidable threat to Hawaii's security. Second, the Japanese community constituted over thirty percent of Hawaii's population. Their removal would seriously cripple Hawaii's work force and radically disrupt the islands' economy and infrastructure. Finally, the Japanese held long standing attachments and friendships in Hawaii. Living and working within a local culture, they had established strong ties with other nationalities. As a result, islanders, both out of economic self-interest and personal ties, spoke out in favor of the Japanese (Ogawa, 1978).

Although most of the Japanese were allowed to remain free, they were under a system of strict control and surveillance. Subject to rules and regulations that were more severe than those imposed upon other civilians. Japanese were required to turn in weapons, were forbidden to engage in fishing activities, restricted in their use of communication equipment, and prohibited from writing or printing attacks against the United State Government.

INTERNMENT

To be sure, the Japanese in Hawaii were much more fortunate than their peers on the mainland; they did not suffer the indignity of mass evacuation. However, it would be a mistake to dismiss the impact of Hawaii's Japanese internment and relocation on the community.

Most of the information in the following section is drawn from the Office of the Chief of Military History (1945).

Before the Pearl Harbor attack, a list of potentially dangerous individuals was assembled. This list was divided into two groups—each containing about 300 persons. People included on List 1-A were to be picked up immediately upon the outbreak of hostilities between the United States and the Axis powers. Everyone on List 1-B was to be put under surveillance and have their activities curtailed.

Once martial law as declared, the apprehension of those on List 1-A commenced. By December 10, 1941, 400 people, three-fourths of them Japanese, were interned at the Honolulu Immigration Building.

The day after the attack, the Sand Island Detention Camp was activated. Within a week after the outbreak of war, about 300 Japanese had been moved from the Immigration Building to Sand Island. For fifteen months this facility was used as a detention site. Later a new camp was created at Honouliuli.

By February, 1942, accommodations were made available on the mainland to confine Hawaii internees. Subsequently, on February 19, 1942, 175 Japanese were sent away to the mainland. Altogether 700 internees, 675 of whom were Japanese, were shipped out of the islands. In addition to these internees, groups of Japanese civilians were evacuated hoping to be united with an interned family member. A total of approximately 930 persons left Hawaii between December 28, 1942 and March 3, 1943, under these conditions.

During the period of martial law, some internees were released on parole upon a Hearing Board recommendation. With the removal of martial law on October 24, 1944, there was no remaining legal authority to hold American citizens of Japanese ancestry in internment. However, Presidential Order 9489 which lifted martial law gave the Commanding General of the Territory of Hawaii Military Area authority to exclude anyone from Hawaii who considered to be dangerous to security for sabotage or espionage reasons.

As of October 24, 1944, 67 citizens of Japanese ancestry and 50 aliens remained at the Honouliuli Internment Facility. The 67 Japanese Americans were sent to Tule Lake on November 9, 1944 and the 50 aliens were gradually released on parole. On V-J day, the 22 aliens still remaining in camp were released. In the last year of the war, 12 Japanese civilians were apprehended and placed in custody pending exclusion from the Territory.

Overall, nearly 10,000 people were investigated and interrogated for security reasons between December 7, 1941 and October 24, 1944. Out of this number, 1,466 Japanese were apprehended. In total, 1,250 people of Japanese ancestry, or less than 1% of Hawaii's total Japanese population, were interned during the war.

In comparison to the mainland, these numbers hardly appear significant. However, numbers alone may not reveal the possible loss in terms of community leadership which the internment created. Because the investigations targeted such individuals as Shinto and Buddhist priests, officers of Japanese organizations, and language school teachers, the relocations essentially robbed the population of is cultural and spiritual resources. Without their leaders, the people, as a whole, suffered a void in dynamism, direction, and guidance.

RUMORS AND TENSIONS

Following the attack, rumors regarding the loyalty of the Japanese were rampant. There were the stories of Japanese seen flashing signals, and of a Japanese fleet waiting to enter Pearl Harbor. There were rumors of Japanese burning secret papers and workers cutting arrows in the fields pointing to Pearl Harbor. Many aggressive words were directed against those of Japanese ancestry, and attempts were made to boycott stores run by Japanese Americans. The situation further deteriorated when news of the Niihau incident reached the other islands.

THE NIIHAU INCIDENT

As related to Lind (1946) and by Allen (1950), Niihau was an isolated island located off the coast of Kauai with a population of less than two hundred, which included three persons of Japanese ancestry. It was cut off from all outside communications, so that the population had no immediate knowledge of Pearl Harbor.

Several hours after the attack, a Japanese plane crash-landed on Niihau. The pilot could only communicate with Ishimatsu Shintani, born in Japan, and Yoshio Harada, a Hawaiian-born Nisei. Whether by threats or promises, he eventually induced Harada to cooperate in gaining control of the island, while Shintani, fearful for his life, went into hiding.

For several days the pilot and Harada directed a reign of terror on the island. It would be correct to say that Niihau was almost occupied and conquered by the Japanese, albeit by an army of one helped by one Japanese American. Several Hawaiians eventually managed to escape by boat to Kauai, but before they could get back with American troops, another native had killed the Japanese pilot. The Nisei then committed suicide.

The Niihau incident was unusual in several ways. The idea of a Japanese pilot taking over an entire island so close to Hawaii strains one's credulity. The cooperation of the Japanese American was another surprise, since in spite of widespread rumors, there was no evidence of Japanese Hawaiians helping the Japanese in their attack on Pearl Harbor. Although the incident was a little known affair, it again portrayed the age-old dilemma of the Japanese group: were they to identify with Japan or America?

RESPONSE OF THE NISEI

In no uncertain terms, Hawaii's Japanese Americans undertook to prove that they were Americans both at home and on the battlefront. Throughout the islands, they worked to demonstrate their Americanization and to eradicate their identity as a Japanese. They stopped speaking Japanese in public, wearing Japanese style clothing, and some individuals even went as far as to change their last name. Any manifestation of being Japanese was abandoned (Ogawa, 1978).

Perhaps the most dramatic response to the war was demonstrated by the second generation. Although the Nisei were essentially products of both Japanese and American culture, they did not hesitate to exhibit their loyalty to the United States by serving in various military units.

When war broke out in 1941, a large number of Japanese Americans were enrolled in the Reserve Officer Training Corps (ROTC) program at the University of Hawaii. Immediately after the attack, this group became part of the Hawaii Territorial Guard which served as a military defense and civilian protection force. On January 19, 1942, however, given orders from Washington they were all honorably discharged. Though relieved of their duties, they still sought to serve in the war and after successfully petitioning the military governor, organized the VVV or Varsity Victory Volunteers. Part of the 34th Combat Engineers Regiment, the VVV was a homefront unit engaged in numerous construction projects which were needed to prepare Hawaii as a major arsenal.

In addition to the VVV, approximately 200 Nisei were serving at the time of the attack in engineering units, later to be called the 1399th Engineering Construction Battalion. The men of this battalion took part in various defense assignments—building bridges, water systems, airfields, and training camps. Eventually 900 Nisei constituted this force, doing important construction work for which they received the Meritorious Unit Plaque.

Before December 7, Nisei were also part of the 298th and 299th Infantry Regiments. However, non-Japanese recruits from the mainland viewed serving with the Japanese Americans disfavorably, and the military decided not to mix the two groups together. A new battalion later called the 100th Infantry Battalion was formed which brought into one unit all of the Nisei recruits, except those in the engineering force.

While Nisei in the VVV, 1399th, and 100th were allowed to serve their country, others desiring to prove their loyalty were barred from military duty. Finally, in 1943, the situation was changed when the military announced that Japanese Americans were eligible to enlist in an all volunteer unit. Within a matter of days, thousands of men joined the 442nd Regimental Combat Team.

Another military unit, composed predominantly of Japanese Americans, was the Military Intelligence Service (MIS), where both Nisei and Kibei proved to be especially vital as Japanese interpreters. It is said that the Japanese Americans belonging to this unit "shortened the war in the Pacific by two years" (Ogawa, 1978:320).

In every instance, the Nisei performed beyond the call of duty. The motto of the 442nd Regimental Combat Team, "Go for Broke," aptly characterized the spirit of the fighting men who repeatedly entered into the most dangerous situations, suffering heavy losses. The 100th Infantry Battalion came to be known as the Purple Heart Battalion and was eventually incorporated into the 442nd Regimental Combat Team. They not only volunteered but sacrificed their lives for their country.

The heroic exploits of the Nisei on the battlefield earned the Japanese Americans an entirely new image. They became a group of valiant martyrs. Because of their record in combat, the suspicions, prejudice, discrimination, stereotypes, and secondary status of Japanese Americans were replaced with social admiration and numerous opportunities.

BREAKTHROUGH: POLITICS

The experience gained on the mainland, in Europe, and in the Pacific meant a changed generation of Nisei who came back from the war. Although young in age, they had their horizons broadened, and many took advantage of the G.I. Bill for further education and training. The *status quo* was about to be challenged, especially in the area of politics.

By 1954 the Nisei war veterans started to challenge the huge Republican majority in the legislature. The close bond established between the Nisei and some of their Caucasian friends who had supported them during harder times developed into a powerful Democratic group that eventually wrested political control from the Republicans. Senator Daniel Inouye (1967) mentions some of these individuals—John Burns, eventually to be governor, Dan Aoki, a 442nd first sergeant; Spark Matsunaga (now deceased) of the 100th Battalion, a member of the Hawaiian delegation to the House of Representatives; Masato Doi of the 442nd, chairman of the Honolulu city council and eventually appointed a circuit judge by Burns. Then, of course, there was Daniel Inouye himself, a war hero who is now a United States senator.

In his autobiography, Inouye recalls the 1954 campaign, in which the young, politically naive group of war veterans began their challenge to the long entrenched Republican political machine. The incumbents raised questions about the loyalty and patriotism of the Nisei, a dubious tactic, since most of these men had recently returned from Europe with the 100th and the 442nd. The cry of communism was another technique used by the Republicans, and in one encounter, Inouye, thoroughly disgusted with the big lie and the big scare, shook his empty right sleeve (he had lost his arm to fight fascists) and said, "If my country wants the other one to fight communists, it can have it" (Inouye, 1967:249).

The Nisei, with the help of their allies, conducted a successful campaign and were able to wrest political control from the incumbents. Since that time, the Japanese Americans have remained a politically significant force.

THE JAPANESE IN HAWAII

For example, in the 1990-91 edition of *Who's Who in Government in Hawaii*, eleven Japanese Americans were mentioned among the twenty-five members of the State Senate, and they comprised over 41 percent of the membership of the House of Representatives. Japanese Americans headed important state departmental posts, including those of education, budget, and finance, and transportation. And, their representation and participation in the educational establishment has been especially strong, so that one common stereotype of the Department of Education (DOE) teacher is that of a person of Japanese ancestry.

Another opportunity to gain a degree of economic and political power was through the International Longshoremen and Warehousemen's Union (ILWU). In contrast to the labor movement along the Pacific Coast, which sought to limit or to exclude the participation of the Japanese and other Asian groups, the ILWU welcomed the ethnics. By 1947 the union claimed a multiethnic membership of more than 30,000 members in a territorial population of 500,000 (Gray, 1973).

THE CURRENT PICTURE

The growth of Hawaii since its admission as the fiftieth state in 1959 has been paralleled by a corresponding increase in problems. Overcrowd-

TABLE 1

Ethnic Representation in the Hawaii State
Department of Education, 1991

Population	Officers (Administrators and Consultants)	Educators (Teachers)	Boards of Education
	By Percent		
Caucasian	21.8	22.6	38.5
Japanese	51.7	52.7	46.1
Filipino	3.0	4.1	0
Hawaiian and part-Hawaiian	8.6	7.4	15.4
Chinese	6.9	6.5	0
Korean	1.6	1.0	0
Negro	0.7	0.6	0
Mixed	4.6	4.0	0
Other	1.1	1.1	0

* Department of Education, State of Hawaii, Personnel by Ethnic Category and Sex, Honolulu, Hawaii, January 10, 1991.

ing, pollution, and high prices have become everyday realities, and the influx of new residents and the constant flow of tourists has contributed to the ever changing island scene. There are attempts to differentiate among the old timers (*kamainas*), the new residents, and those whose stay will be temporary, so that the picture of a dynamic, changing Hawaii is more accurate than that of a slow-paced South Seas island paradise. Even some of the more isolated islands in the chain are sharing in this "progress."

The new immigration has come from several sources. Immigrants from Melanesia, Micronesia, the Phillipines, and Korea have added to Hawaii's ethnic and racial diversity. There has been a steady flow of whites from the mainland, so that by 1990, they were the most populous "ethnic group" with 33.4 percent, and the Japanese proportion had dipped to 22.3 percent.

But much information about the mobility and improvement of the Japanese in Hawaii remains to be gathered. Many leave Hawaii, some temporarily to attend mainland schools, and others emigrate as permanent residents. There is a reverse flow of modest proportions consisting of Japanese Americans coming to live on the islands. Then there is the interisland flow, generally from one of the outer islands to Oahu.

Although not Japanese Americans, there is also a very visible movement of tourists from Japan. It is said that the Japanese tourists "saved" the island economy in the early 1970s because they filled the vacuum created by a drop in American visitors. In 1972 approximately 230,000 Japanese visited Hawaii, an increase of over 50,000 from the previous year (Ishizuka, 1974). The growth continued and between 1980 and 1988 increased by more than 106 percent. By 1989 the number of tourists surged to 1,319,340 with the Japanese spending $2.5 billion for the year or about $7 million per day (Hawaii Visitors Bureau, 1991).

The impact of Japanese ownership in Hawaii has been equally dramatic. In 1986, Japanese bought $1.1 billion of Hawaiian real estate; by 1988 the figure had risen to $2.1 billion followed by $1.2 billion in 1989. Adding construction and development investments, the total for 1989 amounted to $4.4 billion, making Hawaii America's leading state for Japanese real estate purchases on a per capita basis. At least half of the dollar volume generated by commercial, industrial, real, and office space in 1989 came from the Japanese whose possessions included four shopping centers and twelve hotels (Yoneyama and Hooper, 1990:16).

The influx of Japanese tourists and Japanese capital has not been without its problems. In a *Hawaii Business* article dated January, 1990, Yoneyama and Hooper write:

> As investments have multiplied, so have public fears and distrust regarding Japanese investors. Honolulu Mayor Frank Fasi spoke out early in 1988, proposing a ban on sales of residential real estate to foreign investors. Last fall, when Ward Research conducted a telephone survey of more than 400 Oahu residents, two-thirds of the respondents believe that some form of government control was necessary to keep Japanese investment in check. Late last year, Governor Waihee delivered his own analysis of public concerns. During an address before the 18th annual meeting of the Japan-Hawaii Economic Council in Nagoya, Waihee said "while there is no doubt that Hawaii's residents have benefited from an economy that is fueled by dollars from Tokyo, Vancouver, Sydney and Chicago, there is also no doubt that Hawaii's residents are experiencing a sense of loss—loss of their land to others and, more important, loss of control (Yoneyama and Hooper, 1990:16).

The new influx of Japanese from Japan and some of the resultant "new problems" has been a recurring theme in Japanese-American life, whether in Hawaii or on the mainland. For even the most acculturated third or fourth generation Japanese American still has identifiable Japanese features and is generally viewed as such by the majority group. So what Japan does as a nation affects the Japanese American—whether it be Pearl Harbor, or as a staunch Pacific ally, or as purchasers of hotels in Waikiki.

But hopefully there will come a time when the ethnic group will be able to behave autonomously, as individuals with their own needs, expectations, and goals, rather than being compared or mistaken as Japanese from Japan, or measured against the Japanese American from the mainland.

A Hawaiian culture has developed that is a blend of the Pacific Islands, the Asian, the native, and the haole. The proportions of the blend are open to conjecture and probably depend on group identification and position. But even though the influences of the blend may differ, permanent residents of the islands refer to this culture as "local." Although there are ethnocentric connotations to the term, it is also a recognition that the local—whether of Asian, islander, European, or American ancestry—has developed a way of looking at the world that is different from his countrymen across the oceans. As with most cultures, this local blend is difficult to describe, but it is probable that the modern Hawaiian has learned to live in an interracial atmosphere; that they are not too concerned about status, material success, and prestige; and that they have developed a tolerant and a relaxed style of living suited to the ambience of the islands. But the strength of this local culture is under continual testing, just as the tolerance of the native Hawaiians of centuries ago was tested, for Hawaii continues to draw new immigrants, many as aggressive and as sure that their ways are superior as were the missionaries, traders, and businessmen of a past era.

BIBLIOGRAPHY

1. Adams, R. (1933). *The Peoples of Hawaii*, pp. 8-9. Honolulu: The Institute of Pacific Relations.

2. Allen, G. (1950). *Hawaii's War Years*. Honolulu: University of Hawaii Press.

3. Fuchs, L. (1961). *Hawaii Pono: A Social History*, p. 82. New York: Harcourt Brace Jovanovich, Inc.

4. Gray, F. (1973). *Hawaii: The Sugar Coated Fortress*, p. 80. New York: Random House.

5. Hawaii Visitors Bureau (1989). "1989 Japanese Visitors to Hawaii." *Hawaii Visitors Bureau, Asia/Pacific Series*, No. 7, p. 1. The Bureau in 1991 revised the calculation by a decrease of $2.1 billion for 1989 figures of total Japanese tourist expenditure. Instead of $4.6 billion the figure was adjusted to $2.5 billion.

6. Hunter, L. (1971). *Buddhism in Hawaii*, p. 80. Honolulu: University of Hawaii Press.

7. Ibid., p. 81.

8. Inouye, D. (1967). *Journey to Washington*. Englewood Cliffs, N.J.: Prentice Hall, Inc.

9. Ibid, p. 249.

10. Ishizuka, Y. (1974). "Resentment Continues to Grow in Hawaii over Japanese Takeover." *Nichi-bei* Times, April 2, p. 3.

11. Jacobs, P., and Landau, S. (1971). *To Serve the Devil*, Vol. 2. New York: Random House.

12. Kuykendall, R.S. (1967). *The Hawaiian Kingdom, Vol. 3, 1874-1893*, p. 160. Honolulu: University of Hawaii Press.

13. Ibid., p. 172.

14. Lind, A. (1967). *Hawaii's People*. Honolulu: University of Hawaii Press.

15. Ibid., p. 7.

16. Moriyama, A.T. (1985). *Imingaisha: Japanese Emigration Companies and Hawaii, 1894-1980*, p. xviii. Honolulu: University of Hawaii Press.

17. Office of the Chief of Military History (19). *United States Army Forces Middle Pacific and Predecessor Commands During World War II, 7 December 1941 - 2 September 1945, History of the Provost Marshal's Office*, Vol. 24, Pt. 1, p. 11.

18. Ogawa, D.M. (1982). "What Were the Wages of the Early Immigrants?" *Hawaii Herald*, Vol. 3, No. 23, Dec. 3.

19. Ogawa, D.M. (1978). *Kodomo no Tame ni*, p. 79. Honolulu: University of Hawaii Press.

20. Ogawa, D.M. (1973). *Jan Ken Po*, p. 16. Honolulu: University of Hawaii Press.

21. Okihoro, G.Y. (1991). *Cane Fires: The Anti-Japanese Movement in Hawaii, 1865-1945*, p. xii. Philadelphia: Temple University Press.

22. Takaki, R. (1983). *Pau Hana: Plantation Life and Labor in Hawaii, 1835-1920*, pp. 70-71. Honolulu: University of Hawaii Press.

23. Wakukawa, E. (1938). *A History of the Japanese People in Hawaii*, p. 127. Honolulu: The Toyo Shoin.

24. Ibid., p. 169.

25. Yoneyama, T., and Hooper, S. (1990). "The Japanese of Hawaii." *Hawaii Business*, p. 16. January.

26. Ibid., p. 29.

SECTION III

Section III provides a look at the ever present issue of an identity. Japanese Americans, because they do not fit the Euro-American image of what an American should look like, have found that no matter how one acculturates, there remain questions of how really "American" one really is. Identity also includes the role of the Japanese American female.

Related to identity, self concept, and adaptation to the American society is the question of dealing with feelings such as frustration and anger, in the face of racism. How does one adapt to the constant blows to self-esteem, of second class citizenship, of being thrown into a concentration camp and blocked opportunities? Surely, there must have been instances when one wanted to strike back.

I knew that I was different, growing up as a Japanese American child in Chinatown. But, the relationship was not unequal; it was only with the mainstream society, as represented by the whites, that I felt like a second class citizen. I heard my father constantly complain about his treatment from the white owner of his leased hotel; yet I noticed how obsequious he was in face to face contact. The power of the white man was clearly established—I was told to obey my teachers, and by implication, all white authorities—they could never be wrong. They could be dumb (baka), but they were in power. On the other hand his reactions towards the Chinese and other minorities was that of a superior.

My initial protection came from a large family—five older sisters and an older brother. Unfairness in life, racism and inequality were not major concerns in my early years. I felt that whatever problems I was to encounter, I had the support of my brother and sisters.

My first formal encounter with the white world was with elementary school teachers. As a whole they were very supportive; I received more praise and positive reinforcements from them than from my father. In fact, the only negative incident that I can remember with teachers was much later when I was a student at the University of California. I took a Harmony course in the music department; I was not a music major, and did not have the time for my daily homework assignments, so instead of carefully planning and listening to the chordal arrangements, I would haphazardly fill in whatever looked good while

I studied for my other courses. I remember the instructor, Ms Howe, after playing my chords telling the class that, "Orientals don't have an ear for good music." She gave me a failing grade.

Interesting enough, the other Euro-centric remark that I remember was also in the music department. The lecturer indicated that the only acceptable norm for good music was that it be universally appreciated, and that the European masters were the only composers who were worth listening to. Otherwise I generally had excellent instructors, even during the concentration camp period.

The concentration camp still evokes a number of feelings, and they have changed over time. I remember getting angry, but not at the authorities and the directives that put me into camp, but at fellow inmates. The trend to take it out on each other was probably more common than directing our energy and anger at the jailers; faceless, unknown figures in Washington D.C. were too distant, and not easily identifiable as the real enemy. The most common feeling was that of helplessness; that of shi-ka-ta-ga-nai—it couldn't be helped. There were also wise and sympathetic teachers and myriads of activities for high schoolers, so that I was kept busy in everyday activities. Questioning the constitutionality and injustice only came about later in life.

Further, who could I attack, or at least register a complaint? Who could I identify as the person or persons who threw me into a concentration camp? And, what would be the consequences of such an action, given the totally unequal power relationships. Would it do any good?

I repressed my life in camp for many years. It was only in the 1960s that I began to read and study the event, and to question governmental policy. I began to share some of the negative feelings with peers. Previously, we referred to the evacuation in joking terms, or in terms of the people we knew, and what had happened to them. Now there was anger, feelings of betrayal, and of being a victim.

I suspect that my own reactions were similar to many of my peers; silent frustration at being sent to the camps; repression of the incident, followed by a reawakening as more evidence was uncovered concerning our victimization. Finally, there was the awakening that what happened to myself and my ethnic group was not just a historical accident, but was made by people who were ignorant about our group, who were racist, and who felt that it was politically popular position. Therefore, the move for redress was a totally acceptable position to me.

It has been fifty years since the camps; it now remains as one of the most important incidents in my life. Not too many people can claim to have been forcefully incarcerated by a nation with a Constitution such as ours; lived for three years behind barbed wire; remained silent about the injustice for several decades; backed a successful redress campaign; and then incorporated that period into an important part of an identity.

Chapter 12 is based on data drawn from a number of different studies. The studies provide statistical data on the Japanese Americans.

The final chapter explores a number of models in order to understand the different Japanese generations; their identity and their adaptation to minority status.

CHAPTER 11

IDENTITY AND GENERATIONS

THE ISSEI *the Japanese: the certain ones*

Perhaps the only Japanese group in America that was not confused about an ethnic identity were the original immigrant group, the Issei. They were from Japan; they knew and identified with the culture of their upbringing; they were proud of their homeland; their knowledge and use of the English language was minimal; their contact with the majority group was on less than equal terms, and they could not become citizens until relatively late in their lives. With a few exceptions, their major identification was as Japanese, or more commonly as the Issei.

Their Japanese identity was reinforced by their treatment from the dominant community. They were viewed as "Japs," thought to be unassimilable and walled in, or walled out of the mainstream by prejudice, discrimination and segregation. They could only live in specified areas; hold certain types of jobs; could not own land and could not be citizens. Their hopes, in terms of identification as Americans, lay in their American born children, the Nisei. *# only connect to America: Nisei!*

There were differences between the urban and rural Issei, of "ken," class, and background distinctions were sometimes important (i.e. Okinawa), but the idea of achieving an American identity was never an issue. The infamous loyalty questionnaire while in the concentration camps (see Chapter 4) presented problems, but it was clear that ethnic and cultural identity remained as Japanese.

Many Issei became United States citizens after the passage of the McCarran-Walter Immigration Bill in 1952 so that there was a degree of identification with the new country. But by that time they were on their way to senior citizen status, and were not about to lose their Issei identification. Perhaps there was a little more interest in American history; my parents could recite the names of the first few presidents of the United States, but they were more familiar with the "goings on" in Tokyo than in Washington. Their closest friends were other Issei; they ate Japanese food and their language was still Japanese. They celebrated most of the Japanese holidays (and also the 4th of July and Christmas); their favorite newspapers were printed in Japanese and they enjoyed television programs from Japan. They still looked Japanese; they retained their Japanese names and the surrounding community, both ethnic and non-ethnic saw them as Japanese. Very few questioned the Japanese basis of their identity.

THE NISEI

The Nisei faced a different world. They were exposed to the American culture, but were visibly ethnic; they were American citizens but were looked upon as Japanese. In addition, during World War II, they were linked with an enemy nation, so that the development and maintenance of an ethnic identity meant searching for answers which were not easy to come by. If they were American, why were they in camp, and if they were Japanese, why did they feel and act like Americans?

As Hosokawa (1982) writes, the Nisei were constantly in search of an identity. They were exposed to the doctrine of freedom of opportunity and the American dream, yet they encountered a racist society where visibility was more important than desire and ability. Their experiences during World War II, when even the most highly acculturated and the most closely identified with being American, ended up behind barbed wire illustrated the dilemma. Perhaps the most realistic choice for many was to identify as a Japanese American.

Attempts to preserve the Japanese American identity have been made by Nisei groups through the development of the Japanese American National Museum, and a memorial for Nisei soldiers in Los Angeles, and the Japanese American Historical Society in San Francisco.

THE SANSEI

The Sansei, as well as the succeeding generations appear as American as any of their mainstream peers, with the exception of their visibility. Those who live in areas, such as Los Angeles and Hawaii, are more apt to interact with peers who are Japanese and to live in intra-generational settings, so that facets of the ethnic culture are more apt to survive. A few have traveled to Japan in order to experience and to gain some understanding of their ancestral heritage, but the majority have absorbed American life styles and an American identity. Many have married non-Japanese, and perhaps in the long run, visibility may no longer be the critical factor in identity. Perhaps the most appropriate term for the group would be Americans with Japanese ancestry. The rise in the number of children with mixed ancestry creates a dilemma of identity, even for the counting of Japanese Americans in the U.S. Census.

MODELS OF IDENTITY

Individual identity is intimately related to family, group, racial, occupational, community, and national identity. We are all familiar with such identities as "Name, rank and serial number"; the Social Security number, and the Driver's License. Or in social situations, one often starts off with occupation, or in academia, one identifies with a department or profession, so that identification, or the "Who am I"? serves a functional role. And when abroad, one's city, state, nation, and passport serve as identities. Identity in this sense provides information, so that in most situations, the identity which is the most appropriate at a given time is used. As such it is voluntary and functional.

Skin color, physical features and a social definition of race provides the basis for a racial identity. It is difficult to escape a racial identity, although the issue of "passing," especially from pariah status, is not uncommon.

Ethnic identity exists when members choose a cultural, racial or national tie as their primary reference. An ethnic group exists when members consider themselves to belong to such a group. However, it may be also be linked to a racial identity if based on physical features.

Theoretical views of ethnicity range from the primordial—that is, as long lasting and permanent and rooted in the genes (Va den Berghe, 1981), to the situational and structural. The primordial view sees ethnicity as basic to group identity and as such, is passed down from generation to generation. The situational approach sees ethnic identity as essentially fluid so that ethnic boundaries are drawn in the context of external events. As such, it is voluntary.

Bell (1975) gives three reasons for the upsurge in ethnic identification at the present time: (1), the greater intermingling of people and the rise and growth of bureaucracy; (2) the breakup of traditional structures and units, such as the nation and social class; and (3) the politicization of decisions. These changes have lead people to look for smaller, more relevant groups and organizations. Ethnic identity from this perspective is then a choice, rather than a deeply rooted primordial phenomenon, so that its salience may fade in and out depending on the external situation.

Brass (1991) indicates that ethnicity and nationalism are not "givens," but are the creations of elites who draw from the cultures of groups which they wish to represent in order to gain political and economic advantage. He also believes that ethnicity is a modern phenomena intimately connected with modern, centralized states. Matters of descent, birth, and sense of kinship may be important in determining inclusion and exclusion from the group. Ethnic identity also involves subjective self-consciousness, and a claim to status and recognition either as superior or at least equal to other groups. In this sense, "ethnicity is to ethnic category what class consciousness is to class" (p. 19).

ACHIEVING A POSITIVE IDENTITY

Child development models, such as by Erikson (1950) propose the development of an identity through a number of stages, beginning with infancy and ending with maturity. Since identity is achieved through the self in interaction with critical others, can racial minorities achieve a positive identity when they do not possess the requisite attributes considered necessary to participate in the mainstream, and are the targets of prejudice and discrimination?

The simplest answer to the question is, "Of course," since we know many Japanese Americans who have a positive identity and a healthy view of their ethnicity, which includes racial and cultural features. However, we also know that the process is difficult, and at times of crisis proportions, such as during World War II when the decision was not an easy one. My own experiences illustrate this point.

> It was difficult to identify with America while in the concentration camps. The question that was constantly thrown at me, "If you're an American, why are you in the camps with the rest of us Japanese?", never suggested an easy answer. And there was also the reality of having "Japanese" features so that even if I would be released, the outside white world would see me as Japanese. And there was also some pride that the tiny Japanese nation was challenging the might of the Western allies, so an identity based on nationality was not all negative.
>
> However, I also knew that since my life and future was in the United States, I had to face the reality of eventually dealing with the mainstream society. My initial solution was to "pass," that is by changing my name to Harry Lee, so that I would be mistaken for a Chinese.

Therefore, upon release from the camp in Topaz in 1945, I adopted this new name and became a dance band musician. I toured throughout the Midwest territory, primarily in Minnesota and Iowa, constantly afraid of being identified as a "Jap," and burying myself in the role of a musician. I walked, talked and dressed like one.

At one time I remember playing the Tommy Dorsey solo of "Song of India," passing off myself as a Chinese, being Japanese American, and playing before an all white audience. It was a confusing time; I hid my background and my home (how could I admit that my parents and "home" was in a concentration camp?). A particularly difficult time was during vacation when the band would scatter and go home; I told them that my home was in San Francisco, but obviously I could not go there. And spending my vacation behind barbed wire in Topaz was not an appealing option, although I did go back to spend a week with my parents.

There were also many times when I would sit in camp and play the game of "If I were American?," which really meant if I were "white." Now that I look back, it is clear that the negative identity of being a Japanese was an embarrassment; I know that some of my peers turned on their parents and blamed them for their plight, but my adaptation was to dream of being a member of the majority group. Later on, I found that many members of my group, as well as others of Asian ancestry also played with this fantasy.

The internalization of an ethnic identify takes on a variety of forms. We know of Japanese Americans who automatically look for Japanese surnames in a telephone directory when in an unfamiliar city, and go up to talk to strangers with Asian features, just as we know of some who will deliberately avoid anything to do with Asians.

Cultural identity includes language and customs. Gans (1985) also talks about symbolic identity, that is the retention of an ethnic identity by seeing an ethnic movie on occasion, eating sushi, and participating in a yearly Nisei week festival. Many of my peers fit into this category.

The question of having racially different features and its relationship to an identity remains even today. Young Sansei and Yonsei who know little about the Japanese language and culture and may not even qualify as symbolic ethnics, are bemused when they are asked why their command of English is so good, or why they make such good automobiles. Some still find positions such as becoming the head cheerleader, or the lead in a high school play closed. And the opportunities for Japanese Americans is still limited where visibility is an important, but unstated requisite for success.

Nowhere is this point brought home more forcefully by watching television shows from Japan and Korea. There, all of the musicians are Asians, the emcee and the leading lady are Asians, the performers and even the "do-wah" backup singers (all they do is to sing "do-wah") are

Asian, and I am sure that all phases of the show are run by Asians. Yet, even though there probably are as many talented Japanese American performers in America, visibility and stereotypes limit their participation.

In paraphrasing Gordon (1964), there are several ways of looking at the stages in an ethnic identity. The immigrant arrives and may declare:

1. I am Japanese (the Issei).

2. Then, I am a Japanese American (early Nisei).

3. Then, I am an American of Japanese ancestry (Sansei).

4. Then, I am an American (some future generation where assimilation is the desired end).

Or, if the actor prefers a pluralistic perspective, then either Stages 2 or 3, would constitute a last stage. Although self-determination is an important part of the process of achieving an identity, it should be recalled that the reinforcers from the outside world, in this case the mainstream community, also play a significant role. Racism has played a role in affecting the identity of Japanese Americans.

ROLE OF WOMEN

THE ISSEI

One of the historical anomalies when dealing with Japanese Americans is the scarcity of material on the role of women. From the published material, it would appear that the Japanese female, whether Issei, Nisei or Sansei was insignificant, or at best, invisible. Nothing could be further from the reality; it was often the women who provided the stability that kept the families afloat.

The expected role prescriptions for women from the old country were not too helpful in terms of self-development. There was a strong service orientation—first to father, then to husband, and finally to son. And many Issei women fulfilled that role, often submerging their talent and ambition in order to maintain the family. Kikumura (1979:178), in writing about the relationship between her Issei father and mother quotes her mother:

> He was a gambler and a drunk but he was strict when it came to the discipline of women. He would say that a woman must be womanly. She must be subordinate to a man. She is a keeper of the house. In the morning a woman must rise early. He was severe about things like that.

Her mother continues (p. 181):

I'm a Meiji woman so I hold those values, that a woman should place her children's and family's welfare before her own personal wishes. Today people have different ideas. They do what makes them happy. The Issei really put up with a lot—putting up with men that made them sick to their stomachs. But divorce was unheard of. Once you marry someone, it's forever.

Glenn (1986), as a young Japanese American, resented the notion of female subordination. She respected her mother, grandmothers and aunts for their selflessness and hard work, for their contributions to the family and economy through their toil as farm hands, cooks, boarding-house keepers, operatives and assistants to their husbands. But she emphasizes, she did not want to be like them.

She interviewed a variety of Japanese American women and compiled her results in a book titled, *Issei, Nisei* and *War Brides*. She found that on one level, her subjects suffered from triple oppression; that of employment in menial occupations; that of racism, and that of subordination at home to a patriarchal family system. But on another, she found that they were not passive sufferers; that the very difficulty of their lives forced them to struggle for survival, and to develop a corresponding strength and tenacity. They could look back on their lives with satisfaction for what they had accomplished; they had raised their children, gained some measure of independence, and won the respect of their children and community.

Issei women were generally excluded from community involvement; public functions, such as dinners and ceremonies were for men. Women were supposed to stay at home with the children and wait for father to return. The one exception was through the church groups, the fujinkai, where their participation, especially in cooking and serving were particularly welcome. As my mother grew older, she found it more and more difficult to keep on making Japanese goodies for the church, and finally began to beg out of such commitments. But it gave her a chance to mingle with other mothers, both Issei and Nisei, and to interact with more than family and extended family.

Employment was expected of many Issei wives. Male wages were insufficient, especially if the dream was to make enough money to make a triumphant return to Japan so that wives provided much needed labor, both at home and money producing activities on the outside. As Strong (1934) indicates, a majority of farmers, barbers, and small housekeepers used their wives as helpers, while others took jobs as domestics and in laundries.

Domestic service played an important role in the Issei American economy. It was important for a variety of reasons—it took the women outside of the household so that they saw a wider world, and it did not involve any capital investment, language ability, or special skills. It also gave them contact with mainstream households, and there were even close friendships, albeit on a paternalistic level, between employee and employer. The language barrier and the "inferior" position of the domestic sometimes lead to discussions that could be safely made by the employer, even if the Issei could barely understand the monolog.

> I'd been working for a lady for two hours a week for a long time, but she didn't even give me a chance to work. After my arrival, she kept talking and going on and on. For me, housework was much easier because even though I didn't understand English well, I still had to say, "Is that so?," "no," and "yes.". . . . These people just wanted to talk to someone. They didn't care that I couldn't understand English, so I couldn't help them. They just wanted to complain about their son or their son's wife. (Glenn:1986:159).

For some, it was an opportunity to see mainstream life first hand, for others it was another trap—long hours, isolation, and hard physical labor. Most of them took pride in their work, if not in their occupational title. They put in a full day of honest work and were proud of their ability to earn their wages.

Perhaps those women who seldom ventured away from home were the least prepared for changes. Their isolation limited exposure to the new world; conversely, changes in Japan were also unfamiliar so that they remained as aliens in America, as well as unfamiliar with the changes in Japan.

For example, my mother, who never worked outside of home had unrealistic ideas, both about life in the United States and life in Japan. One of her favorite themes for me was to open a "mom and pop" grocery store, because she understood that type of business. Or she could not understand about investments so that she discouraged my father from buying real estate after World War II, or investing in stocks and bonds. Cash in hand was her security. Even more surprising was her visit to Japan in the 1960s which found her completely paralyzed because of the strangeness of the homeland which she had left many decades before. Rather than playing the role of guide for her daughters, she instead became a dependent child.

I suspect that the only "free time" that she had (she had to raise seven children) in her entire life was in the concentration camp. At least, she did not have to cook or to be tied to household chores; she had time to take up poetry and other activities while in Topaz. Perhaps that is why she never overtly complained about her incarceration; freedom is certainly relative.

There were other events which were typical of my mother's Issei life style.

> Mother was marvelous when it came to hard times. She fed clothed and took care of the entire family during the depression years so that we never knew that we were poor. She could prepare meals out of almost nothing, and saved enough so that Christmas and other holidays were joyous occasions.
>
> But when times were better, she still hung onto her old ways. The family would buy her new clothes and appliances that would never be worn or used until the old ones would become unusable. When only she and father would be left at home, she would still buy bargain foods in enormous quantities in order to save a few cents. Her refrigerator was always filled with leftovers; she could not bear to throw anything away.
>
> And she can still remember being in camp. When we finally decided that she could not live alone and had to be put in a home for the elderly, her first comment, upon seeing the institutional like setting was, "Oh, I'm back in a concentration camp." Then she added, "But of course not, there are hakujin (white) people here."

Her main pleasure seemed to be in the progress of her children. I was never sure that she loved her husband; like many Issei, the concept of duty and obligation had higher priority. It is difficult not to have a strong admiration for her; from her "picture bride" marriage, to her ability to manage a large family through most difficult times, to living to a ripe old age. She will enjoy her 103rd birthday at the time of this writing.

THE NISEI

Nisei women also faced a limited world prior to World War II. They belonged to a number of organizations—the church groups were important, and also such mainstream organizations as the YWCA. Employment opportunities were restricted; even though they could speak English and developed a number of business skills, white collar work in white business establishments, and government employment were unavailable. They were almost as restricted as their mothers had been; over a quarter of employed nisei were listed in 1940 as private household workers (Glenn, 1986:76).

A "good" marriage and the raising of children were important. The women were most active behind the scenes; it was their men who were pushed forward to serve as speakers and officers.

In contrast to the Issei, Nisei women began to go to college. My sisters introduced me to a wider world.

One of my older sisters, Kiyo, was the first in our family to go to college. She went across the bay to Berkeley to Cal. She would bring home stories about college life; of meetings at the Asilomar (near Monterey), and the football and athletic heroes at Cal with names like Vic Bottari and Sam Chapman. She would even take me to some football games where I would sit next to the all male, rowdy rooting section. There was no question that I would attend Cal sometime in the future.

Or my oldest sister Tish, married a man from Palo Alto, so that they would take me to games at Stanford. My other sisters would follow the Nisei basketball teams, so that if I went with them (a chaperone at the tender age of 10), my parents would allow them to go to games around the Bay Area. They brought the outside world, narrow as it was, to me. I listened to them talk about good dates and desirable qualities in men, of the frustration of limited opportunities after graduation, and their marriages. Family dinners were often party like with sisters, husbands, boarders and others joining in so that I only had to keep my ears open to find out what was happening, not only in the Nisei world, but in the bigger world.

Nisei women were a product of American, Meiji and localized values. These included education, politeness, hard work, honesty, sobriety, and material success. They often placed themselves midway between the "American" and "Japanese" poles; they liked what was Japanese and what was American in almost equal terms (Glenn, 1986).

In many ways, the evacuation era, and the postwar period, which saw an opening up of the American society, paved the path for Nisei women. Wages in the concentration camps were equal (no one could make more than $19 per month), and job skills, other than domestic labor were acquired. Many left camp for higher education, to join boyfriends and husbands, and to find employment. They found jobs more suited to their background and skills in the East and Midwest.

The transition from camp life to employment on the outside was not an easy one. Leaving camps meant an adjustment, just as entering camp was. One evacuee said:

> I had thought that before evacuation I had adjusted myself rather well in Caucasian society, and I would go right back into my former frame of mind. I have found, however, that though the center became unreal and was as if it had never existed, as soon as I got on the train at Delta, I was never so self-conscious in all my life (Matsumoto, 1989:122).

Life on the outside meant adjustments, often away from the family and the ethnic network, and in new and unfamiliar settings. It was clear that for most, there could be no return to pre-war life as "traditional" Nisei women.

Japanese American women in the 90s, whether Nisei, Sansei or other generations, reflect the ambience of the wider world. They suffer the same inequalities and progress of other women in the society. They publish, write plays, appear in movies, anchor newscasts, and participate in business—avenues that were not a part of female lives several decades before. Just like their ancestors, they marry, and have children, but unlike them, they may marry non-Japanese and may divorce.

In the family of my birth, my sisters have played the major role in keeping the family together. They organize family gatherings, keep in touch with each other, and are the carriers of family traditions. It is interesting that they also involve their husbands in family affairs; my sisters may be unusual, although Yanagisako (1985) also mentions that in her study of Japanese families, it was the women who kept the family and extended families together.

The overall picture of Japanese Americans, whether they be male or female, is that the question of an identity, especially when mixed up with racial, cultural and ethnic features remains an issue of concern. Some resolve it by burying their lives within the ethnic community, while others may take the other extreme and live totally away from fellow ethnics. Most take positions somewhere in between, but all are aware that the relationship between the United States and Japan, an area where they have no control, influences their identity.

The Japanese female role, that of meekness and acquiescence to male dominance, was a stereotype that has certainly been laid to rest when looking at the experiences of Japanese American women. There was pain, suffering, and domineering fathers and husbands, but there was also ingenuity, creativity, and the ability to raise families under trying conditions. The modern Japanese American male has also taken on newer roles, removed from the authoritarian models of past generations. The search for appropriate male and female roles, intertwined with race, ethnic identity and culture in an ever changing society, means that what may be appropriate today may be questionable tomorrow. As a dynamic, these questions may still be appropriate one hundred years from now.

BIBLIOGRAPHY

1. Bell, Daniel (1975). "Ethnicity and Social Change," in Ethnicity, eds. Nathan Glazer and Daniel Moynihan. Cambridge, Mass.: Harvard University Press, pp. 141-174.

2. Brass, Paul R. (1991). Ethnicity and Nationalism. Newbury Park, Ca: Sage Publications.

3. Erikson, Erik (1950). Childhood and Society. New York: W.W. Norton.

4. Gans, Herbert J. (1985). "Symbolic Ethnicity: The Future of Ethnic Groups and Cultures in America," in Majority and Minority. Norman Yetman, ed. Boston: Allyn and Bacon.

5. Glenn, Evelyn Nakano (1986). *Issei, Nisei, War Bride.* Philadelphia: Temple University Press.

6. Gordon, Milton (1964). *Assimilation in American Life.*

7. Hosokawa, William (1982). *JACL in the Quest for Justice.* New York: William Morrow.

8. Kikumura, Akemi (1979). The Life History of an Issei Woman: Conflicts and Strain in the Process of Acculturation. Los Angeles: University of California, unpublished Ph.D. dissertation.

9. Matsumoto, Valerie (1989). "Nisei Women and Resettlement during World War II." Making Waves, ed. by Asian Women United of California. Boston: Beacon Press. p. 115-126.

10. Strong, Edward (1934). *The Second Generation Japanese Problem.* Stanford: Stanford University Press.

11. Van den Berghe, Pierre (1981). *The Ethnic Phenomenon.* New York: Elsevier.

12. Williams, Therea (1986). "International Amerasian Identity: The Case of Third Culture Eurasian and Afroasian Americans in Japan." Los Angeles: University of California, Unpublished Masters Thesis, Asian American Study Center.

13. Yanagisako, Sylvia (1985). *Transforming the Past Tradition and Kinship among Japanese Americans.* Stanford: Stanford University Press.

CHAPTER 12

PRESENT STATUS

America at the end of the 1900s is different from the America that started the 1900s, just as the early Issei immigrant of yesterday bears little resemblance to the third and fourth generation Sansei and Yonsei of today. The theme has been that of change—changes in the dominant society and changes in the Japanese American community; changes in the relationship between Japan and the United States, and changes between the Japanese Americans and the American society. There have been bad times and good times, frayed relationships and those of a more friendly nature. There is little doubt that these changes will continue, so that the roller coaster ride will continue, hopefully with more ups than downs.

Japanese Americans as a group have lived through these changes; there are even some individuals who have been on the roller coaster through all of these years. My mother, who arrived in 1914 is still alive and has lived through the bad times and the good times, and her wise remark is that, "good times are better."

The purpose of this chapter is to present data showing the present status of the ethnic group. It will be interesting to see if a researcher, probably of mixed Japanese ancestry, will present data on the status of the Japanese American at the close of the 21st century. Will there be an identifiable Japanese American group a century from now, and what will the data show?

NUMBERS AND DISTRIBUTION

TABLE 1
Population Increase by Race—1980 vs. 1990

Race	1980 (%)	1990 (%)	Population Increase (%)
Total	226,545,805	248,709,873	9.9
White	188,371,622	199,686,070	6.0
Black	26,495,025	29,986,060	13.2
American Indian, Eskimo of Aleut	1,420,400	1,959,234	37.9%
Asian Pacific Islander	3,726,440	7,273,662	107.8
Chinese	806,040	1,645,472	104.1
Filipino	774,652	1,406,770	81.6
Japanese	700,974	847,562	20.9
Asian Indian	361,531	815,447	125.6
Korean	354,593	798,849	125.3
Vietnamese	261,729	614,547	134.8
Hawaiian	166,814	211,014	26.5
Samoan	41,948	62,964	50.1
Guamanian	32,158	49,345	53.4
Other Asian Pacific Islander	N/A	821,696	45.1
Hispanic Origin	14,608,673	22,354,059	53.0

Source: U.S. Department of Commerce News. (June 12, 1991) Table 1.

Table 1 shows the total population of the United States for 1980 and 1990; the population by different ethnic group and the percentage increase from 1980 to 1990. The Japanese population was 700,974 in 1980 and 847,562 in 1990, a 20.9 percent increase. It placed them behind the Chinese and the Filipino in terms of total numbers, and the population increase of 20.9 percent between 1980 and 1990 was the lowest of any Asian American group.

Table 2 shows the population distribution of Asian Americans by region. Over 75 percent of the Japanese population lives in the West; while most of the other Asian American groups also live in the West, with the exception of the Asian Indian, their proportions are less than for the Japanese.

TABLE 2

Distribution by Region

| Population | Percent Distribution (1990) | | | |
	Northeast	Midwest	South	West
Total U.S.	20.4	24.0	34.4	21.2
Total Asian*	19.2	10.9	15.8	54.1
Japanese	8.8	7.5	7.9	75.9
Chinese	27.0	8.1	12.4	52.4
Filipino	10.2	8.1	11.3	70.5
Korean	22.8	13.7	19.2	44.4
Asian Indian	35.0	17.9	24.0	23.1
Vietnamese	9.8	8.5	27.4	54.3

* Includes all Asian, not just those listed separately.

Source: U.S. Department of Commerce News. (June 12, 1991). Table 3C.

Table 3 shows the States with the largest percentage of Asian and Pacific Islanders. As expected, California with 36.9 percent has the largest percentage of the Japanese population, followed by Hawaii with 29.2 percent.

IMMIGRATION, NATURALIZATION, FOREIGN BORN, AND ENGLISH SPEAKERS

TABLE 3

States with Largest Percent of Asian Pacific Islander (1990)

Population	CA	NY	HI	TX	IL
Total U.S.	12.0	7.2	0.4	6.8	4.6
Total Asian Pacific Island	39.1	9.5	9.4	4.4	3.9
Chinese	42.8	17.3	4.2	3.8	3.0
Filipino	52.0	4.4	12.0	4.6	2.4
Japanese	36.9	4.2	29.2	1.7	2.6
Asian Indian	19.6	17.3	0.1	6.8	7.9
Korean	32.5	12.0	3.1	4.0	5.2
Vietnamese	45.6	2.5	0.9	11.3	1.7

Source: U.S. Department of Commerce News. (June 12, 1991). Table 5B.

Table 4 shows immigration figures for Asian groups from 1951 to 1988. The high points of Japanese immigration were prior to 1980 with over 46,000 in 1951-1960; about 40,000 in 1961-1970, and over 49,000 in 1971-1980. The figures for 1984 and 1988 are for individual years and if combined may show similar rates, although in general, Japanese immigration numbers are much smaller in comparison with other Asian groups.

TABLE 4

Immigrants Admitted by Selected Regions and Countries of Last Residence—1951-1988.

Regions	1951-1960	1961-1970	1971-1980	1984	1988
All	2,515,479	3,321,677	4,493,314	543,903	643,025
	(100%)	(100%)	(100%)	(100%)	(100%)
Asia	153,249	427,642	1,588,176	247,775	254,745
	(6.1%)	(12.9%)	(35.3)	(45.6%)	(39.6%)
Japan	46,250	39,988	49,775	4,517	5,085
China*	9,657	34,764	124,326	29,109	34,300
Hong Kong	15,541	75,007	113,467	12,290	11,817
India	1,973	27,189	164,134	23,617	25,312
Korea	6,231	34,526	267,638	32,537	34,151
Philippines	19,307	96,376	354,967	46,985	61,017
Vietnam	335	4,340	172,820	25,803	12,856
Africa	14,092	28,954	80,779	13,594	17,124
	(0.6%)	(0.9%)	(1.8%)	(2.5%)	(2.7%)
America	996,944	1,716,374	1,982,735	206,111	294,906
	(39.6%)	(51.7%)	(44.1%)	(37.9%)	(45.9%)
North**	377,952	413,310	169,939	15,659	15,821
Mexico	299,811	453,937	640,294	57,820	95,170
Caribbean	123,091	470,213	741,126	68,368	110,949
Central	44,751	101,330	134,640	27,626	31,311
South	91,628	257,954	295,741	38,636	41,646
Europe	1,325,727	1,123,492	800,368	69,879	71,854
	(52.7%)	(33.8%)	(17.8%)	(12.8%)	(11.2%)

* Beginning 1957 China includes Taiwan.

** Canada and Newfoundland.

Source: U.S. Department of Justice, Immigration and Naturalization Service. (August, 1989). *1988 Statistical Yearbook of the Immigration and Naturalization Service.* Table 2.

Table 5 shows naturalization figures for various Asian groups for 1980, 1984, and 1988. Because of the low number of Japanese immigrants, their figures for naturalization are also low. Overall, Asian groups become naturalized American citizens at a higher rate than immigrants from non-Asian countries

TABLE 5

Persons Naturalized by Region and Selected Asian Countries of Former Allegiance

	1980	1984	1988
All Regions	157,938	197,023	242,063
	(100%)	(100%)	(100%)
Asia	67,402	87,261	114,849
	(42.7%)	(44.3%)	(47.4%)
China	12,524	——	——
Mainland China	——	9,143	10,509
India	6,552	8,294	9,983
Japan	1,759	1,108	1,041
Korea	14,703	14,019	13,012
Philippines	17,683	23,487	24,580
Taiwan	——	2,758	5,716
Vietnam	1,828	11,039	21,636
Europe	35,191	34,898	36,351
	(22.3%)	(17.7%)	(15.0%)
Africa	2,587	4,276	7,122
	(1.6%)	(1.6%)	(2.2%)
North and Central America*	41,785	54,808	65,096
	(26.5%)	(27.8%)	(26.9%)
South America	10,065	13,092	16,972
	(6.4)	(6.6)	(7.0%)
Oceania	637	709	779
	(0.4%)	(0.4%)	(0.3%)

** Includes Canada, Mexico, Caribbean and Central America.

Source: U.S. Department of Justice, Immigration and Naturalization Service. (August, 1989). 1988 Statistical Yearbook of the Immigration and Naturalization Service. Table 51.

Table 6 shows the proportion of foreign to native born populations for various Asian groups. As expected, the Japanese have the highest percentage of American born residents, 77 percent, in comparison to the other Asian groups. Other Asian groups, such as the Indian, Korean, and Vietnamese show that over 90 percent of their population is foreign born

Table 7 shows the estimated number of the student population between 5 through 14 years of age where there is limited English proficiency. The proportion of all Asian student groups with limited English proficiency is low, and especially low in the Japanese American population when compared to the "Spanish" population.

HEALTH STATUS

Table 8 shows the leading causes of death between Japan and the United States. Heart disease and cancer were the leading causes of death in the United States, whereas cerebrovascular disease and cancer were the leading causes of death in Japan. Table 9 shows that the Japanese American cancer rate in Los Angeles County is between the rates for Japan and the total U.S. It should be noted that the rates of suicide in Japan are

TABLE 6

Percentage Distribution by Immigrant Status and Year of Immigration, Men 25-64 Years (1980)

| Group | Native Born | Foreign Born | Foreign Born by Year of Immigration | | | |
			1975-1980	1970-1974	1965-1969	Before 1965
Chinese	23.9	76.1	31.0	22.3	19.4	27.3
Filipino	19.8	80.2	27.8	27.9	21.9	22.3
Japanese	77.0	23.0	49.6	16.9	8.7	24.3
Indian	4.7	95.3	36.7	34.8	18.7	9.9
Korean	6.4	93.6	48.5	32.1	10.4	9.1
Vietnamese	1.6	98.4	95.0	3.1	1.2	0.6
White	93.0	7.0	14.3	10.0	12.8	62.9

Source: U.S. Commission on Civil Rights. (October, 1988). *The Economic Status of Americans of Asian Descent: An Exploratory Investigation.* (Clearinghouse Publication 95). Table 4.1.

TABLE 7

Estimated Number of Student Population with Limited English Proficiency, Aged 5-14 (in thousand).

Languages	1980		1990		2000	
U.S. Total	2,394.2		2,795.9		3,400.0	
Japanese	13.3	(0.6%)	14.0	(0.5%)	15.3	(0.4%)
Chinese	31.3	(1.3%)	33.0	(1.2%)	36.2	(1.0%)
Filipino	33.2	(1.4%)	35.0	(1.2%)	38.3	(1.1%)
Korean	12.2	(0.5%)	12.8	(0.4%)	15.3	(0.4%)
Vietnamese	24.9	(1.0%)	26.2	(0.9%)'	28.7	(0.8%)
Spanish	1,727.6	(72.2%)	2,092.7	(74.8%)	2,630.0	(77.4%)
Portuguese	23.8	(1.0%)	25.1	(0.9%)	27.5	(0.8%)

Source: Trueba, H.T. (1989). *Raising Silent Voices: Educating the Linguistic Minorities for the 21st Century.* Table 1.1 (Adopted originally from National Advisory Council for Bilingual Education 1980-91). New York: Newbury House.

TABLE 8

Leading Causes of Death in Japan and the U.S. (number of deaths per 100,000 persons)

Cause of Death	1980	Japan[1] 1980	U.S.[2] 1987
Heart disease	106.3	336.0	312.4
Cancer	139.2	183.9	195.9
Cerebrovascular disease	139.7	75.1	61.6
Cirrhosis of the liver	14.2	13.5	10.8
Motor vehicle accidents	10.1	23.5	19.8
Other accidents	15.0	23.3	19.2
Suicides	17.7	11.9	12.7
TOTAL*	622.0	878.3	872.4

* All causes including those not listed separately.

Source: [1]Norbeck, E. & Lock, M. (eds.). (1987). *Health, Illness, and Medical Care in Japan: Cultural and Social Dimensions.* Honolulu: University of Hawaii. Table 3. [2]U.S. Department of Commerce, Bureau of the Census. (January, 1990). *Statistical Abstract of the United States.* (110th ed.). Table No. 115.

TABLE 9

Incidence Rate and Mortality Rate of All Types of Cancer by Race, Ethnicity and Gender, Los Angeles County

	Japanese	Chinese	Anglo	Black	Latino
Cancer Rate per 100,000					
Male	278	251	397	465	285
Female	237	203	348	307	252
Mortality Rate per 100,000					
Male	155	156	203	281	156
Female	100	100	144	162	115

Source: Scott, J. (July 11, 1991). Cancer Watch. *Los Angeles Times.*

slightly higher than in the United States, but the figures question the stereotype of the Japanese as a suicide prone culture.

Table 9 shows the incidence and mortality rate of cancer in Los Angeles county by race, ethnicity, and gender. Both the male and female Japanese cancer rates rank fourth among the five comparison groups. The Japanese American cancer rates of 278 for males and 237 for females compares to the rate of 139 in Japan and 312.4 for the total U.S. Japanese and Chinese male and females have the lowest mortality rates in comparison to the Anglo, Black and Latino.

Table 10 shows the number of live births by race, by teenage mothers and unmarried mothers for selected years. Births to teenage mothers is generally low among the Japanese as well as most of the Asian groups. Births to unmarried mothers is also low in comparison to Whites, Blacks and those of Hispanic origin.

Table 11 shows the birth rate by ethnicity. The data lumps all of the Asian groups together; the percentage of children born to Asian women is the lowest among the four comparison groups. The old stereotype, that "Asians breed like rabbits," is not supported by data on birth rates. The increase of Asians is primarily through immigration.

EDUCATION, INCOME, POVERTY, AND UNEMPLOYMENT

Table 12 shows educational attainment by ethnicity. The Japanese median years of school completion of 12.9 ranks below the Filipino, Chinese, and Korean groups. The percent completing high school is high, but the percent with four or more years of college also falls below some of the other Asian groups. However, the figures do not show whether the

TABLE 10

Live Births by Race

Race	Number of Births (1,000) 1985[1]	1986[2]	1987[1]	Births to Teenage Mothers % of Total 1985[1]	1987[1]	Births to Unmarried Mothers % of Total 1985[1]
Total	3,761	3,757	3,809	12.7	12.4	22.0
White	2,991	2,970	2,992	10.8	10.4	14.5
Black	608	621	642	23.0	22.6	60.1
American Indian, Eskimo, Aleut.	43	43	44	19.1	18.9	40.7
Asian Pacific Islander*	116	119	129	5.5	5.5	10.1
Chinese	18	18	19	1.1	1.1	3.7
Filipino	21	22	24	5.8	6.0	12.1
Japanese	10	10	10	2.9	2.7	7.9
Hawaiian	7	N/A	7	15.9	15.4	N/A
Hispanic Origin	373	389	406	16.5	16.3	29.5

* Includes races not shown separately.

Source: [1]U.S. Department of Commerce, Bureau of Census. *Statistical Abstract of the United States 1990.* Table No. 87;
[2]U.S. Department of Commerce, Bureau of the Census. *Statistical Abstract of the United States 1989.* Table No. 89.

TABLE 11

Children Born per 1,000 Women Aged 15-44 by Ethnicity, United States, 1980

Group	Children
All United States	1.43
White	1.35
Black	1.80
Hispanic	1.81
Asian	1.16

Source: Robert W. Gardner, Bryant Robey, and Peter C. Smith. "Asian Americans: Growth, Change and Diversity," *Population Bulletin* 40. No. 4 (Oct. 1985): Figure 4.

TABLE 12

Educational Attainment by Ethnicity

Race	Median Year of School Completed[1]	Percent High School Graduates[2] (Persons > 25 Yrs.)			Percent 4 or More Years of College[2] (Persons > 25 Yrs.)		
		Total	Male	Female	Total	Male	Female
Japanese	12.9	81.6	84.2	79.5	26.4	35.2	19.7
Chinese	13.4	71.3	75.2	67.4	36.6	43.8	29.5
Filipino	14.1	74.2	73.1	75.1	37.0	32.2	41.2
Korean	13.0	78.1	90.0	70.6	33.7	52.4	22.0
Vietnamese	12.4	62.2	71.3	53.6	12.9	18.2	7.9
White	12.5	N/Z	N/A	N/A	N/A	N/A	N/A
Total U.S.	N/A	66.5	67.3	65.8	16.2	20.1	12.8

Sources: [1]U.S. Commission on Civil Rights. (1986). *Recent Activities Against Citizens and Residents of Asian Descent.* Table 6.
[2]U.S. Department of Commerce, Bureau of the Census. *(1988).* We, the Asian and Pacific Islander Americans. Table 7.

years of schooling were in the United States or abroad, which may be more relevant in terms of occupation and income. In general, all Asian groups with the exception of the Vietnamese, show higher rates of education than for the total United States.

Table 13 shows the undergraduate, graduate and total enrollment at UCLA for 1975, 1980, 1985 and 1990. Japanese undergraduate enrollment of 1279 was the highest in 1975, with each subsequent five year period showing a drop so that in 1990, there were only 830 Japanese students enrolled. Graduate enrollment showed a relative steady state from 1975 to 1990. The drop may be due to the decreasing number of Japanese in the total population.

Table 14 is drawn from a study by Fugita and O'Brien (1991) comparing responses regarding college graduation of Nisei and Sansei from Gardena, Sacramento and Fresno, all cities in California. The percent of Sansei college graduates is over twice as high than the Nisei in all three of the areas. The 70 percent of college graduates from Sacramento and Fresno indicates a highly educated sample.

Table 15 shows the mean annual income by gender and ethnicity, and average family income by birthplace and ethnicity for 1980. The Japanese mean annual income of $21,466 for males was the highest of all comparison groups; the mean annual income for females of $10,385 ranked second among the six comparison groups.

TABLE 13

UCLA Fall Enrollment by Ethnicity
(Number of Foreign Students*)

		1975	1980	1985	1990
Total	U	21,560 (599)	22,004 (770)	22,901 (578)	24,207 (460)
	G	10,253 (1,013)	10,274 (1,295)	9,845 (1,331)	10,550 (9,072)
	T	31,813 (1,612)	32,278 (2,065)	32,746 (1,909)	34,757 (1,938)
American	U	115 (0)	73 (0)	137 (1)	245 (1)
Indian	G	47 (1)	34 (2)	57 (2)	43 (0)
	T	162 (1)	107 (2)	190 (3)	288 (11)
Black	U	1,068 (24)	935 (10)	1,437 (14)	1,595 (8)
	G	563 (54)	472 (57)	368 (28)	493 (27)
	T	1,631 (78)	1,407 (67)	1,805 (42)	2,088 (35)
Hispanic	U	1,181 (167)	1,248 (22)	2,348 (16)	3,811 (23)
	G	599 (83)	578 (77)	613 (75)	805 (98)
	T	1,780 (167)	1,826 (99)	2,961 (91)	4,616 (121)
Asian	U	2,621 (228)	3,721 (351)	5,073 (306)	6,898 (288)
Pacific	G	1,302 (403)	1,164 (489)	1,606 (655)	2,209 (885)
Islander	T	3,923 (631)	4,885 (840)	6,679 (961)	9,107 (1,173)
Japanese	U	1,279 (40)	1,191 (45)	1,044 (40)	830 (47)
	G	267 (56)	330 (65)	328 (62)	316 (89)
	T	1,546 (96)	1,521 (110)	1,372 (102)	1,146 (136)
Chinese	U	871 (114)	1,214 (109)	1,648 (147)	2,456 (154)
	G	418 (202)	510 (258)	746 (387)	1,088 (537)
	T	1,289 (316)	1,724 (367)	2,394 (534)	3,544 (691)
Korean	U	193 (10)	566 (25)	760 (42)	1,459 (34)
	G	55 (30)	133 (63)	209 (111)	326 (138)
	T	248 (40)	699 (88)	969 (153)	1,785 (172)
White	U	15,115 (222)	13,590 (249)	13,083 (173)	11,015 (127)
	G	7,029 (380)	6,092 (434)	5,909 (329)	6,027 (284)
	T	22,144 (602)	19,682 (683)	18,992 (502)	17,042 (411)
Other	U	1,460 (41)	2,437 (138)	812 (57)	643 (13)
and No	G	1,107 (92)	1,934 (236)	1,296 (242)	973 (184)
Response	T	2,567 (133)	4,371 (374)	2,108 (299)	1,616 (197)

Source: UCLA Office of Academic Planniong and Budget. Ethnic Survey 1975, 1980, 1985 and 1990.

U, G and T represent Undergraduate, Graduate and Total, respectively.

TABLE 14

College Graduates by Generation and Area (N = 581)*

	AREA							
	Total		Gardena		Sacramento		Fresno	
Generation	N	Percent	N	Percent	N	Percent	N	Percent
Nisei	309	25.6	105	23.8	102	29.4	102	23.5
Sansei	272	64.7	80	50.0	100	71.0	92	70.7
TOTALS	581	43.9	185	35.1	202	50.0	194	45.9

*Includes only respondents, 25 years or older.

Source: Adapted from Fugita, Stephen S. and O'Brien, David J. (1991) *Japanese American Ethnicity.* Seattle: University of Washington Press, p. 85.

The average family income of the native born Japanese of $38,324 ranked third behind the Chinese and the Koreans; the average family income of $25,094 for the foreign born ranked behind the Filipino, White, and Chinese populations.

In general, the native born Japanese, Chinese and Korean show higher incomes than for the White population, while only the foreign born Filipino shows higher income than foreign born whites.

Table 16 shows the poverty rate by place of birth, year of immigration and ethnicity for 1980. The total poverty rate of 4.2 percent of the Japanese is the lowest among all comparison groups; the native born rate of 2.6 percent is again the lowest, while the 12.5 rate for the foreign born ranks relatively high. The year of immigration is also related to poverty rates, with those arriving prior to 1965 with the lowest rates of poverty.

Table 17 shows the percent in the labor force and rates of unemployment in the United States and Los Angeles County by ethnicity for 1980. The percent of Japanese in the total United States and Los Angeles County labor force is relatively consistent, ranging from 67.8 to 71 percent, while their rate of unemployment, 3 percent, is the lowest among all comparison groups.

Table 18 shows the occupational types by ethnicity for 1980. The highest percent of the Japanese are employed in the Technical, Sales, and Administrative area with 34.2 percent, followed by Professionals and Managers, 28.5 percent. The relatively low number in farming, 4.4 percent, an area which was the entry point for most Issei, still shows a higher percentage than for the total United States farming population.

TABLE 15

Mean Annual Income by Gender and Ethnicity, and Average Family Income by Birth Place and Ethnicity (1980)

	Japanese	Chinese	Filipino	Korean	Vietnamese	White
Mean Annual Income (Age 25-64)[1]						
Male	21,466	17,777	16,973	18,978	11,303	19,712
Female	10,385	6,852	11,412	8,547	8,490	8,490
(Male-Female Ratio)	(0.484)	(0.554)	(0.672)	(0.450)	(0.751)	(0.431)
Average Family Income (Dollars)[2]						
All* (Relative to White)	35,207 (1.33)	28,377 (1.07)	28,514 (1.07)	25,234 (0.95)	15,859 (0.60)	26,535 (1.00)
Native Born* (Relative to Native Born White	38,324 (1.44)	39,805 (1.50)	21,190 (0.80)	38,610 (1.46)	(N/A)** (N/A)**	26,514 (1.00)
Foreign Born* (Relative to Native Born White	25,094 (0.95)	26,230 (0.99)	29,400 (1.11)	24,895 (0.94)	15,873 (0.60)	27,006 (1.02)

*Asian-group families include only those whose head and spouse are of the same race and nativity.
**No significant data available.

Sources: [1]U.S. Commission on Civil Rights. (1986). *Recent Activities Against Citizens and Residents of Asian Descent.* Table 7.
[2]U.S. Commission on Civil Rights (1988). *The Ecnomic Status of Americans of Asian Descent: An Exploratory Investigation.* Table 3.1. (Estimates based on the 1980 Census of Population, 5 Percent "A" Public Use Sample.)

Table 19 shows Asian business firms owned and gross earnings by ethnicity for 1982. The Japanese rank second to the Chinese in terms of the percent of businesses owned and gross revenue.

MARITAL DISSOLUTION, JUVENILE DELINQUENCY

Tables 20, 21 and 22 are symptoms of disorganization. Table 20 shows divorce rates by ethnicity, birth and age for 1980. The native born Japanese have the lowest rates of marital dissolution of all comparison

TABLE 16

Family Poverty Rate (1980) by Place of Birth, Year of Immigration and Ethnicity

	Japanese	Chinese	Filipino	Korean	Vietnamese	White
Total[1]	4.2	10.5	6.2	13.1	35.1	6.6
Native Born[2]	2.6	3.7	15.8	3.5	N/A	6.6
Foreign Born[2]	12.5	12.1	5.2	12.8	34.0	9.3
Year of Immigration						
1975-80	13.9	28.1	9.4	19.6	35.1	23.3
1965-74	14.1	6.8	3.8	7.2	18.8	5.1
Before 1965	9.8	4.8	4.3	7.4	N/A	7.7

Sources: [1] U.S. Commission on Civil Rights. (1988). *Recent Activities Against Citizens and Residents of Asian Descent.* Table 11.
[2] U.S. Commission on Civil Rights (1988). *The Economic Status of Americans of Asian Descent: An Exploratory Investigation.* Table 3.3. (Estimates based on the 5% Public Use "A" Sample of the 1980 Census.)

TABLE 17

Percent in Labor Force and Unemployment Rates in the U.S. and Los Angeles County, by Ethnicity (1980)

Ethnicity	U.S.[1]		Los Angeles County[2]	
	Percent in Labor Force	Unemployment Rate (%)	Percent in Labor Force	Unemployment Rate (%)
Total	62.0	6.5	65	6
Asian	66.6	4.7	—	—
Japanese	67.8	3.0	71	3
Chinese	66.4	3.6	64	4
Filipino	72.5	4.8	75	3
Guamanian	69.9	6.8	—	—
Hawaiian	64.7	7.0	66	7
Asian Indian	65.4	5.8	66	5
Korean	63.9	5.7	64	4
Samoan	60.2	9.7	—	—
Vietnamese	57.3	8.2	44	7

Sources: [1] U.S. Department of Commerce, Bureau of Census (1988). *We, the Asian and Pacific Islander Americans.* Table 8.
[2] United Way. (1985). *Pacific Rim Profile.* Page 8.

TABLE 18

Percent Occupational Types by Ethnicity (1980)

	Japanese	Chinese	Filipino	Korean	Vietnamese	U.S.Total
Professional & Managerial	28.5	32.6	25.1	24.9	13.4	22.7
Technical, Sales, & Administrative	34.2	30.1	33.3	27.4	26.7	30.3
Service	12.8	18.6	16.5	16.5	15.3	12.9
Farming, Forestry & Fishing	4.4	0.5	2.8	0.9	0.9	2.9
Precision Production, Craft & Repair	10.0	5.6	8.3	9.9	14.5	12.9
Operators, Fabricators & Laborers	10.1	12.7	14.0	20.4	29.3	18.3

Sources: U.S. Department of Commerce, Bureau of Census. (1988). *We, the Asian and Pacific Islander Americans.* Table 7.

groups; in contrast, the foreign born Japanese rates of divorce are among the highest. It should be an area for further research.

Table 21 shows the referral of juveniles to the Los Angeles County Probation Department by ethnicity for 1983 through 1989. The number of Japanese juveniles referred to the probation department is extremely low, especially after 1984 when it was the lowest among all comparison groups.

Table 22 shows the referral of Japanese juveniles to the Los Angeles County Probation Department, and its disposition. The number of referrals is of course very low, and most of the cases were closed or given informal probation. Only two individuals in 1986 and one in 1989 were sent to the California Youth Authority. At least in terms of official statistics, the problem of juvenile crime and delinquency is not a major problem in the Los Angeles County Japanese American community.

Table 23 shows party identification by family income for the Japanese American sample drawn by Fugita and O'Brien (1991) from Gardena, Sacramento, and Fresno. Overall, the Japanese Americans preferred Democratic Party affiliation (52.4%) over that of the Republican Party (33.7%). However, there is a change as income rises; those with incomes

TABLE 19

Asian Business Firms Owned and Gross Earnings by Ethnicity (1982)

	Business Firms Owned		Gross Earnings	
	Number	(Percent)	Dollars (in millions)	(Percent)
Asian Pacific Islander	204,211	100	15,731	100
Japanese	49,039	24	2,731	17
Chinese	52,839	26	6,075	39
Korean	31,769	16	2,677	17
Filipino	26,464	13	747	5
Asian Indian	25,539	13	1,661	11
Vietnamese	5,234	3	215	1
Hawaiian	3,305	2	86	1
Other Asian	8,977	4	1,105	7
Other Pacific Islander	1,045	1	434	3

Source: U.S. Department of Commerce, Bureau of the Census. (1988). We, the Asian and Pacific Islander Americans. Table 5.

TABLE 20

Marital Dissolution* Rate by Ethnicity, Birth Place and Age

	Japanese	Chinese	Filipino	Korean	Vietnamese	White
Native Born						
Age 25-64	8.5	11.5	16.3	15.8	N/A	12.5
Age 25-34	11.6	13.8	18.5	17.5	N/A	15.2
Foreign Born						
Age 25-64	9.5	4.2	6.5	7.2	7.3	9.6
Age 25-34	8.1	3.5	6.9	7.7	6.4	14.0

*Marital Dissolution Rate: the number of women who were divorced or separated in 1980 by the number of women in that age category who were ever married.

Source: U.S. Commission on Civil Rights (1988). The Economic Status of Americans of Asian Descent: An Exploratory Investigation. Table 3.4. (Estimates based on the 5% Public Use "A" Sample of the Census).

TABLE 21

Referrals of Juneniles to Los Angeles County
Probation Department by Ethnicity

	1983	1984	1985	1986	1987	1988	1989
White	6,534	5,990	5,405	5,507	5,016	4,456	4,773
Hispanic	6,868	6,496	6,222	6,864	7,597	8,909	14,561
Black	6,144	4,959	4,397	4,911	5,059	5,146	7,623
American Indian	55	38	24	39	35	17	24
Chinese	7	11	56	34	34	41	42
Japanese	9	9	15	15	14	7	7
Filipinos	33	45	47	91	144	77	102
Other	625	512	736	635	777	774	1,068
Unknown	1	0	2	59	45	196	173

Source: State of California Department of Justice. *Crime Justice Profile, 1983, 1984, 1985, 1986, 1987, 1988 & 1989.*

TABLE 22

Referrals of Japanese Juveniles to
Los Angeles County Probation Department,
by Probation Department Disposition and Court Disposition

	1983	1984	1985	1986	1987	1988	1989
Number of Probation Referrals	9	9	15	15	14	7	7
Probation Department Disposition							
Closed	4	4	5	3	1	3	1
Transferred	0	0	0	0	0	0	0
Informal Probation	1	1	4	5	4	3	1
Petition Filed	4	4	6	7	9	1	5
Petitions Filed by Juvenile Court Disposition							
Closed/Dismissed/Transferred	1	0	0	1	0	1	5
Remanded to Adult Court	0	0	0	0	0	0	0
Informal Probation	0	0	0	0	0	0	1
Non-ward Probation	0	0	0	0	0	0	3
Wardship Probation	3	4	6	4	9	0	2
California Youth Authority	0	0	0	2	0	0	1

Source: State of California Department of Justice. *Crime Justice Profile, 1983, 1984, 1985, 1986, 1987, 1988 & 1989.*

TABLE 23

Party Identification by Family Income, for the Japanese American Sample (N = 587)

Family Income	Party Affiliation		
	Democrat	Independent/Others	Republican
$0–9,900	46.7	21.7	31.7
10,000–19,999	53.3	19.9	25.5
20,000–29,000	58.5	9.8	31.6
30,000–49,999	53.7	13.4	32.9
50,000–over	25.0	6.8	68.2
TOTAL Sample	52.4	13.9	33.7

Source: Adapted from Fugita, Stephen S. and O'Brien, David J. (1991) *Japanese American Ethnicity.* Seattle: University of Washington Press, p. 142.

over $50,000 were affiliated more with the Republicans (68.2%) than with the Democrats (25.0%).

Table 24 shows the amount of discrimination faced by the Nisei and Sansei in the Fugita and O'Brien (1991) study. The Nisei have faced much more discrimination than the Sansei; the percentage of Sansei who have faced minimal or no discrimination (69.9% and 17.2%) is one indication that at least for the Japanese American, discrimination still exists, but at a relatively low rate. Overall, over three quarters, or 78% of the respondents reported minimal or no past discrimination. I am unclear as to how back the respondents were asked to remember; would the wartime evacuation be counted as discrimination?

In summary, the data shows the following about the Japanese Americans:

1. That they are a slow growth, English speaking population, with low rates of immigration.

2. That they are concentrated in California and Hawaii.

3. That they are a relatively healthy population in terms of live births and mortality rates.

4. That they have a high percentage of high school graduates; that enrollment in college is also high, but somewhat lower in comparison to the Chinese, Filipino and Koreans.

TABLE 24

Percentage of Respondents Agreeing with Statements About Past Experienced Discrimination (N = 634)*

Generation	Amount of Discrimination Experienced as an Adult			
	Great Deal	Considerable	Minimal	None
Nisei	12.9	18.4	60.2	8.7
Sansei	3.1	9.7	69.9	17.2
TOTAL	7.9	14.0	65.0	13.0

Source: Adapted from Fugita, Stephen S. and O'Brien, David J. (1991) Japanese American Ethnicity. Seattle: University of Washington Press, p. 149.

5. That their mean annual income and average family income is high; that male annual income is twice the female income.

6. That there are differences in the poverty rate between the native and foreign born; the native born rate is the lowest among all comparison groups.

7. That the majority of the employed are in the Technical, Sales, and Administrative category followed by the Professional and Managerial.

8. That symptoms of social disorganization are low as measured by divorce rates and juvenile delinquency.

9. That the majority are affiliated with the Democrats, but that the tendency is to become Republican with a rise in income.

10. That discrimination exists, but a relatively low level.

BIBLIOGRAPHY

1. Fugita, Stephen and O'Brien, David (1991). Japanese American Ethnicity. Seattle: University of Washington Press.

2. Gardner, Robert, Robey, Bryant and Peter Smith (1985). Asian Americans: Growth, Change and Diversity." Population Bulletin 40, 4, October, Figure 4.

3. Norbeck, E. and Lock, M., eds. (1987). Health, Illness and Medical Care in Japan: Cultural and Social Dimensions. Honolulu: University of Hawaii Press.

4. Scott, J. (1991). "Cancer Watch", Los Angeles Times. July, p. A-1.

5. Trueba, H.T. (1989). *Raising Silent Voices*. New York: Newberry House.

6. State of California, Department of Justice. Crime Justice Profile, 1983 through 1989. Sacramento.

7. University of California Academic and Budget Office. Ethnic Survey, 1975, 1980, 1985, and 1990. Los Angeles: University of California.

8. United States Commission on Civil Rights (October, 1988). The Economic Status of Americans of Asian Descent: An Exploratory Investigation. Washington, D.C. Clearing House Publication. Tables 3.1, 3.3, 3.4.

9. United States Commission on Civil Rights (1986) Recent Activities Against Citizens and Residents of Asian Descent. Tables 1, 6, 7.

10. United States Department of Commerce, Bureau of the Census (1990) Statistical Abstracts of the United States. Table 87, 89.

11. United States Department of Commerce, Bureau of the Census (1988). We the Asian and Pacific Island Americans. Table 5, 7, 8.

12. United States Department of Commerce News (June 12, 1991). Table 1, 3C. 5B.

13. United States Department of Justice, Immigration and Naturalization Service (August, 1989). 1988 Statistical Yearbook of the Immigration and Naturalization Service. Table 2, 51.

14. United Way (1985). Pacific Rim Profile. Los Angeles.

CHAPTER 13

SUMMARY, CONCLUSIONS

It is difficult to summarize the experiences of any one individual over the course of his or her lifetime; it is even more difficult to chart the course of an ethnic group over a hundred year period. For we are dealing with diversity and change—changes in values, attitudes and behaviors of a minority group, numbering at various times well over a half million, and its interaction with the American society, itself made up of millions, including other racial minorities and ethnic groups. The purpose of this final chapter is to provide a summary based on theoretical issues which reflect the changes both in the ethnic group and with its interaction with the more powerful, host society.

DIVERSITY

One constant issue when analyzing the Japanese American experience is the diversity within the group, even though there may have been some common experiences that have, on the surface, created strong bonding patterns. This diversity is reflected in a discussion that I held with a group, now in their 60s, who spent their high school years from 1942-45 behind the barbed wire fences in Topaz (Kitano, 1991). Nineteen ninety two will mark the 50th anniversary of the forced evacuation, and although they spent their adolescent years together behind barbed wire, their present lives reflect a variety which defy simple categorization.

> It was a surprise to see a gathering of recognizable and familiar faces. We recognized each other instantly even though I had not seen some of them since my release from Topaz over four decades ago. But there was an ease and familiarity which brought back a comfortable style of

interaction, even though time had certainly wrought changes in all of our lives.

We discussed a number of issues and the nine of us, six females and three males—all presently in our 60s, but teen-agers while in Topaz, talked about our past and present lives.

Marriage and Family

Three of the females were still married, while the other three were divorced. Two of the males were still married, while one was divorced. The image of intact families among the Nisei did not hold for this group, and discussions of other peers that we knew lent credence to the idea that not all marriages were made in heaven.

Several of the marriages were to non-Japanese, and expectations and relationships of their Sansei children showed a wide variation. One common thread was that of a college education for their children; this was a high priority that came down from the Issei, to the Nisei, to the Sansei.

Their children showed an equal diversity. Some held professional positions, others were interested in community causes, some were still living at home and others were trying to find themselves. The majority of their children were interracial in terms of friends, dating and marriage; there was a general feeling that the children would find their own paths, in spite of what the parents desired. Parental desires in terms of marriage for their children were also varied; some wished that they would marry other Japanese; others thought that happiness and love were the most important.

One of the families spanned three generations living in the same household; others had a variety of family styles. Some were involved in placing their surviving parents in an elderly facility.

Integration, Pluralism

All of the group were highly acculturated; language, dress, housing, and life styles would fit into any mainstream setting. And they led a variety of different lives; some totally with Caucasians; others heavily involved with the ethnic community. One taught in Harlem, and the others lived in other parts of the country before coming "back home" to the San Francisco Bay Area. One family reflects this diversity—the oldest son is married to a Caucasian, another lives in Japan with a Japanese wife, while the youngest child is pursuing a doctorate in history. The one common bond was the experience in the concentration camp, and all agreed that this experience was the common denominator that held the group together.

Predictions

One of the most interesting discussions centered around the way we behaved as high schoolers in Topaz, and whether we could have predicted how we would turn out. There was very little predictability among the males; one was a cutup while in high school and I thought of him as a most happy fellow, joking and laughing constantly. But to my surprise, he indicated that camp life was a miserable experience and that he wished to forget about his adolescent years. He then earned a PhD, and became a much decorated colonel, in Korea and Vietnam. His serious demeanor was in sharp contrast to what I remembered of him back in Topaz High.

Another had been an athlete and had continued his career, as a football player in an Eastern College and as an athletic instructor at a community college. The idea that a Nisei, especially of his small size would make a career as an athlete (although he was an excellent football player), was a surprise.

The lives of the women were even less predictable. They were young, vulnerable, innocent, and more or less "typical young Nisei ladies," of that era. Some were quiet and shy, others were more active in high school, but most of us remained quite ignorant of each other's background while in camp because we all dressed alike, ate alike and lived alike. Finding about the different backgrounds for the first time came as a surprise to me; some had come from very privileged families while others from more traditional Issei families, but all of this was lost to me when in high school.

However, seeing them now—marriage, children, divorce, responsible motherhood, continued education, searching questions, a youthful enthusiasm and a willing to share seemed far from what I remembered of this group many decades ago. Time, place, setting and age surely shape behavior in ways that are difficult to predict.

Generation and Ethnic Identity

There was agreement that identity as Japanese Americans, or as Americans of Japanese ancestry remained. In addition, other identities included being Nisei, or as from Topaz. There was agreement that one could not hide the past, nor to ignore their identifiable physical features. There was some movement towards re-establishing a cultural identity, if not for themselves, at least for their children who were encouraged to take Japanese language classes and courses in Asian American studies.

As can be gleamed from meeting with this group, there were a wide variety of expectations, experiences and adaptations after their release from camp, and their current lives reflect this variety. If we add to their experiences the thousands of other Japanese Americans of different ages and generations; of those whose upbringing and socialization was in non-camp settings, and those who had grown up in non-ethnic communities, then the problem of developing explanations for the total group grows even more complex.

I also held a discussion with a Sansei group in Stockton, California (Kitano, 1990), which was at one time considered rural, but now defies that simple category. There are still Japanese Americans in farming, but at the time of the meeting in 1990, farmers were having a difficult time so that the trend of children leaving the farms was likely to continue. The overall theme was that although there remained ethnic ties, the relatively small size of the Japanese American community meant that there was much more contact with non-Japanese on a regular basis. But there remained live ethnic organizations, such as churches, the JACL and other interest groups. It would have been difficult to detect any significant differences in terms of dress, content and discussion styles from similar age groups of Japanese Americans in Los Angeles or San Francisco.

THEORETICAL MODELS

There are a variety of models which attempt to explain the interaction between an immigrant group and the host society. As one would expect, none fit the group perfectly, yet each fits part of the group. So if we talk about identity, acculturation, and assimilation, we can certainly cite the experiences of some of the Sansei; when we talk about a bi-cultural model, we can include some Nisei and Sansei. And if we talk about a separate, ethnic experience, the Issei come to mind, and if we talk about domination, the Issei experience qualifies. The wartime evacuation was an example of domestic colonialism, and other models that provide partial explanations include the dual economy model and the middle-man minority. Structural models, focussing on economic and social opportunities, as well as world wide issues provide additional insight, while the development of human capital may more closely fit the current generation.

It is clear that no one model or one theory can fit the entire group. The most common differential is that of generation, so that we will discuss models pertinent for each generation. Generations will also allow us to illustrate the continuity between the various groups—that is, what the Issei passed on to the Nisei, and in turn, what the Nisei passed onto the Sansei.

THE ISSEI

Of all of the Japanese Americans, the Issei were the least directly affected by acculturation. They came into an American society that was unwilling to provide them with access to the mainstream, which meant that they were kept in the lower part of a stratification system through the

boundary maintenance mechanisms of prejudice, discrimination and segregation (see Chapter 3). In the early years, they lived under a caste-like system and were denied access to the mainstream.

However, they came with an intact culture; hostility from the host society lead to structural and cultural pluralism, and a cohesive ethnic community. By the time that some of the structural constraints were liberalized in the 1950s (i.e. citizenship), most were already set in their life patterns and changes in their life styles were minimal.

The model that is the most appropriate for the Issei is that of caste, domination, structural pluralism, cultural separation, minimal acculturation, and a strong ethnic identity. They maintained their language, culture and values; their voluntary associations were with fellow Issei; they belonged to Issei organizations and most of their occupations were "typically Issei." The professionals, such as doctors, lawyers and dentists served primarily in the ethnic community; small business meant "mom and pop" establishments, real estate, barbershops, cleaners, inn-keepers, and the like. Service occupations included gardening, housework and day labor. Government and Civil Service Jobs were scarce as was employment in mainstream private corporations.

Retirement and elderly status was within the ethnic community and family. Although it may be a stereotype—that Asian families take care of their own, and do not need outside assistance, impressionistic evidence indicates that families prefer to take care of their elderly, and that the ethnic community has developed their own facilities. Senior citizen's housing and nursing home facilities with names such as the Keiro Nursing Home, and Little Tokyo Towers are available in Los Angeles, and other Japanese communities with adequate resources have also developed their own facilities.

Taking care of the elderly Issei has been a priority among many Nisei. My family is probably typical.

When my parents reached retirement age (my father ran an apartment), they were lucky enough to have their own house. So my sisters took care of most of their other needs; they would drop in, take them shopping and include them in our family outings. In turn, my mother would still prepare food for New Years and for her church, so that we were continually exposed to important facets of the Japanese culture, Issei style. But after my father died and my mother became more dependent, there was the thought of a twenty four hour care facility. She at first resisted; finally she was placed in a small private care facility run by a Korean lady. It was interesting that she did not want to be placed with other Japanese, even though there were openings in San Francisco's Japanese town. It was my hunch that her primary interactions were within the family, and that she never got used to interacting with other Japanese on a voluntary level even though she went through the concentration camp experience. The private care facility turned out well, however, their license was not renewed so she eventually ended up in a much larger integrated institution. She does not appear to miss Japanese meals, nor does she seem to miss interacting with fellow ethnics, even though her language ability in English is minimal. It may well be that after a certain age (probably after one reaches the century mark), variables like ethnicity, ethnic identity, the ethnic culture and racism are no longer major factors.

THE NISEI

The Nisei lived under a variety of conditions, including domination and structural separation in the early days; then in common with the Issei, the wartime incarceration. After their release they saw the opening up of the society so that their education and training, or their human capital, has lead to occupational and social mobility.

The life of the early Nisei, prior to World War II was a continuation of the Issei experience, although they had one theoretical advantage for life in America, that of citizenship by birth and an American education. Nevertheless, they faced similar barriers under the model of domination—prejudice, discrimination and segregation. As indicated in Chapter 3, they were even labelled the "second generation Japanese problem," because even if they went on to higher education, there were limited job and social opportunities. However, there was agricultural employment and employment in the Issei community; they developed their own organizations and lived their lives within the ethnic community. It was a period of structural pluralism in terms of occupation and social contacts, but they were also exposed to the host society. There began several streams within the Nisei; those whose major goals were assimilation, integration and acceptance into the mainstream; those who felt that there was no future in the United States and went to Japan, and those who felt that the maintenance of ethnic solidarity and ethnic cohesion were the major priorities. Many vacillated between the goals, others were confused, while most resigned themselves to fate, living day to day, and letting events take care of the future.

WARTIME EVACUATION: DOMESTIC COLONIALISM

The wartime evacuation can be aptly summarized as a period of domestic colonialism. As Blauner (1972: 396) indicates, the colonial model has the following main features:

1. The racial groups forced, involuntary entry into their situation. The Japanese American group had no choice; they were forced to live behind barbed wire.

2. The impact of the interaction is much more dramatic than the slower process of acculturation. The colonizing power carries out a policy "which constrains, transforms, or destroys indigenous values, orientations and ways of life." The Japanese were forced to give up their life previous lives and life styles; there was the planned destruction of anything to do with being "Japanese," and placing leaders and those suspected of having strong ties with Japan in separate institutions. Those who were thought to be more "American" were given leadership positions, and governmental clearance was also based on loyalty to the United States. Acculturation was to camp norms, often at variance with previous Japanese values and, also in many cases, non-functional in the larger society. However, there was also exposure to a variety of occupations within the camp settings which was different from their restricted positions in pre-World War II America.

3. Colonization "involves a relationship by which members of the colonized group tend to be administered by representatives of the dominant power. There is the experience of being managed and manipulated by outsiders in terms of ethnic status." All administrative positions were in the hands of government appointed Caucasians; there was unequal pay differentials between the "outsiders" and the "insiders," even though the jobs were similar, such as in teaching. Housing, food and other amenities of life were clearly segregated on a "less than equal" basis.

4. There is racism. One group is seen as inferior, exploited, controlled and oppressed by the dominant group. The Japanese were the only "enemy" group that faced mass incarceration, and the racist stereotypes provided ample ammunition for "Jap" bashing.

Although the entire evacuation was a tragedy, the one blessing was that it lasted only from 1942 to 1945. It is easy to imagine the effect on any population if they were forced to live under colonial conditions for a lifetime, or for several lifetimes. Even over this short duration, some Japanese Americans were effected by the experience and internalized feelings of inferiority, low self esteem, dependence, and a colonized mentality.

The post war period saw an opening up of the system so that barriers, especially of a legal nature began to be removed. What was previously an iron ceiling—impenetrable and strong, began to be replaced by a glass ceiling—one could see the top but could only look. It was the period of integration, of Civil Rights, of equal opportunity, of the fall of anti-miscegenation laws so that there was a degree of structural and social assimilation.

Many Nisei are now at the point in their lives where they would like to provide a legacy for future generations. One of the most ambitious projects has been the Japanese American National Museum, which opened in Los Angeles in 1992. The goal of raising $25 million towards the museum would have been unrealistic decades ago, but the interest and the ability of the group to work on this ambitious project can be read as one indication of change in the ethnic community. Other Japanese communities have also developed histories and exhibits, lead primarily by the Nisei. It is refreshing to see older Nisei giving back to the community; individuals such as George Aratani and Herb Kawahara and their all-Nisei committees have lead drives to fund such diverse projects as the Japanese American National Museum, and the Japanese American Endowed Chair at UCLA.

The majority of the Nisei are now approaching or are already in their retirement years. Issues of the elderly are of primary concern so that health, housing, hospitalization, retirement, and the role of the family and ethnic community are topics for discussion. One of the answers seems to be the development of ethnic facilities, some with governmental assistance, for the elderly Nisei and the few, surviving Issei. There is a degree of irony to these ventures; when the Japanese Americans did not want or need government assistance, they became wards of the government and were put into the concentration camps. Now that some may need assistance, the federal government may be less responsive.

THE KIBEI

The Kibei are technically Nisei, that is born in the United Sates to Issei parents, but they differ in that their developmental years were spent with relatives in Japan. Because they differ in terms of age and reasons for leaving their families in American, sex, time and experiences in Japan, as well as relationships with their families, it is difficult to arrive at meaningful generalizations of this diverse group. Leighton (1945) estimated that the Kibei numbered over 9 percent in one of the concentration camps of World War II so that their numbers were not insignificant.

The practice of sending at least one child back to Japan was most popular between 1920 to 1941 which coincided with the period of nationalism and patriotism in Japan. As a consequence, many returned to the United States with strong Japanese identities. This placed them in conflict with the Nisei who were going through the process of acculturation and working towards an American identity. Some of the conflicts that occurred in the relocation centers were the result of Kibei-Nisei clashes. Their fluency in Japanese served the United States in the war against Japan.

The practice of sending children to Japan for a part of their developmental years has not continued so that the Kibei population has remained static, and is currently indistinguishable from their Nisei peers. One impression is that they may have participated in ethnically oriented activities such as judo, kendo and other forms of Japanese martial arts more than the Nisei, and that as a group, they were less acculturated and were more restricted in terms of educational and occupational mobility than the Nisei. But these differences have not carried over to the Sansei generation. The most appropriate model for this group would be pluralism and a bi-culturalism.

THE SANSEI

The Sansei have continued to come closer to the host society; they live in widely scattered areas and attend a wide variety of schools. There is no one dominant Japanese American Community—the Little Tokyos are primarily for business, and for tourists, but many ethnic organizations remain. Social, athletic and religious organizations are available for those who wish to participate.

Corporate pluralism (Gordon, 1978) has become a part of professional life. There is a recognition that an individual, or a small ethnic group does not have access to policy makers. Therefore, the Japanese American has joined with fellow Asians in a number of organizations in order to have their collective voices. Some are national in organization—the National Asian Pacific American Families Against Substance Abuse (NAPAFASA) combines the various Asian American groups in order to provide prevention, assistance and education towards substance abuse. Other organizations are occupational and professional; there are the Asian American Psychologists and the Asian American Social Workers; there are also Asian American educators, civil service workers and a wide variety of occupational, alumni, recreational, interest, and service organizations. It is a recognition that corporate pluralism is an acceptable way of organizing in order to gain access to decision makers.

There are a variety of models to cover the Sansei. There is structural pluralism— organizations primarily for Japanese Americans, but also of a pan-Asian variety, and there still are businesses and services that are a carry over from the Issei and Nisei era. So if need be, a Sansei can still participate primarily in ethnic organizations—birth can be by a Japanese American physician, marriage to a Japanese American, and burial by a Japanese American mortician in a Japanese American cemetery. The primary difference between the Sansei and previous generations is that his or her choice is voluntary; one can participate fully, partially or not at all in ethnic activities. Choices in the mainstream may be more limited; many structural barriers have been eliminated, but there are areas, such as in the movies, television, and big business where there is a glass ceiling.

There are Sansei who follow the acculturation, integration and assimilation model. They find that some previously closed organizations, such as sororities and fraternities have openings, and careers in big business, in law and in politics are possibilities, which is a change from the expectations of their Nisei parents and Issei grandparents. Many structurally assimilate by marrying non-Japanese so that they "melt away" from the ethnic group. Even the symbolic aspects of ethnic identity may disappear with each move succeeding generation, especially among those who marry out of the group.

Then there are Sansei who follow a bi-cultural model; they may go to Japan to learn more about their ancestral heritage; take Japanese language classes, and are interested in the Japanese history and culture. But they are also American, so that they are comfortable in both cultures.

There are a number of other Japanese groups in the United States. There are the new Issei (shin-Issei) who have come to America since the change in immigration legislation in 1954. Some have come as quota immigrants, others as relatives of citizens, and others who were eligible under the refugee relief act of 1956. More recent immigration has been the result of the elimination of national quotas where there is a preference for relatives and skills deemed important for America.

The new Issei are a diverse group, and their background experiences in Japan reflect these differences. Some grew up in war-torn Japan after World War II, and experienced deep poverty and hard times, while others are products of modern day Japan, and are in some ways, even more "modern" than their American born peers. Their spending styles, their dress and their mannerisms tend to shock some of the more conservative Japanese Americans. In common with other immigrant groups, they tend to retain their ethnic language and culture, which may be different from the culture that the original Issei brought with them decades ago. They prefer to interact with fellow ethnics, but their American born Nisei children have and are going through the acculturation process, similar to that of the Nisei of another era. The major difference is that they do not have to face the structural barriers that hindered and limited the opportunities of their earlier peers, so that they are in a position to move rapidly in the direction of the host society if they so desire. In addition, in spite of spates of Japan "bashing," their ancestral homeland commands respect so that a bi-cultural identity is not unusual.

We have found no studies focussed on the new Issei and new Nisei; it is presumed that they have adapted to the host society with minimal stress.

Other groups include the war brides; an estimated 25,000 were in the United States by 1960. Background experiences were varied, and their lives in America were also characterized by differential experiences. This group had structurally assimilated, most were married to American servicemen, but were unfamiliar with America. Acculturation meant a variety of adjustments—to husbands, to in-laws, to life as the wife of a serviceman, to American born and educated children, to American neighborhoods, schools, and communities, and sometimes to divorce. Much of this was done without the support of family, old friends and neighbors, and with language difficulties and cultural differences. The ethnic community did not extend an unconditional welcome to this group; there have been stories and plays about marital discord and friction.

Their children, as well as the many other children of interracial marriages, constitute a group that has structurally assimilated. They have "melted," but in a variety of different ways. Little research information is available on this varied population; it is presumed that some have moved towards the host society, others in the direction of the ethnic culture, whereas others may be assessing the need for a subgroup of their own.

Then there are the Japanese tourists and businessmen who have retained most of the trappings of their national culture. The stereotyped tourist arrives in groups, flies on Japanese airlines, stays at Japanese owned hotels, but loves to shop in America because the prices are cheap and the yen to dollar ratio is so favorable. There is little interaction with most of America so that they remain as Japanese from Japan, both structurally and culturally.

The Japanese businessman (kaisha), especially if he (most, if not all of them are males) is here on a temporary assignment, lives a pluralistic existence. In large cities, such as in New York and Los Angeles, they can retain their Japanese life styles with minimal social interaction with the Japanese American community and the host society. He may work with

Americans, and interact with them on a business basis, but he is most likely to prefer to spend his free time at Japanese clubs, bars, restaurants, and organizations that cater primarily to the Japanese from Japan. Their wives may have some difficulty in adjusting to the new country.

There are Japanese (not Japanese American) programs on TV, in areas such as Honolulu, the San Francisco Bay Area, and Los Angeles with news and entertainment programs direct from NHK and Tokyo. Karaoke bars, which are now invading the host society were initially popular with the shin-Issei. Even though their school aged children attend American schools, the temporary visitors have also developed their own Japanese schools, with a curriculum based on models from Japan.

Perhaps the most influential import from Japan is not its people, but its capital, its goods, and its management styles (Ouchi, 1984). The influx of cameras, electronic equipment and automobiles has spread throughout the nation and the world, and decimated American competitors. The sight of Japanese money buying up desirable properties in Waikiki, New York and Los Angeles has raised the specter of a "Japanese invasion," albeit a green, rather than a yellow one, and has raised anti-Japanese sentiments, especially among those who see their unemployment as a result of Japanese competition. The tragedy for the Japanese American is that they do not gain any direct positive benefits from this invasion, but become easy targets and scapegoats for the misplaced hostility.

CHANGE

A Los Angeles Times article, "It's Taps for Scout Troop 41" (Hamilton, 1991), provides an apt summary of the changes in the Japanese American Community. The former Cub and Eagle Scouts of Troop 41 are now in their 70s, and there are not enough new members to keep the Troop going. So a group that started in 1931 in Pasadena, who talked in Japanese to their parents, but who built campfires and sang "God Bless America"; who survived the depression and the World War II internment experience, has been disbanded. There are not enough young Japanese Americans to keep the troop going so that after 60 years, the survivors of the original scouts have gathered to celebrate the occasion.

WHERE ARE THE JAPANESE AMERICANS?

When compared to their fore-fathers who came as immigrants many years ago, the current Japanese American is better equipped to deal with stress, racism and the scapegoat role. The barriers of discrimination and segregation have been lessened; there is an opening up of the structures of the mainstream as well as opportunities within the ethnic community; the group is competitive in education and income, and there are a variety of professionals and businesses to serve the community.

There has even been a small crack in "show business"; Pat Morita, Nobu McCarthy and Mako are familiar faces, while Philip Gotanda has written a variety of plays, such as "Song for a Nisei Fisherman," "The Wash," and "Fish Head Soup." But, the tendency to type cast and to use Caucasians in leading roles limits the role of Japanese Americans, as well as other Asians in show business.

Television has seen news anchors on the West Coast; Tritia Toyota, JoAnn Ishimine and Wendy Tokuda add much to Los Angeles television. The lack of Asian males in a similar capacity has yet to be addressed. Kristy Yamaguchi's Gold Medal performance in the Winter Olympics stands as another source of ethnic pride; it probably has sent scores of young Nikkei onto the ice skating rinks. It is also interesting to note that her main challenger, Midori Ito, was from Japan. I was in Japan at the time of Ms. Ito's retirement, and noted that on Japanese television, there was almost no mention of Kristy's triumph.

Japanese Americans have electable politicians, and although their ancestral homeland is not loved, it is respected. No longer is there a one dimensional analysis of acculturation and Americanism; one can be comfortable with multiple identities, so that both an American and a Japanese American identity is possible.

Change in the main has been positive. But there is some ambivalence and regret about some of the changes. Perhaps the most important has been the change in values that encourages a more individualistic outlook on life. I know and have experienced some of the stifling effects of living in the old ethnic community, but there was also the positive side that gave group life and group reputation a high priority. It meant that what one Japanese did, positively or negatively, affected the entire community. We were proud of the accomplishments of those who represented the "best"; we were also embarrassed at the shortcomings of those who violated the norms.

The result was community cohesion and caring beyond the individual self. My father gave to the community, even though it meant that his family would have to do with less. It is a value system that is difficult for those of us who have grown up under more individual circumstances to understand, yet the meaning of an ethnic identity would be valuable if it included a sensitivity and caring for those in the community who were less fortunate and less "successful."

In many ways, my own experiences provide a summary of Japanese American concerns with the issues of generation and ethnic identity.

My Issei parents, especially my father, provided a constant Japanese influence. He would remind me that I was Japanese; I would never directly challenge him, but in my early years, I truly believed that I was American. I hated Japanese food; never seriously studied the Japanese language, even though I had to attend Japanese language school, and mocked the language teacher because of her Japanese accent.

However, I lived in San Francisco's Chinatown and I knew that I was not Chinese, and constantly heard the term "Jap." There was one Chinese girl, Dorothy Lee, who would pinch me and call me "Jap"; I tried to avoid her as much as possible, and my only rejoinder to her was that I was an American.

The World War II concentration camp experience made it clear that to the United States Government I was Japanese. Living in Topaz for three years in an all ethnic setting, with the exception of Caucasian administrators made it even clearer that I was Japanese, a second class citizen, but with an additional identity as a resident of Topaz—a concentration camp. I repressed that identity for many years.

From that time on I tried a number of identities; musician, Chinese, student at the University of California, Berkeley, and even trips to Japan to see how it life would be in the ancestral homeland. Living in Japan reinforced my American identity; I immediately knew that I was not Japanese; I walked, talked and behaved like an American, and I prized my U.S. Passport. Comparisons were usually in favor of the United States, especially in terms of office space, heating and plumbing facilities, and general life styles.

Strongest support of my Japanese American identity came when I began my professorial career at UCLA in 1958. Word got around that there was a Nisei professor at the University; I was called upon constantly by the ethnic community to give lectures, seminars and panel discussions. The basic question in the community in those years was one of identity; "Who am I," or Who are we?," conferences were quite popular.

A historian colleague, Roger Daniels, was instrumental in breaking through my reticence concerning my experiences in Topaz. He suggested that we co-sponsor a conference commemoration the 25th anniversary of the "Wartime Evacuation." I thought at that time that it was a risky proposition; after the announcement of the conference, I received several phone calls from members of the ethnic community indicating their opposition, since it was better to let "sleeping dogs lie." It was the first such conference held at a major university, and it turned out to be successful.

In 1992, the fiftieth year since the evacuation, UCLA hosted a year long conference, with a variety of activities, including art shows, plays, seminars and lectures. In my address at the opening ceremony which included Mayor Tom Bradley of Los Angeles, Congressman Norman Mineta, and Chancellor Charles Young of UCLA, as well as many former evacuees, I felt proud that I had survived the camps, and had experienced a unique event in American history. I was also proud to be associated with a university that recognized the enormity of the event, and was willing to assume sponsorship.

So given my experiences, I have arrived at a number of identities. I am a member of the Nisei generation, a Japanese American, a former resident of Topaz, and a professor at UCLA. Perhaps my search for an identity has been resolved.

So, as we near the end of the twentieth century, and look back at the past, it appears that the Japanese American has done rather well. The interaction with the dominant culture, never ever very smooth, has been of a more positive nature. The term, "Japs," is no longer bandied around as a common epithet, and overt racist remarks against Japanese Americans are causes for censure. Perhaps the total racial climate has changed, although there are also constant reminders that racism remains an unresolved American dilemma. But would any Japanese American trade where they are now with where they were five decades ago?

BIBLIOGRAPHY

1. Blauner, Robert (1972). *Racial Oppression in America*. New York: Harper and Row.

2. Gordon, Milton (1978). *Human Nature, Class and Ethnicity*. New York: Oxford University Press.

3. Hamilton, Denise (1991) "It's Taps for Scout Troop 41", Los Angeles Times, July 27, p. B-1.

4. Kitano, Harry H.L. (1991) Meeting with Amy Tamaki Doi, John Juji Hada, Sadame Hara Kojimoto, Sachi Kawahara Masaoka, Sam Nakaso, Daisy Uyeda Satoda, Asaye Ashizawa Takagi and Aileen Yamate in San Francisco, July 28.

5. Kitano, Harry H.L. (1990) Meeting with Nelson Nagai, Kenneth Yamashita and several other Japanese Americans in Stockton, July 7.

6. Leighton, Alexander (1945). *The Governing of Men*. Princeton, New Jersey: Princeton University Press.

7. Ouchi, William (1984). *The M-Form Society: How American Teamwork Can Recapture the Competitive Edge*. Reading, Mass.: Addison-Wesley.